Jane Remer

D1450450

Changing Schools through the Arts

HOW TO BUILD ON THE POWER OF AN IDEA

ACA BOOKS
American Council for the Arts
New York, New York

93 92 91 90   10 9 8 7 6 5 4 3 2 1

Book and Jacket Design by: Celine Brandes, Photo Plus Art
Edited by: Lisa Parr

Printed by BookCrafters

Director of Publishing: Robert Porter
Assistant Director of Publishing: Doug Rose

Library of Congress Cataloging-in-Publication Data:

Remer, Jane.

   Changing schools through the arts: how to build on the power of an idea / by Jane Remer : foreword by John Goodlad. — Rev. ed.

   ISBN: 0-915400-86-3

   1. Arts—Study and teaching—United States. I. Title

NX304.R45 1990
700'.7'073—dc20   90-1293
                                                              CIP

This publication was made possible
by the generous support of
the Ahmanson Foundation

Dedication

In Memoriam - Kathryn Bloom

Kathryn Bloom was born on October 15, 1919 in Brownsville, Texas. She died on November 23, 1988 in Petoskey, Michigan. In the sixty-nine intervening years, Kathy lived a rich, imaginative and significant life. Wherever she went, she made a difference. She has left me a legacy of experience and an inheritance of wisdom, and I shall always cherish both.

Kathy's career began in 1944 when she taught art in Owatonna, Minnesota. She went on to lecture at the Minneapolis Institute of Arts and to supervise art education at the Toledo Museum of Art. In 1957, as an arts consultant for the national Association of Junior Leagues, she traveled the country evaluating community-based arts programs and recommending new and improved educational services. From 1963 to 1968 she was named director of the Arts and Humanities Program of the U.S. Office of Education where she administered a groundbreaking research program for the improvement of education in the arts and humanities. At the same time, she was special advisor to two commissioners of education (Francis Keppel followed by Harold "Doc" Howe), representing them in dealings with the Arts and the Humanities Endowments and other federal agencies. In September 1967 she took partial leave from OE to act as a consultant on the arts in education to the JDR 3rd Fund and its president, John D. Rockefeller 3rd. A year later Mr. Rockefeller appointed her director of the Fund's new Arts in Education Program. She occupied that position until 1979 when the program was terminated, a year after its founder's sudden death.

Kathy took early retirement in 1982, bought a house, moved to the Midwest and adopted a dog, Daisy. Toward the end of her life, she kept herself moderately busy and quite content by working with the Little Traverse Conservancy, designing display panels and writing a newsletter. She never looked back on her life in New York or the field that she was largely responsible for creating: the arts in education. She accepted no engagements, answered few letters and even fewer phone calls.

Fortunately we kept in steady touch, mostly by phone. Kathy finally succumbed to cancer, and the last letter I have from her, a month before she died, is typical. She was resigned, at peace, philosophical and matter-of-fact. When I learned of her death from a long-time friend who had been with her to the end, I was not shocked, just profoundly saddened and bereft. This great lady, this wonderful mentor, this amazingly good friend of sixteen years, had slipped away without a bang or a whimper. The silence was deafening.

And so, I take this occasion to pay tribute to her. Let me tell you about Kathy, the person, as I knew her. She was full of contradictions. She was a risk-taker and a daredevil; she could also be prim, proper and quietly formidable. She was a humorist and a clown; she was also deadly serious about her work and dangerous when she felt "the integrity of the idea" of the arts in education was threatened. She was warm, generous and thoughtful, and she loved to dance, yet she hated parties and social gatherings. She was a powerful and compelling public speaker who was always as nervous as a cat before any conference engagement.

All in all, her influence on people was astounding. Idiosyncratic, assertive, often combative, this fiercely articulate woman could as easily alienate her potential allies as charm her outspoken adversaries. Some people may not have liked her, but they always had a healthy respect for her abilities and her intellect. Kathy, however, was not interested in popularity contests; she had a strong and healthy ego. She also had a job to do. To get a better idea of just how peripatetic and influential she actually was, at least from the mid-sixties to the end of the seventies, I suggest you study the Interpretive Chronology of Major Events in the Arts in Education in the Appendix of this book.

It is important to incorporate here what I said about Kathy in the Acknowledgments to the first edition of this book in 1981. I had made sure to read the copy to her before letting it go to print, and I was relieved when I got her okay. Kathy was uncomfortable with gushing love letters, and I cut it pretty close:

"My respect for and gratitude to Kathryn Bloom are infinite. It was she who created an unparalleled opportunity for me to search for new ways to integrate the arts into the education of every child. During the six years that we worked together, her strength, vision and unfailing sense of good humor taught me the true meaning and value of partnerships and mutual support.

"Kathy was never afraid to break the mold or bend the rules. In the true spirit of the American pioneer, she kept clearing paths and taking chances. She believed that foundations should be 'stalking horses,' unafraid to test new ideas, win, lose or draw. While she admired the risk-takers and even the impulsive, she was always a hard taskmistress with her staff. You could speculate, experiment and deviate all you wished, but you had better produce; the program's survival depended on it, as did her faith in you.

"She was for me and for many others in the field an inspiration, an anchor and a goad because she was never satisfied. Whatever had been accomplished and before we had had a chance to catch our breath, her question was always: What's next? 'What's next' was usually just around the bend, and Kathy had the uncanny and often unnerving ability to pick it up and run with it.

"Looking back at the events of the past three decades, one may be tempted to say, 'They were giants in those days.' Throughout her long and distinguished career, she was certainly one of them. In fact, if anyone deserves the title of 'elder statesperson' in the arts in education movement, it is Kathryn Bloom."

Aria da Capo

She *was*, indeed, a giant in her day.

Jane Remer

August 1990

Contents

1   *Setting the Stage*   *1*

5   *Networking and Collaboration:*
     A Strategic Design for Change   *87*

6   *A Day in the Life of
an AGE Demonstration School:
P.S. 152 Brooklyn*   *99*

8 *Pieces of the Puzzle: Potential Sources of Leadership, Advocacy and Support*   **151**

Appendices

List of Exhibits

Foreword

This book is about the arts in schools and how to establish a firm place for them there. Throughout its pages, Jane Remer presents a convincing case for the role of the visual arts, music, dance, drama, architecture and aesthetics in educating boys and girls. Her argument ranges over the value of the arts for their own sake to their usefulness in enhancing other fields and in kindling the interest in learning of students not otherwise identifying with the expectations of schools. She is convincing.

But Jane Remer is also "streetwise." She has been in and around schools for years as educator, mother of two, foundation executive and consultant. She knows that ideas, however good, do not get into schools by immaculate conception. A long and sometimes painful process is involved. The curriculum is always full; instructional time is finite. For centuries, mathematics and language arts (reading, spelling, writing and so on) have dominated elementary school programs, today averaging well over 50 percent of the instructional week—and up to 70 percent in some schools. Everything else is usually regarded as secondary. Rhetoric alone, however convincing, will not bring the arts into schools. Strategies are required.

In addition, then, to addressing the role of the arts in schools, this book presents strategies for getting them there. These strategies combine a considerable amount of extant knowledge about processes of change with less well-established insight into the particular potential of the arts for facilitating school improvement. The result is a volume that contributes on two fronts: on one hand to our growing understanding of how best to effect educational improvement in schools and, on the other, to our awareness of the importance of arts experiences in childhood and youth education.

It is this combination that makes Jane Remer's book special. There is a substantial body of literature in education and other fields on effecting change. There are also many treatises on the arts and their place in educational institutions. But books combining the two are virtually non-existent.

Remer's narrative moves in and out of a series of experiences with school districts seeking to place greater stress on the arts in education. I pass quickly over the various motivations involved. It is sufficient to say that responsible persons perceived in the arts opportunities to enhance the education of children and youth. Top leadership in these districts also recognized the potential of using the arts as a vehicle for general school improvement. Jane uses these situations to enrich and illustrate her observations on what appeared to her to enhance school improvement through the arts. The result is an almost unprecedented illustration of principles drawn from research and theory but not often enough accessible to those who manage and teach in our schools.

The proposition that the arts are basic in the education of our young has been argued effectively in relatively recent books directed to both the general public[1] and educators.[2] All states make reference either to the arts or to the aesthetic development of children and youth in the guides they prepare for local school districts. And parents, it appears, want it all for their children when it comes to education—goals encompassing the arts as well as mathematics, language arts, science, social studies, physical education and vocational education.[3] To provide only reading, writing, spelling and arithmetic in schools is to ignore both a historical and a contemporary mandate.

Ms. Remer reiterates the familiar justifications. But like some others who believe in arts education, she perceives the role of this domain as being much more than a designated subject or group of subjects. Because, for example, the arts in some form are always an accompaniment of what people in other times did or in other places do, they constitute a significant part of history and geography. They become not only a field in themselves but also an inseparable part of the rest of humankind's knowledge and

---

[1] American Council for the Arts in Education/Arts, Education and American Panel. *Coming To Our Senses*. New York: McGraw-Hill Book Company, Inc., 1977.

[2] Hausman, Jerome J., ed. *Arts and the Schools*. New York: McGraw-Hill Book Company, Inc., 1980.

[3] Findings from *A Study of Schooling*, a comprehensive look at a representative sample of schools in seven regions of the United States. For preliminary information regarding this study, now in process, see Goodlad, John I., Kenneth A. Sirotnik, and Bette C. Overman. "An Overview of *A Study of Schooling*," Phi Delta Kappan 61, No. 3 (November 1979), 174-78.

skills. The arts, then, are not only a specialized field of study and performance but an integral part of general education for all. One does not argue for the need to understand civilization without implicitly arguing for the arts. This view pervades Remer's book and her reiteration of a fundamental premise is in itself a contribution.

Her larger contribution, however, resides in the insight she provides regarding how to establish the arts in schools while simultaneously using them as a vehicle for school renewal. I deal with the second of these two processes first. In recent years, students of educational change and improvement have become increasingly aware of what are becoming known as "networking" strategies. Individuals and groups of present or potentially similar interests are linked together in ways designed to maximize commonality otherwise not likely to be joined and shared.

This is not a new technique, but the history of its use in schooling is short. The elements are familiar. The units to be linked can be scattered geographically but share some common goal such as using the arts to look afresh at ways to rejuvenate schools grown staid through the preservation of long-established practices. Some central agency establishes itself as a hub. The hub simultaneously builds a bridge to each of the units to be linked and then promotes ways to link each unit to each of the others. Envision a wheel with spokes from the hub to each unit and a rim connecting the units. Begin to employ terms conveying family relationships or common membership such as Family of Schools or League of Cities. Common expectations are conveyed.

Envision further the infusion of different and perhaps countervailing ideas into the whole. New and alternative drummers convey messages that differ from those dominating current practices. The alternative messages become the new norms. Those espousing the new norms become role models for persons who have similar beliefs but, perhaps, live in a daily environment not conducive to the cultivation of these beliefs. What were once somewhat countervailing and perhaps threatening beliefs become fashionable beliefs. One is able to believe differently without appearing bizarre. Ideas once considered provocative become ideas considered to be in vogue.

The above is a simplistic summary of the strategy of change employed by the individuals and institutions described in what follows. The organization with which Jane Remer and Kathryn Bloom—to whom the former gives great credit—were affiliated and which served as the "alternative drummer" was the JDR 3rd Fund in New York. The units with a spark of mutual concern seeking a catalyst were school districts from New York City to Seattle, Washington. These institutions and others came together for mutual satisfaction and accomplishment. Jane Remer describes the process and its effects.

The common enterprise was to make the arts more central in school programs and to improve school programs through the arts. Usually, however, such enterprises ebb and flood. The arts have tended to remain peripheral in school programs in part because their teaching has been relegated to specialists. My own studies, referred to earlier, suggest that elementary school teachers, for example, do not feel as well prepared to teach the arts as they do language arts and social studies. Consequently, they welcome into their classrooms persons who claim specialization in arts education. The presence in schools of persons who take over from regular classroom teachers all responsibility for teaching the arts has certain negative consequences. Regular teachers do not feel a responsibility for the arts; the arts become special.

The approach recommended and described by Jane Remer moves the arts from a peripheral to a central place in the classroom. The classroom teacher and the arts specialist work together in making the former increasingly autonomous and self-dependent in arts education. Teaching the arts and infusing all other subjects with the arts becomes part of the repertoire of classroom teachers. A constituency for the arts is built inside of the schools.

Finally, let me say that Jane Remer's book is one of the few case studies available to us for increasing our understanding of processes of school improvement through a vehicle that itself is indigenous, not foreign, to schools. The arts for schools have been articulated and legitimated by all fifty states. But rhetoric is not enough. The strategies described in this book can help convert rhetoric to practice. But, more, they can help schools and school districts engage in that reconstruction of schooling that many of us are convinced is necessary to the very preservation of our unique society.

John I. Goodlad

Acknowledgments

I would like to thank ACA and its president, Milton Rhodes, for their support of this project, and I am grateful to the Ahmanson Foundation for its grant toward production expenses. I particularly want to thank ACA's publishing director, Robert Porter, who gave me invaluable feedback along the way. His thoughtful and persistent questioning of several of my assumptions helped me to sharpen and focus my thinking and my writing. It has been rewarding, too, to work with David Bosca, Lisa Parr and Doug Rose in the research, editing and production process.

I am indebted to ACA's former arts in education director John McLaughlin, who believed in the need for this second, revised edition. John and several of my colleagues, including Junius Eddy, Charles Fowler, Harlan (Rip) Hoffa, and Lonna Jones, supplied me with some important reactions to and information for the arts in education chronology. Junius and Rip, in particular, provided tremendous support when my energy and experiential knowledge base flagged.

My thanks also go to the Exxon Education Foundation, the JDR 3rd Fund and the New York Foundation for the Arts for their financial and administrative support of the first edition of this book. My gratitude extends to Ted Berger, Edythe Gaines, John Goodlad, members of the League of Cities and a host of friends and other colleagues in the field. I will always feel obliged to Tom Quinn, my editor at McGraw-Hill, who instantly recognized the potential value of the original version of the book in 1979.

Setting the Stage

BUILDING ON THE POWER OF
A PROMISING IDEA: ALL THE ARTS FOR
ALL GOD'S CHILDREN

We need to expose all of the children in our schools to all of the arts, and to do so in a way that enriches the general curriculum rather than reinforcing the segregation of the arts.

John D. Rockefeller 3rd

All the arts for all God's children, not just the privileged few. It was original-ly Mr. Rockefeller's idea. It has since become a cause, a rallying cry for a growing number of people who have converted this idea into comprehen-sive arts in general education programs. These people recognize the value of the arts for their own sake and for their usefulness as tools for teaching and learning. They also understand the catalytic effect the arts can have in the complex process of school change and development. The ranks of these people include chief school administrators, school board members, principals, supervisors and classroom teachers. They also include arts specialists, guidance counselors, librarians, school aides, parents and community volunteers—not to mention artists, arts administrators, college professors and university deans. And of course, there are always the children.

This book is about people. It tries to account for the promise that a powerful idea held for them. This promise—the arts as content and metaphor for learning and as catalysts for improving the school climate and environment—somehow galvanized them into collaborative action, compelled them to work in concert and inspired them to convert abstract theory into concrete programs with comprehensive goals.

I have based much of the book on my recent experience with Project Arts Connection in New Orleans and on the individual and collective experience of six diverse urban school districts known as the League of Cities for the Arts in Education, whose membership included Hartford, Little Rock, Minneapolis, New York City, Seattle and Winston-Salem. I will describe and analyze a somewhat unorthodox educational effort that began in 1973 under the auspices of the John D. Rockefeller 3rd (JDR 3rd) Fund's Arts in Education Program, which was founded in 1967. I will document the origin of the idea of school development through the arts and briefly examine its latest manifestation in New Orleans. I will trace the history of the League, set forth and define the components of AGE (arts in general education) programs and describe the main strategies devised or discovered to translate theory into daily practice. I will also identify some of the problems encountered, discuss some of the lessons learned and suggest areas for further study and action.

I write the book from my perspective as a practicing professional and an investigative reporter with a professed bias. For the record, however, I do not claim that this approach to the arts in education is the only one around, nor do I think it has a "corner on the market." I do not even believe it is the easiest way to go. But I am convinced that it works—under certain conditions. It is based on the belief that schools and the people in them, especially principals and teachers, are capable of defining their own educational philosophy and shaping their own destiny. Since they are held responsible for the consequences, they should have a say and, therefore, a stake in the action. Grassroots involvement in planning, execution and assessment of programs is key. So are networking, collaboration and continuing rounds of negotiation and consensus in the decision-making process.

School development is not an altogether new idea, and the arts are no strangers in the education of the young. What *is* new is that the League recognized and now others are accepting the fact that the arts—all of them—can play an animating and liberating role in helping school people to help themselves. They have found that when they choose the arts as the focus for change, they are challengedto create more elastic structures in which they have the freedom to take chances, to be different, to find new ways to solve old problems. And they have found that through networking and collaboration at the national and local levels, they can meet some of their very basic human and professional needs and find the necessary security and support as they take the risks to change.

What is also new is that League programs and Project Arts Connection offer tangible proof of the flexibility and adaptability of the model process the participants themselves helped to invent. While they all have certain basic elements in common, the programs actually represent several unique variations on a theme. They were designed in light of local conditions and constraints and reflect the important differences of size, structure, geographic location, socio-economic-ethnic mix and historical and cultural tradition. They offer at least seven examples for study and many options from which to choose, either in whole or in part.

What is perhaps most significant is that League programs managed to wed the content of the arts and the school development process to broader educational and social purposes. By so doing, they devised strategies for strengthening the school system itself and improving its image and relationship with the general community. In these days of austerity budgets, social unrest and harsh attacks from some quarters on public schooling, that is no mean feat.

THE ORIGINAL PURPOSE OF THIS BOOK

When the Fund's Arts in Education Program ended in August 1979, the League experiment was just beginning to yield promising results. I realized then that if I did not try to document our work, we might never be able to share our experience with a wider audience. With the encouragement and backing of the Exxon Education Foundation, the JDR 3rd Fund, the New York Foundation for the Arts, and League members, I decided to write a book which would:

— set the record straight about the contribution made by the League, the Fund and many others to the idea of school change and development through the arts

— pay tribute to some of the major and seminal thinkers, dreamers and doers in the field

— be specific about some of the "how to's," providing a comprehensive framework for program planning along with a

variety of field-tested guidelines, criteria and some interpretative generalizations about lessons learned
— strike a blow in defense of the American system of universal
public education, compulsory notwithstanding, because it has
been maligned for decades mostly by those who do not understand it, work with it or send their children to its schools

THE PURPOSE OF
THIS BOOK—TODAY

Ten years ago, I wanted it all. So did JDR 3rd Fund Arts in Education Program Director Kathryn Bloom and my colleagues in the League of Cities for
the Arts in Education. We wanted *all* the arts, for *all* the children in *entire*
school systems, *nationally*. We knew we had an emerging model for changing schools through the arts, but we never had a chance to prove it conclusively. John D. Rockefeller's death in 1978, the termination of our program the following year and our inability to interest another institution to
act as a sponsor or coordinating hub caused the League's collapse in 1980,
four years after it was formed.

Ten years ago, my statements, assertions and interpretations of the
facts could have been corroborated, questioned or refuted by visits to
League sites, observations of programs under way and discussions with
the people involved. Today, I can refer you to New Orleans.

Today, there are individual schools, cultural institutions and arts agencies that are still committed to the arts in education philosophy, but there
is little evidence of the original, comprehensive district-based programs in
the six cities. Few of the original foot soldiers and leaders are still active.
Some people, such as Kathy Bloom, have died, many have retired, others
have moved on to different jobs in unrelated fields.

With the League's original demonstration base all but gone, you may
wonder why I chose to spend the time and effort on a revised and expanded edition of this book. The persuasive proof, after all, was supposed
to be in the pudding. Since none of the original programs appear to be
going strong today, why not write off the whole effort as a short-lived success but an ultimate failure. Before proceeding with my reasons for the update, I will address this issue of program attrition.

The JDR 3rd Fund's Arts in Education Program was essentially a research and development effort that was carefully documented and disseminated over a twelve-year period. We launched and supported many collaborative projects that were designed to explore and demonstrate the
feasibility of the varied and complex aspects of comprehensive arts in

education programs. Mr. Rockefeller felt it was our responsibility to spread the word about what did and did not work to a large and growing audience of educators and arts professionals.

The League was one—and a significant one—in a developmental series of these carefully-designed, labor-intensive (from the Fund's point of view) experiments. Together with our educational colleagues, we were conceptualizing, planning, developing and field-testing a model process, a prototype from which we hoped that we and many others could learn some valuable lessons from our mistakes as well as our successes. If projects and programs continued on their own following the research and development phase, as many of them did, that was a welcome but secondary bonus. Our job was to work with others and help them set up and demonstrate the value of an idea. Once this job was done, we knew from history and our own experience that it was the local community's responsibility to nurture and maintain the effort it had presumably learned to appreciate as a result of being engaged in the process.

The League's arts in general education programs, like most innovative efforts that depart from the accepted norm, depended on the vision, courage and stamina of a group of unusual people in leadership and decision-making positions who decided or were persuaded, for whatever reason, to make the arts a priority in their lives and their work. These people rarely stayed put longer than two or three years; the turnover of superintendents, curriculum supervisors, principals and teachers was constant and often staggering. The instability in the arts community was no less astonishing.

These programs also depended on the JDR 3rd Fund's staff acting in the capacity that John Goodlad and other scholars in the field have labeled "the alternative drummer" for educational change. Again and again, one or more of our staff was summoned to rescue a program in mortal jeopardy. Under the impressive banner of the Rockefeller name, we were able to get the attention of newly-motivated superintendents and school boards and convince them of the value of the arts. We helped district personnel fight off devastating budget cuts, tax-levy defeats, shifts of principals and teacher layoffs. We were also able to shore up the morale and determination of what is known in education parlance as the "infrastructure"—the shock troops and the foot soldiers, without whom no program exits. When the Fund disappeared and the essential core of movers and shakers in each site eventually dwindled to a precious few, programs faltered and ultimately faded away.

There are many lessons to be learned from this, among them that networks cannot survive without a hub, and the role of the external change agent is delicate but critical. Another important finding is that popular enthusiasm, backed by hard dollars, for the arts in education and a lasting commitment to the idea of comprehensive school development through the arts are scarce and fragile commodities. They are hard to come by and even harder to keep intact. To the extent that innovative efforts such as these are dependent on the right people being in the right place at the right time, they can perhaps never be fully institutionalized.

In addition to the original impetus for the book, there are other reasons for the revision, even though (or perhaps precisely because) the League no longer exists:

— The League's planning and development process was as important as the product, and it has proved replicable. The New Orleans school district, using the first edition of this book as a guide, built its impressive Project Arts Connection on the League model.

— The experience of the League and the lessons learned have had a profound influence on federal, state and local legislation, language and program design. The guidelines, criteria and strategies in the original book are still widely used. The rationale, the definitions and the various checklists are referred to regularly. And, in the intervening ten years, I have developed and field-tested a significant amount of new material that expands on and amplifies the original processes and approaches.

— The original text is in wide use around the country in school districts, colleges, universities, arts organizations, cultural agencies and the like. I use it regularly in my own consulting work. Several of my colleagues complained to me when they discovered it was out of print and no longer available.

— There is a whole new generation of arts in education professionals in the field who deserve to know about and be able to use our experience in their work. They should be able to learn from the history of the field and not be unwittingly condemned to repeat its mistakes.

I also believe it is important to place the League's work in the context of American educational history, especially now that school-based management teams, the linchpin of our arts in general education (AGE) strategy for school development through the arts, are back in vogue in cities such as Pittsburgh, Rochester, Seattle, Toledo, Miami and New York. I have come to believe that if you promote a good idea (before its time), and you live long enough, you may come back into fashion.

Of course, school-based management wasn't original with the League. It is based on the populist notion of decentralization of bureaucratic power that can be found throughout the reform literature of the sixties and early seventies. Both Edythe Gaines and John Goodlad considered it an excellent strategy for broadening and strengthening the base of local power and control to include teachers and parents in the decision-making process. They also believed, as I did, that it would improve school climate, governance, operation and accountability. We never for a moment claimed that restructuring, by itself, or even school change through the arts would directly affect basic skills or improve standardized achievement test scores.

In any case, I am glad to see school-based management and local community control as an idea whose time has come, again. Perhaps it will make the AGE school development approach more appealing to educators, arts professionals and parents since we are, once more, in step with the current pedagogical party line.

PLUS ÇA CHANGE. . .

I had other reasons for updating the book. It gave me a chance to look back over the decade to see what, if anything, had happened in the field that directly affected all the arts and all the children. Notwithstanding the emergence of the Getty Center for Education in the Arts, with its focus on the visual arts, and all the rhetoric of enlightenment and reform, I have come to the conclusion that there has been little systematic, systemic change in arts education that has taken root behind the classroom door. John Goodlad, professor and director of the Center for Educational Renewal at the University of Washington, apparently agrees. In a recent letter to me he wrote:

> The circumstances requiring attention to the arts in schools probably are worse today than when you and your associates in the Fund were doing your good work. The governors' slogan, 'Better Schools Mean Better Jobs,' does not leave much room for the arts. I would say that the situation has declined, particularly in middle to upper middle class school districts where parents are so geared to achievement test scores and getting their children into the best colleges and universities. . . . In brief, there clearly is a need for [an updated version of] your book.

A quick glance at my bookshelves and my files gives the deceptively comforting appearance of significant activity in the arts in education field since 1979. By my count there are at least eight task force reports and studies, several books, a monograph series, about half a dozen national or regional conference reports and a magazine devoted exclusively to the discussion of current topics and events. Mixed in with the material on the arts are national studies on schooling and reform. With the exception of Goodlad's work, not one of the documents calling for school reform contains the word "arts." The recent meeting of the nation's governors with

President Bush is no exception: the national agenda proposed covers a great deal of territory; it is silent about the arts.

In some respects, we are dealing with a *status quo ante*. Our schools mirror society and its ills, but we still expect them to solve problems of great magnitude that are not of their making. Crime, drugs, AIDS, teen-age pregnancy, the alienation of the poor "underclass" and the racist perceptions of a have/have-not world produce an uneasy climate for schooling. They certainly do not provide a receptive environment for the arts. Actually, apart from the brief Kennedy-Johnson era of relative optimism and plenty in the sixties, followed by a more conservative but still abundant seventies, we have returned to the more typical national *modus operandi* in which other social and political problems always seem more pressing and there is never enough money for the arts.

Ten years has not changed American attitudes about the fundamental value of the arts to our society or to our schools. Consider the following remarks made by former NEA Chairman Frank Hodsoll, who was an arts in education champion, and you will discover just how un-American the arts really are unless they can ultimately be defended in terms of a patriotic strategy for the nation's economic and political survival:

> Why, one could ask. Why have we done this [broaden the Arts in Education Program and make education one of the principal areas of the NEA's large grant and multiple match Challenge Program]? Because we believe that the arts that the Endowment supports—virtually all of our cultural heritage and most contemporary expression—should be a part of the lives of all Americans. . . . By telling us about the civilization of America and the civilizations that have contributed to America, these arts tell us about what it is to be an American. And if we have a more profound sense of what it is to be an American, *we will be better enabled to compete with other nations as Americans—politically and economically as well as culturally.*[1] [Italics mine.]

If Frank Hodsoll, who did so much for the arts in education during his tenure at the Endowment, felt compelled to speak of the arts in these terms, is it any wonder that they still struggle in vain for an unencumbered place in the sun on the American free enterprise landscape? Do we really need further proof that even in the corridors of American arts leadership and cultural influence, the arts are still not valued for their own intrinsic

---

[1] From the transcript of the speech delivered at the National Arts Education Research Center at New York University/IBM Corporation Conference in New York City, November 28, 1988.

sake but are prized only to the degree to which they facilitate the achievement of other utilitarian social, economic or political ends?

THE PRIMARY LESSON I HAVE LEARNED:
GET THE ARTS IN—
ANY WHICH WAY YOU CAN

These days, the vision of school change through the arts informs much of my work, but it has receded into the background. Instead, I find myself having to go back to "arts basics." I have begun to say, again and again, that since there is precious little quality arts activity of *any* type—never mind scope, sequence, history, aesthetics and criticism—to be found in the vast majority of our public schools, we had better concentrate all our energies on getting them there, any of them, in any order, for as long as possible, *any which way we can.*

The recent tendency of some state arts agencies and other granting organizations to denigrate (and categorically refuse to fund) programs that feature "mere exposure" to outstanding artists, performances and exhibits is most unfortunate. Since when and by what reasoning has the impact of first-rate artists and art works on young and old been deemed trivial or inconsequential?

There is another lesson that I have learned in the last decade: we are better off looking at the arts in education ideal as an upward-spiraling continuum rather than a linear scope and sequence curriculum. Using the continuum metaphor, exposure takes its rightful place somewhere on the developmental timeline that acts in this case as a check on those who, in their zeal, have a tendency to throw the baby out with the bath water. In addition, from this perspective, the ideal is less daunting because it becomes the cumulative result of a comprehensive series of related arts instructional activities, experiences and events —both in and out of school— that includes exposure to the arts as well as study of the history of various art forms, performance, production and creation.

In my definition, comprehensive means all-inclusive. It also implies balance—of kinds of activities, experiential approaches, instructional methods, ranges of art forms, types of instructors, ethnicity, cultural values and the like.

ONCE MORE, DEAR FRIENDS, INTO THE FRAY

To prepare for this edition, I designed and sent out a questionnaire to over one hundred colleagues in the field, including members of the League of Cities. I hoped to get a variety of perspectives on the last ten years and information about the status of various arts in education efforts. The results of this survey are summarized in the Appendix. I also talked with or interviewed several people, read or re-read major books, pamphlets, reports and studies that have been published since 1977, and went to New Orleans and Baton Rouge, Louisiana to gather information on Project Arts Connection, the latest variation on the League's theme.

I have done some major surgery on the sequence of chapters in the original edition and a fair amount of new writing, especially of the how-to-do-it variety throughout the book. I have combined, reordered, retitled and reworked several of the original chapters. New material includes most of this chapter, the conclusion (which contains the Louisiana story and some of their program guidelines), and the chapter entitled "Who Shall Teach the Arts?" This last expands the original text about the role and prospects for arts specialists, classroom teachers and artists and adds guidelines, checklists and frameworks for planning AGE programs. Also new, and for what I believe to be the first time anywhere, is an interpretive chronology of selected key events and landmarks in the arts education field over the last fifty or so years. This, too, can be found in the Appendix, which has been completely revised.

A decade later, I still feel we are outnumbered and overwhelmed by as large a margin of legitimate competing forces and rival issues as I believed we were at the beginning of the eighties. Glasnost and perestroika have diminished the international threat, but we now face domestic social, economic and health issues of monumental proportions. As bad as I thought the budget crunch was for the arts ten years ago, it has worsened considerably, especially under the current leadership at the U.S. Department of Education. From the hundreds of millions spent on the arts in the sixties, down to the tens of millions dispensed in the next ten years, the DOE's current expenditures are now reduced to a comparative trickle.

Summing up, I think it is a tribute to the obstinacy and tenaciousness of the field that the arts in general education movement has survived the conservative eighties. I think we just need to keep on keeping on, and I hope this book helps along the way.

And now, once more, dear friends, into the fray.

BELLING THE CAT: WHAT IS AGE?

AGE is a concept, an instructional framework and a psychological contract.

Paul Hoerlein, Administrator
Seattle Public Schools

If I could tell you what I mean, there would be no point in dancing.

Isadora Duncan

A decade ago, people asked me for a one-line definition of AGE, the acronym for the League's approach to comprehensive arts in general education programs. They insisted they knew more about what it was not than what it was. Many, especially those of us who have been busy doing it for nearly two decades, are still stumped for an easy answer. Ask ten different principals, for example, and you'll get ten different responses. To say that it stands for an arts in general education program that has a set of guidelines and criteria for planning and development is accurate, but it begs the question. To add that it proceeds from the belief that the arts are basic to a quality education and that ideally all children should experience all of them is fine, but still vague and wordy. It is time to try to bell the cat.

AGE is not a finite body of knowledge, a discrete discipline or a subject such as aesthetic education. It is not contained in one textbook or packaged neatly in a box of instructional materials. It is not one thirty-hour in-service course or a unit to be followed in a teacher's guide, with the correct answers at the back. It is not a curriculum bulletin, an artist residency, or a "hands-on" workshop experience. It is not a course of study available at a discount from your local bookstore. AGE is, or can be composed of, all the above. The beauty of AGE is that it has certain basic ingredients, but the scope, sequence, instructional methodology—the entire program design—is up to you.

Underlying the AGE approach is a concept, a philosophy, a way of looking at schooling and the arts that alters the standard patterns for teaching and learning. It is an attitude, a set of ideas, a process and a program. It goes by many names, such as Arts for Learning, Arts in the Basic Curriculum and Arts in Basic Education, but it has certain common qualities, elements and characteristics, all of which are covered in this book.

AGE is a collaborative effort that relies on networking. It means that people plan and work together, share ideas, information and resources and make connections. It is a holistic or comprehensive way of dealing with a school and its community by studying the institution's structure and operation and figuring out how the arts, artists and other arts providers can become more prominent, more pervasive and more useful in the education of the young.

Paradoxically, the notion of AGE is populist, purist and pragmatic. It combines the notion of all the arts for everyone with the conviction that the arts have value for their own sake as well as for reaching other desirable ends. But AGE is primarily a grassroots approach. It focuses on schools, classrooms, principals, teachers, artists and students. It provides people in the schools with a way of re-examining educational truisms, tradition and practice. It also offers school people and those who work with them another route to self-renewal because the arts stimulate and nurture insight, creativity, pride and a sense of joy. And because the arts can be fun, AGE contributes to a climate of spontaneity and gives people a sense of comfort and well-being.

AGE, then, is fundamentally a way for schools to develop or change through the arts. But in AGE, unlike some school improvement efforts, the principals, teachers and parents in the schools work together to plan and bring about the changes they consider necessary and appropriate. It is not imposed from the top down by a faceless and remote bureaucracy.

So as not to leave you completely bewildered and adrift in a sea of abstractions, I offer you my most recent attempt at a one-line description of AGE, a new rationale for the arts in general education, and an operational definition of the four modes of instruction in AGE programs, which I recently prepared for a New York City task force on arts in education policy and practice.

AGE *is* a long-range process that unites the concept of local school governance with a comprehensive developmental program that offers first-rate, regular, school and community-based teaching and learning experiences in all the arts for all the children, kindergarten through high school.

A RATIONALE FOR
THE ARTS IN GENERAL EDUCATION

The place of the arts in education should need no justification. They are invigorating, life-giving, healing. They express our thoughts and feelings. They are nourishment for the spirit and the intellect. But since the arts do need defending behind the classroom door and in the school corridors, here are some practical reasons for the arts in the school program:

The arts are useful for the education of all children because they

— are valuable and valid for their own sake (pure arts)
— illuminate other art forms (interarts)

— illuminate other subject areas and are illuminated by them (interdisciplinary)
— bring the community's cultural resources into the classroom (linkages)
— bring the students, their teachers and their parents out into the community (linkages)
— involve parents and guardians in school governance and volunteer activities
— identify, respond to and serve the needs of special populations (gifted, talented, handicapped, etc.)
— provide a means, a common ground to break down racial stereotypes, barriers and prejudices (multiculturalism, diversity)
— provide the impetus and the content for positive changes in teaching and learning (curriculum and staff development)
— act as catalysts for comprehensive schoolwide improvement

My current operational definition of the arts in education is essentially a restatement of the comprehensive definition that appears throughout this book, but I am now more explicit about the concept of "infusion."

AN OPERATIONAL DEFINITION OF THE ARTS IN EDUCATION

The Four Modes of Instruction in Comprehensive Arts in General Education Programs

ARTS FOR ARTS' SAKE: study of, about, and in the individual disciplines, including but not limited to music, visual arts, drama, dance, creative writing, poetry, film, video, architecture, etc.

ARTS AT THE SERVICE OF OTHER STUDIES: arts concepts, ideas, themes, material, strategies and processes introduced or integrated into the study of other (primary focus) disciplines serving to illuminate and reinforce other concepts, themes and ideas

OTHER STUDIES AT THE SERVICE OF THE ARTS: educational concepts, ideas, material strategies and methodologies from other disciplines introduced or integrated into the study of one or several art forms

ARTS AS AN EQUAL PARTNER IN A HOLISTIC, HUMANITIES/GLOBAL EDUCATION OR MULTICULTURAL APPROACH: the arts relate to or correlate with the study of other topics, trends, movements in world history; as such they inform and are informed by this larger context

While definitions are useful, this is probably a case where seeing is only partly responsible for believing because AGE can be even more intangible—an atmosphere, an attitude, a state of mind. As John Dewey maintained, it is the doing that leads to complete understanding and the active engagement in the process, over time, that builds confidence, mastery and, finally, the conviction that comes with ownership.

So perhaps, although a completely satisfying one-liner still eludes me, I had to write this book and then revise it ten years later because I have some concrete guidelines and criteria to offer you as guidance for building your own AGE programs. I also feel I need to lay out the process for you to study and use, if you choose, because you can trust it; I have culled it from the experience of school people, arts administrators, artists and others who were, and still are, "in the trenches."

I now know, thanks to Project Arts Connection in the New Orleans Public Schools, that the AGE concept can stand the test of time. I also know that John D. Rockefeller 3rd, Kathryn Bloom and Edythe Gaines always insisted that we try to spread the word to as many people as possible. In the spirit of that tradition, I offer you this book as a guide and reference.

From Rhetoric to Reality

SIX SCHOOL DISTRICTS BUILD A MODEL FOR CHANGE THROUGH THE ARTS

NEW YORK CITY: BIRTHPLACE OF THE CONCEPT OF SCHOOL DEVELOPMENT THROUGH THE ARTS

Balancing the Equation: Edythe Gaines and the Learning Cooperative

In the fall of 1972, I joined the New York City Public School's Learning Cooperative. Having worked for so many years outside the system in, for example, Young Audiences and the Lincoln Center Education Department, I knew it was time to learn more about schooling from the inside. I also wanted to discover some solutions to the stubbornly persistent and often frustrating problems that confronted artists and educators when they tried to work together.

My job at the "Coop" was to design and coordinate an Urban Resources Linkage Prototype. Translated, that meant I was to invent ways for teachers to use the historic sites and resources of the financial, business and cultural institutions clustered around Federal Hall in Lower Manhattan.

In addition, I served as a special assistant on the arts to the Coop's director, Dr. Edythe J. Gaines, a dynamic and visionary educator who had come up through the ranks as teacher, principal and community superintendent and had developed a well-deserved reputation as an innovator and a strong advocate for the arts.[1]

I credit Edythe, her executive assistant, Nola Whiteman, Ed Rubin, and the rest of the small, devoted Coop staff with giving me an insight into the practical, political and bureaucratic aspects of public education that no textbook or university could ever hope to duplicate. In the crucible of the Coop we learned the difference between "glamour stock," "scatter-shot" approaches and those that, when sound and sustained, could make a positive contribution to schooling. We learned about the art of creative money management in a sprawling public institution that is essentially labor intensive with little discretionary leeway. We also learned tolerance and respect for minority or dissenting opinions and how to achieve collaboration, if not harmony, through negotiation and consensus. Our mission was to serve the field, not individual egos, and the bottom line—the acid test—was the benefit to children.

AGE was the product of a marriage of like minds and spirits in the JDR 3rd Fund's Arts in Education Program and the Coop, both of which no longer exist. The Fund's history and legacy have been amply documented in *An Arts in Education Source Book: A View from the JDR 3rd Fund* (New York, 1980). The Coop's contribution to the concept of constructive school change and development through the arts deserves attention here.

---

[1] Edythe Gaines considered the arts as basics and made them a priority throughout her distinguished career as a teacher, a principal of a junior high school on Manhattan's Upper West Side and a community superintendent in the Bronx. At the Learning Coop, she set up an arts and culture linkage prototype and raised money to support its operation. She made sure that every citywide conference or major event sponsored by the Coop featured the arts. When she moved to the Board of Education as the head of the Division of Planning and Support (Curriculum and Instruction), the AGE program partnership with the JDR 3rd Fund prompted her and Chancellor Irving Anker to declare the arts a priority in New York City education, for the first time in the city's history. Her successor, Arnold Webb, continued the strong commitment to the arts and became an active participant in the AGE program and the League of Cities. Since then, except for a brief period under one of several succeeding chancellors, no chancellor and no one responsible for curriculum and instruction at the Board of Education has designated the arts a system-wide priority. Furthermore, as of this writing (June 1990) the central board has phased out its support for the AGE program; it remains to be seen what action the new chancellor will take.

Solving the Problem of "Bigness": Networking and Collaboration

The Learning Cooperative was established in 1971 as an arm of Chancellor Harvey Scribner's office. Supported by modest public and private funds, its official function was to facilitate school decentralization by acting as a "switching station" that provided services to the field. Part of its mandate was to identify successful programs and help foster innovative efforts by bringing together various educational, cultural, municipal, business and private groups "to recreate excellence in the city's public schools."

New York is not just another urban center but another country, and the Coop's charge was immense. Its task was to serve, directly or indirectly, over nine hundred schools, more than one million students and approximately sixty thousand teachers and supervisors. The job was further complicated by the newly organized system of dual governance that placed responsibility for the senior high schools and certain special services at the Central Board; responsibility for the elementary, intermediate and junior high schools was distributed in thirty-two quasi-independent community school districts located throughout the five boroughs.

Faced with the question of how a small group of professionals could take on the whole system, the staff proposed that the Coop consider itself the hub of several separate but functionally-related networks. To solve the problem of "bigness," smaller compatible groups would be identified, organized and linked together with appropriate community resources and provided with consulting, technical and fundraising assistance. In addition, a few program prototypes would be designed to field-test new ideas, and results would be shared with practitioners and the community at citywide dissemination conferences. Demonstration and other exemplary programs and practices would be documented and made available for inspection to the field.

Design for Change: The Arts in General Education (AGE) Manifesto

"Design for Change," a special supplement to the New York City Public Schools' staff bulletin (May 15,1972) is a relatively little-known four-page document that describes the mission of the Coop and outlines the concepts of total school development and comprehensive system-wide change. "Design for Change" provided the conceptual framework for the Urban Resources Program and later became the "manifesto" for AGE. The League of Cities adopted and refined its main ideas. Its influence now extends to other school districts and state education departments that have unwittingly absorbed some of the basic principles into their own arts in education programs.

"Design for Change," although cooperatively authored, was essentially Edythe Gaines' brainchild. The following summarizes the core of its philosophy:

The new educational system is a network of interrelated and interacting component parts of which the core school is a key part. The core school is one in which a pupil is enrolled and accounted for, where he spends a significant amount of time, where he is assisted with "brokering" the other parts of the education network and where he is provided with certain foundational learning (e.g., basic literacy).

Key concepts in this document were program prototypes, demonstration ("beacon light") schools, networks, linkages between schools and the community's resources, an on-going leadership and staff development effort, an information and feedback system and citywide dissemination conferences. Underlying these concepts was Edythe's strong belief in individualized and humanized education, choice of teaching and learning style and environment and education as an integrative process. Parent and community involvement in schooling was considered a strategy for increasing public support and broadening the range of instructional opportunities for students and teachers.

"Design for Change" did not try to prescribe specific programs, educational support services or even a master strategy for system-wide overhaul. It presented an interactive framework with a progressive credo that redefined education as a matter of choice, process and individual style. It regarded the school as a center of teaching and learning with dynamic linkages to other schools and the general community. The individual was to use the system and the community as a resource, and success was to be measured by comparing a student's achievement against his or her personal goals and prior abilities. The Coop staff hoped that practitioners would convert these abstract ideas and beliefs into effective practice. One central strategy, however, was spelled out:

Change is never comfortable and therefore is rarely welcomed. Quite the contrary. Usually it is resisted either overtly or covertly. Consequently, change will not occur unless it is deliberately planned for. We plan to include in each program or proposal a specific mechanism whose function it is to set in motion a specific set of strategies by which the changes we are aiming for are likely to be brought about . . . . That is the revolution we seek!

"All the Arts for All the Children": A Joint Venture between the New York City Public Schools and the JDR 3rd Fund

By June 1973, when I joined the Fund's Arts in Education Program, Edythe Gaines had become executive director of the school system's newly-formed Division of Educational Planning and Support, with the Learning Cooperative as its operational arm. Banking on her long-standing advocacy of the arts in education, Kathy Bloom and I proposed a collaborative project for the city's schools. Once we agreed on the general nature and purpose of our joint venture, Edythe asked me to prepare a position paper and a comprehensive plan of action.

I developed the plan for New York City in consultation with key personnel from the Central Board, the local school districts, the schools and the arts and cultural community. I incorporated the basic principles of "Design for Change" and built on the important lessons Kathy and her staff had learned during the Fund's six-year experience with comprehensive and smaller-scale pilot projects all over the country. I also took into account the Fund's pioneering work with the Bank Street College of Education and a few of the city's elementary schools, notably P.S. 51 and P.S. 3 in Manhattan. Above all, the plan was designed to build on the strengths and, where possible, sidestep the limitations of the nation's largest school system. Somehow, we had to make the project work within the context of contemporary urban life: fiscal crises, racial and ethnic diversity, union power and a complex set of bureaucratic agencies and procedures.

The plan laid out the goals, characteristics and processes for school development through the arts (see Exhibit 1). It did not prescribe a specific instructional program, a curriculum development or teacher-training effort. It promised no large amounts of incentive money. The participants were expected to develop their own school programs by allocating existing resources. We were planning to rely heavily on networking and collaboration as strategies to furnish answers to questions about program content, design and implementation.

Toward that end, I assembled and prepared new materials that included:

— a rationale for the arts in general education
— a description of the characteristics of effective arts in general education programs at the school and district levels
— criteria for elementary and secondary school participation in the program and guidelines for the selection process
— criteria for the effective use of cultural resources and artists in the schools and the community
— strategies for the formation of a network of demonstration, cooperating and consultative schools
— a general description of the school development process
— a definition of the roles, functions and responsibilities of all participants
— a statement that the main source of funds for the program would come from existing central and local school budgets (Instead of a major grant, the Fund's main contribution

would be to provide technical, consulting and management assistance and small amounts of seed money for planning and development. Although the plan operated on the theory of a zero-based budget at the outset, a substantial amount of school district and outside funds for planning, leadership training, staff development and artist services were quickly secured.)

Although the program was to be launched in a relatively few schools in largely uncharted waters, we hoped that in time an arts in general education school-development prototype (in other words, a model process) would emerge that could apply to many local schools and school districts and perhaps to other school systems around the country.

This was not the first collaboration for the Fund but it was the first working partnership. Kathy Bloom had already joined forces on ambitious projects with the school systems in University City, Missouri and Jefferson County, Colorado, for example. In both cases, the Fund had made major grants over several years supported by technical and consulting assistance from the fund's staff. The New York City AGE approach was unusual because Edythe Gaines refused to accept any major grant money. She was determined to join the Fund as a senior partner in what would amount to a major research and development effort, to determine whether and how the arts could become the organizing principle and catalysts for overall school improvement.

The Coop's Beacon Light School network had deliberately left the choice of the philosophical goal, the instructional focus and the strategies for achieving them up to each school. In the arts in general education program the instructional framework made the goal explicit: "all the arts for all the children." Superintendents, principals, staff, union representatives, parents and student leaders who wished to work together toward this end were encouraged to stand up and declare themselves.

Unusual Aspects of
The New York City Schools/
JDR 3rd Fund AGE Program Partnership

While a review of the original position papers, working documents and rationale for New York City's AGE program reveals the important legacy of the Fund's prior experience, the New York City program marked a turning point because it was unique in several significant ways:

1. For the first time, the Fund and a major urban school system officially agreed to become partners in the planning and development of a comprehensive arts in general education program. This partnership was established through an

E X H I B I T 1 _____

THE ARTS IN GENERAL EDUCATION: THE GOAL, THE FIVE MAIN CHARACTERISTICS, THE CHANGE THEORY AND THE PROCESS

THE GOAL OF ARTS IN GENERAL EDUCATION PROGRAM is found in its program subtitle, "All the Arts for All the Children." Defined more specifically in the original plan, it was "to improve the quality of education for all children by incorporating all the arts into the daily teaching and learning process . . . ."

THE FIVE MAIN CHARACTERISTICS OF AN ARTS IN GENERAL EDUCATION PROGRAM that were to be translated into comprehensive programs and instructional activities were spelled out:

— High-quality, continuous instruction in various aspects of each art form for all students at all grade levels

— Interdisciplinary teaching and learning opportunities in which the arts are related to each other and to other areas of the curriculum

— Programs and services that make effective use of the community's artists, arts and cultural resources, in and out of school

— Programs in the arts for children with special needs (e.g., the gifted and talented, the handicapped, the educationally disadvantaged, the multilingual)

— Programs in the arts using the services of artists and arts organizations to reduce the damaging effects of personal and racial isolation

THE THEORY FOR SCHOOL CHANGE AND DEVELOPMENT THROUGH THE ARTS AND THE PROCESS BY WHICH THE SYSTEM WAS TO HELP BRING IT ABOUT WAS SUMMARIZED:

— The individual school is the most efficient, manageable and logical social unit for educational change.

- Individual principals are the educational as well as the administrative leaders of their school communities. They can effect positive changes in schooling by regularly involving supervisors, teachers, parents and students in the decision-making process and the implementation of school programs.
- School planning committees provide an effective vehicle for local management of arts in general education programs and generate ownership, practice in the decision-making process and administrator and teacher satisfaction.
- Change is difficult, especially if the alternatives proposed deviate substantially from the prevailing norm. Thus, schools cannot and should not go this route alone since they need the support of other schools, the community district, the central board and other public and private agencies and organizations outside the school system.
- All schools in the system are told of a new program opportunity, given guidelines and criteria for participation and invited to submit proposals. Screening committees review proposals, visit schools and gather relevant information. Schools are ranked and selected for participation based primarily on broad school-community commitment to program purpose and the actual or potential ability to carry out program intent.
- Citywide and/or districtwide networks of "like-minded" schools form for mutual support, problem solving and the sharing of information and resources.

— These networks of principals, supervisors and teachers are coordinated by a "hub" or management team that provides technical and consulting assistance, orchestrates support services and identifies and secures the human, financial and physical resources that the schools have determined are essential to progress.

— Over time, these networks serve as tangible demonstrations of a particular idea or concept translated into effective practice. They provide a talent bank of authentic resource professionals and a source from which information about their experience in leadership training, staff, curriculum and child development, school reorganization, community relations and fundraising can be captured and shared with a wider audience.

— Ideally, demonstration networks increase their membership so that they become large enough to notice but still small enough to manage. Members also participate in other coalitions that have similar purposes or help form affiliated networks that establish functional relationships with the core group and its hub.

— Expansion of the original network and linkages with others eventually create a "critical mass" of schools that inspire and help still more schools follow their example. Given the right encouragement, recognition and support, a significant number of schools in a system will improve the nature and quality of educational opportunities they provide for all their students.

exchange of correspondence that clearly defined commitments, roles and functions.

2. Defying philanthropic tradition, the Fund made no major grant to the school district, nor did it mention any specific time frame for program implementation. Instead, it provided money for developmental activities (conferences, site visits, planning meetings, publications), provided technical and consulting assistance and participated actively in every phase of the program from conceptualization to the design of plans and strategies for management, implementation, documentation and dissemination. This was also the first time that a staff member of the Fund was authorized to participate in the day-to-day operation of a program from the beginning.

3. We were testing the hypothesis that the arts would somehow galvanize the process of total school development and result in better schooling for children and youth. We also wanted to discover whether and in what ways AGE schools could develop and improve themselves through networking—cooperating with other schools and with the support of an array of agencies, organizations and people within and outside the system.

4. In the Fund's earlier projects, the development of programs placed primary emphasis on teacher training, curriculum development and the involvement of artists and artist-teachers. In AGE, these were critical strategies for achieving the overarching goal of school development through the arts. By employing these strategies in a school whose principal exerted dynamic leadership as a member of a school-based planning team, we would be able to integrate the arts into the teaching and learning process and thereby alter the entire climate and operation of the school.

5. The most distinctive characteristic of the New York City AGE program was its emphasis on an organized approach to school change. Through the cost-effective strategies of networking and collaboration, the goal was to develop several prototypes for documentation, inspection and adoption by other schools and school districts.

Planning the Program: Comprehensive and Thorough

Planning for the arts in general education program began in July 1973. The joint venture was announced in May 1974; schools were identified by January 1975 and full-fledged activity in the schools began in 1975-76. A great many people had spent a year and a half on a variety of preparatory and training activities long before the program became operational and school-based. To be sure, the size and complexity of the school system contributed to the amount of time and energy consumed in the process, but so did the nature of the process itself. On the basis of experience, the aim was to use time as an agent in creating public awareness, involvement and support.

There were essentially three stages in the planning process. The first nine months involved drafting the position paper, designing the comprehensive plan and organizing a "project management team."

The second nine months concentrated on leadership-training activities and seminars for members of the Central Board and the Learning Cooperative; the development of guidelines and criteria for participation in the project; and the identification of schools and community resources. During this period, national consultants such as researcher John Goodlad, evaluator Robert Stake and CEMREL (Central Midwestern Regional Educational Laboratory) Aesthetic Education Program Director Stanley Madeja were among those who participated in "think tanks" at the Coop. Members of the Coop's staff also visited the CEMREL laboratory in St. Louis and JDR 3rd Fund project sites in University City, Missouri, and Oklahoma City, Oklahoma. Costs for consultant fees and expenses and site visits were underwritten by the Fund.

The next six months were devoted to school-staff orientation and organization of the network. During this period, the principals and AGE planning teams from each of the schools identified their needs and resources, decided on their program objectives and strategies for implementation and revised their budgets accordingly. Regular network meetings were held and representatives from the city's arts and cultural institutions were invited to help plan certain aspects of school programs.

Main Features of the School Identification Process

Recognizing the complexity and demands of the AGE program, we were often tempted to pick the principals we all thought we could count on as winners. AGE was, after all, a demonstration program, not a turn-around or compensatory effort, and we were under no obligation to satisfy federal guidelines or deal with standard bureaucratic red tape. After weighing all the pros and cons, however, we decided it would be wisest to "go public." We made a formal announcement of the program at the Central Board; we sent guidelines and criteria to all the schools in the city and invited them to submit brief "proposals" (which were actually declarations of intent). We held an orientation meeting for those who wanted more specifics about our plans.

Our reason for going public was that participation in this unusual venture, whether by school people, artists or other community representatives, should be voluntary, not by designation from superiors or outsiders. We also wanted assurance that the school was committed to the program's overall philosophy and purpose. We knew from the extensive experience that programs and expensive package deals imposed on schools rarely take root because they bypass the very people on whom "success" depends.

We based our final recommendations for the AGE school network and the classification of schools within that group on four main sources of information: simple written proposals and supporting materials; site visits to the schools; firsthand knowledge and experience of the project management team and an ad-hoc steering committee; and the advice from members of the teachers' unions, supervisors' organizations and others familiar with the schools and the program's objectives.

The Screening Process

The first step in the screening process was the review and ranking of the thirty-two written proposals that were submitted. The project management team and at least three members of the screening committee read each proposal, which was then checked against our guidelines and ranked on a prepared form listing the program criteria. We added written comments where appropriate and then transferred the "raw data" onto a profile sheet for each school.

Next, arrangements were made for members of the project management team and the screening committee to make site visits to those schools that met the project guidelines for "demonstration" status (elementary, intermediate or junior high schools in districts with more than one school applying). Since the "raw scores" for the proposals from all thirty-two schools were unusually high (none fell below the median level), we decided that single schools from a district or from the senior high school division would automatically be eligible for either "cooperating" or "consultative" status.

Checklists were prepared based on the same criteria used for proposal ranking for site visits. The observer teams were given instructions on what to look for and inquire about in the contending schools and again asked to rank each school according to the items on the list.

These sheets were then compiled into school site-visit profiles, and the "raw scores" were added to the original profile sheets. The project management team reviewed the materials, made its final determinations and presented them to the screening committee for discussion. The results were presented to and discussed with Edythe Gaines, who approved the roster. We had accepted all thirty-two schools.

Original Categories of Schools in the AGE Network

When AGE began, the thirty-two schools were arranged in three interconnecting networks. As the program developed, this structure turned out to be impractical and unrealistic. Eventually, after several reorganizations, all schools were absorbed into one group as "demonstrations," with the understanding that each was in a different stage of, as we called it, "the process of becoming." For the record, however, here is how we began.

DEMONSTRATION SCHOOLS Demonstration schools receive intensive technical assistance in all areas of program planning and development. They are the first in line for leadership training and other staff and curriculum development activities, modest financial support and the dissemination of program results. They participate in monthly network meetings, serve on committees and task forces and assist in documentation, dissemination and evaluation. Principals and staff are available as consultants, and their schools are open for observation and study.

COOPERATING SCHOOLS Cooperating schools receive less intense but high-quality technical assistance in program planning and development. They participate in many of the planning activities and training sessions scheduled by and for demonstration schools and receive regular information about program progress through the network. They are the second in line for dissemination of program results and receive modest financial support.

CONSULTATIVE SCHOOLS Consultative schools have a supportive and advisory role in the project. They provide technical assistance to other project schools and have the opportunity to participate in a variety of program and staff-development activities.

Criteria for Participation in Age

For those interested in the nitty-gritty of the selection process, Exhibit 2 outlines the criteria that were originally established for program participation. They have since served as guidelines for many school districts nationwide, including the League of Cities. In the last ten years, the criteria have

V**IEWPOINT**

"What better way to improve the quality of school life than through the arts in education? It is an instructional approach and a social framework that has given me a new way of looking at my whole school."

(Principal)

also been used for a foundation's school awards program, a state arts council's arts in education program grant application, a university research study on the impact of arts on school climate and environment, and in the New Orleans Project Arts Connection.

Results of the Citywide
School-Identification Process

The school-identification process took four months and consumed the time and energy of many people from the school system and the community. In the end, it turned out to be well worth the investment and produced some unexpected results.

The original AGE plan called for four demonstration schools from two districts (a pair in each district) and an unspecified number of cooperating schools. The decision to accept thirty-two schools was based largely on the project management team's ability to assume increased administrative responsibility. It was also made in recognition of other factors such as the high quality of leadership, support and commitment from the schools and the community that kept surfacing during the selection process. Finally, it resulted from our discovery that much of what the program was hoping to achieve was already happening in pockets of several of the city's schools. What was needed, however, was a more comprehensive and systematic approach to total school development so existing programs and services would become more sophisticated and reach all the students at all grade levels.

Perhaps the most influential reason for enlarging the network grew out of the realization that we needed a broader base of community awareness and support for the novel idea of school change through the arts. The original plan was based on the conviction that programs of this kind, which call for serious changes of attitudes and behavior, should start small, be carefully nurtured and be permitted to grow gradually and organically. The theory was sound but it did not take into account that "small" is a relative term and, in a city the size of New York, four schools are almost invisible. In addition, a larger field would provide more options from which others could study and choose.

Therefore, we modified our plans and organized a network of thirty-two "demonstration," "cooperating" and "consultative" schools representing thirteen of the city's thirty-two community districts and the senior high school division. This network was large enough to notice but still small enough to manage and had the additional advantage of broad geographical, socioeconomic, racial and ethnic diversity and balance—critical considerations in New York City and any other urban center.

There were other important outcomes of the citywide selection process. First, as many as thirty-two schools, a few of which were unknown to us, were apparently willing to make a serious and somewhat blind commitment to the abstract notion of school development through the arts, although there was no ready-made program to install and no large sums of money or additional personnel were dangled as incentives. The extent and nature of this commitment were all the more impressive because it was backed up by superintendents, school-board chairpersons, teacher-union representatives, PTA presidents and heads of student governments, all of whom were required to join the principal in signing off on the proposals.

Second, as word spread about the program, an increasing number of public and private philanthropic organizations and other community agencies made commitments to it because a few thought it was a coherent approach to school improvement, some saw it as another source of advocacy for the arts and everyone felt that at last they would be able to get through the "maze" at the Board of Education. Others were encouraged by the idea that perhaps now they would have an impact on not just one or two isolated schools but on an organized, visible group.

Finally, through constant dialogue and exchange of information among the project management team, the divisions and bureaus at Central, the community districts, the schools, the arts and cultural resources and the Fund, an informal communication network was established. This network helped sustain the program in its early days and contributed to its survival.

Biting the Bullet: A Bloodless "Revolution" With the Arts as the Instruments of Change

Many people in the arts world and in the field of education feel strongly that the arts should be taught for their own intrinsic value and should not be perceived as tools, catalysts, agents or instruments for school change. Three issues appear to bother these people:

First, they believe the arts are somehow sacred and not to be tampered with; when the arts are used for other purposes, especially social ends, they will be bastardized and distorted beyond recognition. I, for one, do not consider the arts or artists so fragile and vulnerable.

Second, the notion that all the arts are or should be the province of all the children threatens not only the patrician definition of what is "fine" or "high" aesthetically, but adds insult to injury by maintaining that the arts are within everyone's reach. Arts for the people is a populist but still not very popular idea.

E X H I B I T   2

INSTRUMENTS FOR RANKING SCHOOL PROPOSALS AND SITE VISITS

A. CHECKLIST OF CRITERIA FOR REVIEW OF SCHOOL PROPOSALS

1. Quantity, quality, variety and general availability of existing arts programs
2. Plans for improving and expanding existing arts programs and for incorporating all the arts into the general education program for all students
3. Evidence of or plans for an interdisciplinary teaching and learning approach
4. Identification and use of existing, in-house resources indicated in these plans
5. Identification and use of community resources, especially arts and cultural
6. Evidence of effective school leadership
7. Evidence of staff involvement in school programming and project planning and development
8. Extent and nature of district and community awareness of, and commitment to, the school and the project
9. Capability of school and district to implement plans and programs
10. Other strengths or weaknesses (written comment)

B. CHECKLIST OF CRITERIA FOR SCHOOL SITE VISITS (observations and interviews)

1. General impression of the school climate and environment
2. Level of openness and receptivity of the school to the visitor/observer
3. Use of existing space, materials and equipment for current programs
4. Quantity and quality of existing arts programs
5. Quantity and quality of interdisciplinary programs
6. Extent of the school's involvement with community resources, especially arts and cultural

7. Extent and nature of general student-body participation in arts and interdisciplinary programs and cultural events

8. Familiarity of the principal with the program's goal, objectives, strategies for implementation, evaluation and dissemination

9. Familiarity of school staff with the program

10. Extent of district and community support of the school and the project

11. Extent of parent and community involvement in the school

12. Other strengths or weaknesses (written comment)

C. OTHER THINGS TO LOOK FOR WHEN VISITING A POTENTIAL SCHOOL OR WHEN GATHERING RELATED INFORMATION FROM RELIABLE SOURCES (observations and interviews)

1. The nature and scope of the school's commitment to the idea of educational change through the arts and to participation in the program as evidenced by the school administration, staff and parents. Superficial familiarity with the program is not sufficient.

2. Nature and degree of involvement of the school staff and parents in the proposal-writing process. If the principal is the only one who has been responsible for the proposal, without the advice and consent of his or her staff, prospects for total school involvement and support of the program are dim.

3. The style and effectiveness of the principal as an educational leader and an able administrator. Evidence of teamwork and participation of the staff and parents in the decision-making and evaluation process is important.

4. The attitude of the staff toward the principal, each other, parents and especially the children. Openness, respect, warmth and courtesy are important qualities to identify.

5. The general tone, energy and atmosphere of the school as a pleasant, attractive and exciting place in which to live and learn. If the school is dark, and the walls and classrooms are barren, or if it gives the impression of a rigid, stratified society, prospects for success are minimal in a program that requires collaboration, flexibility and creativity.

6. General enthusiasm, even impatience, to participate in the program and candid recognition of areas of need in which technical and other assistance would be useful.

7. Evidence of open lines of communication throughout the school and its community.

8. The kind and quality of teaching and learning taking place in the classroom. Children should look actively involved in what they are doing and at ease with their peers, teachers, visitors and surroundings.

9. Evidence of a wide variety of teaching and learning styles and program choices in the school.

10. Evidence of the arts and creativity in the halls, the classrooms and throughout the school; presence of artists in residence and other community resource personnel.

The third issue underlies the first two: the arts for change implies an erosion of or an attack on the status quo, and this danger, imminent or far off, real or imagined, is enough to unsettle most people, myself included, who instinctively prefer to cling to the security of what is rather than take too many risks for the sake of what might be. Probing the unknown may produce rewards; it can also unleash anxiety and upheaval.

Changing schools means changing people. Since most people resist change unless, as "Design for Change" maintained, "it is deliberately planned for" by the people who will effect and be affected by the process, the prospect of it will not be welcomed and its course will be blunted. Although we had built ownership and cooperative action into the plan, we really weren't sure whether we had covered all the bases. We also

11. Evidence of untapped resources in the school and community with potential for program development. Many schools do not always recognize or use most effectively the human talent and other resources that exist in their own environment and in their immediate neighborhood.

12. Evidence of on-going staff and curriculum development programs and activities.

13. Use of existing space and facilities for learning and resource centers, labs and parent and teacher conference rooms. A well-stocked, colorful and well-used library is also significant.

14. Potential areas of trouble such as lack of school board and community support, teacher-union difficulties, inflexible schedules, conflicting priorities and educational objectives.

15. Depth of understanding of potential importance the arts have for improving the quality of education for all children as evidenced by discussion of the project as a school-development effort, not a cultural-enrichment or arts-exposure program.

16. General capability of the school to design, implement and evaluate the plans, programs and activities described in their proposal.

wondered how the "powers that be" would react to the radical idea of a cluster of schools taking charge of their own destiny.

In brief, planning the program, identifying and corralling resources and selecting schools had been challenging and time-consuming but relatively painless. Our ideas were attractive but largely theoretical, and our language was sometimes numbingly rhetorical. When it finally came time to test our unorthodox approach in the schools, it became clear that we were in for a long, hard journey. But Edythe Gaines kept urging everyone to "bite the bullet" and proceed undaunted on our joint "adventure." Kathy Bloom agreed; she maintained we had everything to learn and nothing to lose except a few hours of sleep at night. That was a small price to pay for discovery.

Fifteen years ago, I could not have written this book. Many people around the country have had to go through and often invent parts of the process to make it tangible—for them, for me and I hope for you. My hat is off to all those out there who "bit the bullet" and used the arts as ammunition for better schools.

THE LEAGUE OF CITIES FOR THE ARTS IN EDUCATION: SIX VARIATIONS

How Members Were Identified: One By One

How did the Fund get involved with the districts that formed the League? They were not picked out of a hat, nor did we send out requests for proposals; they came to us, one by one, through a gradual process of self-selection. The formation of the network was also a result of opportunity and, to a degree, necessity. We had no plans and no grand design for it at the outset, and we certainly didn't dream that the New York City plan would have such instant appeal, much less such easy applicability, to five other diverse districts. The Fund embarked on networking chiefly because it was the next logical developmental step in its own programmatic history.

Why those particular six cities? Their participation was the result of people who were interested in the arts and education knowing people who were trying to do something about it. News of the New York City program had begun to spread rapidly through the nation's formal and informal arts-in-education communication networks and as a result of Kathy Bloom's many keynote speeches and the staff's panel presentations and workshops at local and national conferences. I had documented every step of the process on which we were embarked, and these descriptive materials, program guidelines and criteria were widely disseminated. But the six League districts surfaced mainly because someone who knew us personally or knew of and respected our work either cornered us at a meeting, picked up the telephone and insisted on talking to one of the staff or wrote a personal letter.

I have already described the New York City "connection." In Minneapolis, Kathy Bloom and I knew the then-superintendent, John Davis, and I knew two of his staff consultants from my work at Lincoln Center and as an evaluator of their nationally recognized Urban Arts Program. In Seattle and Little Rock, the first overtures were made by representatives of their Junior Leagues. (Kathy had worked as the arts consultant for the national association and maintained many contacts within the organization.) In Hartford, Edythe Gaines took the idea with her when she became their new superintendent. In Winston-Salem, the first approach was made by Kathy's friend on the local arts council who was also a prominent citizen in the community.

The most difficult question has always been why the League was confined to six cities when there were other school systems asking, and certainly eligible, to be included. As a private foundation, we could not take on the whole country; we had neither the time, the money, the staff nor the mandate from our board of trustees. As an operating foundation, the Fund was attempting to fulfill its self-described role as a stalking horse, and the League was considered a small research and development field experiment. We hoped it would become an enduring demonstration of an unusual educational approach to the arts that would provide food for thought, a model for study and adaptation and a source of technical assistance.

The Fund's Criteria for a Partnership: Ten Characteristics of School Systems that Have Developed Effective AGE Programs

While many of the first contacts for information and help from the Fund came from people outside the school system, our practice was to accept formal requests for assistance only from the school superintendent or a chief administrative officer.

Following an official request, members of our staff would spend several days in a site meeting with key people in the school system and the community and visiting the schools. We would describe the Fund's mission and the AGE concept and offer a rationale for the arts in education. We would distribute our working papers and describe the status and experience of our projects to the superintendent and his or her cabinet, to the members of the local Board of Education and to the movers and shakers in the local arts and business community.

The purpose of these visits was simple: both "parties" needed to get to know each other and to establish at least a minimal level of trust. It was important to find out, firsthand, whether the chemistry as well as the landscape was right for a partnership. Kathy Bloom would not commit the Fund's resources to any venture unless it had a reasonably good chance of success. Although the approach and methods were informal, what was sought was concrete evidence of certain characteristics or the potential to develop them before any formal commitment was made.

In developing partnerships, the Fund looked for certain traits that were summarized in a paper I wrote in May 1974. It was based on the patterns I was able to tease out of the Fund's prior six-year experience with pilot projects around the country and those that were emerging from our new-born venture with the New York City schools (see Exhibit 3).

The Unusual Nature of Partnerships

When each of the school districts and the Fund felt satisfied that collaborative action would be mutually advantageous, a formal partnership was established through the exchange of letters of agreement between Kathy and the superintendent. These letters specified the nature, terms and conditions of the relationship (see Exhibit 4).

One of the unusual features of this contractual agreement was the nature of the Fund's support, which was primarily technical and consultative and only incidentally financial. However, there were two departures from the Fund's no-grant policy. The first was New York City where, because it was our own backyard, Mr. Rockefeller felt very strongly about the city's public schools. Small $500 planning grants were made to each of the original twelve demonstration schools, and the costs for national consultants, special conferences, retreats and publications of national significance were frequently covered. The second exception was in the form of two small grants ($6,000 and $5,000) to each League school district (matched in cash, in-kind and indirectly) to hire and train arts-in-education program supervisors. Called the Arts in Education Administrative Fellowship program, this project was designed for the Fund's Coalition of States network as well as for the League. It is described in more detail in Chapter 9.

The Need and Opportunity for a National Network: Formation of the League

By 1976, in addition to my administrative duties and appearances at national meetings and conferences, I was working almost every day as part of the Project Management Team with the New York City program and paying two and sometimes three visits a year to each of the other five districts. It became abundantly clear that although our budget would hold out, my stamina might not. We had established the Coalition of States for the Arts in Education. which indicated the value and the feasibility of our organizing another national consortium of urban centers with a similar common goal. Thus in April of that year, we invited teams of key administrators, program coordinators and other decision-makers—about forty in all—from each of the six cities to Chicago to discuss the possibility of forming a network. We wanted to determine whether they, too, would see the advantages of forming a consortium whose potential benefits promised to outweigh any real or imagined threat to individual autonomy or integrity. Although we agreed to form the League at our first conference, it took several business meetings and site visits to come to an understanding of one another's speech patterns, establish a common vocabulary and navigate the often choppy waters of contrasting styles and temperaments. But in a relatively short time the group built the trust and confidence essential to cooperative action.

After that first meeting, we managed to define and write our mission statement and sketch out a framework for the organization, structure and operation of the new League of Cities for the Arts in Education. The Fund agreed to continue to work in a consulting and technical capacity with the individual districts, coordinate the network and provide the main financial support for business meetings, conferences and site visits. League members agreed to participate in all activities planned in cooperation with the Fund. They would serve on task forces and special committees, organize site visits and, wherever possible, supplement the Fund's financial support from their own local resources. They established a steering committee and later a core group of decision-makers representing each district to hammer out the details on policy, structure and organization and to chart each step in the network's development.

At first it seemed that as League coordinator I would have more, not less, of an administrative workload and an even heavier travel schedule. Gradually, the network created an efficient mechanism for mutual assistance, moral support and leadership training, and I was able to reduce the number of site visits I had previously felt obliged to make. In the sense and spirit of "two heads are always better than one," the League's large and small group meetings addressed and resolved, practically and immediately, through negotiation and consensus, more issues than any one person could ever hope to deal with in a lifetime.

I am now certain that there is no equal to the group discussion process, no matter how stormy, slow or painful, for sparking ideas, generating creative and collective solutions to knotty problems, and building a sense of group ownership, pride, and conscience. I am also convinced that the amount of money required to bring people together from different parts of the country is small compared with the benefits derived. Networking, even nationally, is a cost-effective mechanism for professional growth and development.

The League's Mission Statement and Declaration of Intent

The Mission Statement and Declaration of Intent were written and adopted unanimously by members of the League and read as follows:

MISSION STATEMENT   The goal of the League of Cities is to support and facilitate the efforts of its members as they seek to improve the effectiveness of education and the quality of life for all children and youth by

E X H I B I T   3 ─────────

TEN CHARACTERISTICS OF SCHOOL SYSTEMS THAT HAVE DEVELOPED EFFECTIVE ARTS IN GENERAL EDUCATION PROGRAMS

As has been stated frequently by one eminent educator, reading, writing and arithmetic do not, in themselves, constitute an education; rather, they are the tools that one needs to become educated. We believe that the arts are also important tools for schooling and that quality education can result when the arts are incorporated in the teaching and learning process.

We have observed that when an entire school system embarks on an arts in general education program, certain kinds of changes take place in the schools and in the community. While not all the characteristics of change described here appear in every situation, they do identify main features that summarize the common identity of school systems with which we have been associated.

1. A COMMITMENT TO QUALITY EDUCATION FOR ALL CHILDREN

The school system has a commitment to improving the quality of education for all children and has established a mechanism for systematic change and innovation.

2. A COMMITMENT TO QUALITY EDUCATION THROUGH THE ARTS

A significant number of chief school officials, administrators, teachers and parents subscribe to the belief that teaching and learning through the arts improves the quality of education for all children. They regard education as a creative living and learning process and feel that the arts provide a powerful motivation for this process. They have found that by incorporating the arts into all aspects of schooling, children develop positive attitudes toward learning, a stronger sense of themselves and a keener awareness of the world around them.

3. THE CREATIVE USE OF EXISTING HUMAN, FINANCIAL, AND PHYSICAL RESOURCES

The school system allocates a significant amount of time, effort and money to the planning and development of arts in education programs. Local public funds provide the main base of support for school programs; private funds are used primarily for research and development purposes. Existing facilities in the schools and the community are fully utilized.

4. A COHERENT, COLLABORATIVE APPROACH TO PROGRAM PLANNING AND DEVELOPMENT

Programs are planned, developed, operated and assessed by those who participate in them. Consequently, these programs relate to the actual strengths and needs of the district and individual schools and make use of the appropriate resources in the schools and community. Professional consultants in the arts and education are involved in the planning and development process.

5. AN ORGANIC PROGRAM DESIGN WITH FIVE MAIN OBJECTIVES

Though they will vary from district to district and school to school, effective arts in general education programs have at least five related objectives or points of emphasis in common:

a. Interdisciplinary teaching and learning
b. Strong programs in all the arts for all children at all grade levels
c. Effective and regular use of community cultural resources, including services provided by artists and arts institutions
d. Special programs for special populations
e. Use of arts activities to reduce personal and racial isolation

6. A CONTINUING CURRICULUM AND STAFF DEVELOP-MENT EFFORT

Program planning and development occur simultaneous-ly with curriculum and staff development workshops, seminars and meetings. These activities encourage the development of new learning skills, teaching strategies and materials that are appropriate to the content and structure of new programs. The instructional staff, artists and community volunteers have access to new or existing arts resource materials and can test them out in actual classroom situations or other learning environments.

7. AN ON-GOING INTERNAL AND EXTERNAL SYSTEM OF DOCUMENTATION AND EVALUATION

Evaluation of the school's efforts in program planning and development are continuous, largely internal, and ad-dress questions of effectiveness in terms of the goals and objectives the district and the schools have set for them-selves. Judgments about quality and achievement are made by those best in the position to render and make use of them, and modifications are made as soon as they are needed. Educational research and evaluation consult-ants or outside agencies are used to help determine the effectiveness of the overall program.

8. AN EFFECTIVE COMMUNICATIONS NETWORK

A conscious and systematic effort is made to share infor-mation about the school's arts in education programs, and problems and prospects are discussed within each school, with other schools and cultural institutions and with community advisory groups. As a result of this process, other schools wishing to move in similar direc-tions are encouraged to do so more effectively.

9. A BROADENED AND HUMANISTIC CONCEPT OF SCHOOLING

In the course of incorporating all the arts into an entire school system, the concept of schooling broadens and teaching and learning become more humanistic. School buildings and classrooms are transformed into attractive living and working environments; the content of the curriculum is significantly altered; teachers develop new capabilities and patterns of instruction; and a working partnership is formed between the schools and the community.

10. AN INCREASED COMMITMENT TO AND UNDER-STANDING OF THE CHANGE PROCESS IN EDUCATION

The process of educational change is often slow and difficult. It calls for imaginative leadership and cooperative working arrangements among many different sectors of the community. It also requires patience, fortitude and broad public awareness and commitment. School systems that have developed effective arts in general education programs have not only improved the quality of teaching and learning in their schools but have developed a greater understanding of the change process. This process is most effective when the individual school is viewed as a social unit and the most powerful agent for progressive change in education.

E X H I B I T   4

CONTENTS OF A TYPICAL PARTNERSHIP LETTER OF AGREEMENT BETWEEN THE SCHOOL DISTRICT AND THE JDR 3RD FUND

THE SCHOOL DISTRICT MADE:

1. A commitment by the superintendent and the school board to the goal of all the arts for all the children and to the development of a comprehensive program that would start in a few demonstration schools and gradually expand throughout the district.

2. A commitment to the idea of networking, collaboration and school development through the arts.

3. A commitment of local district staff, time and resources for program planning and operation and the assurance that additional funds would be sought from public, private, local, state and federal sources to supplement tax-levy funds.

IN RETURN, THE FUND AGREED TO:

1. Provide consulting and technical assistance from its staff instead of an outright cash grant.

2. Underwrite staff travel and expenses, certain "outside" consultant services by local and national authorities in the arts and education and attendance by district representatives at special meetings, conferences, and site visits.

3. Provide information about the Fund's experience with other arts in education projects, act as liaison between the district and other arts in education efforts and function as a clearinghouse of information.

incorporating all the arts in the teaching-learning process and to make results available to others.

DECLARATION OF INTENT   The following cities—Hartford, Little Rock, Minneapolis, New York, Seattle and Winston-Salem, in collaboration with the JDR 3rd Fund—have begun to plan and implement comprehensive school-development programs in order to reach the common goal of "all the arts for all the children." These cities have found it useful to meet together regularly under the auspices of the Fund to share information, resources and effective strategies for planning and implementing comprehensive arts in general, or basic, education programs.

The League intends to enable participating school districts to:

— raise the level of awareness of schools and communities about the value and effectiveness of the arts as a vehicle for school change, tools for living and learning and areas of study in their own right

— demonstrate how the total climate, environment and organization of a school can be changed through the arts so that it becomes a place conducive to better teaching, learning and living

— make better use of the arts, artists and the arts process as one of several ways to achieve educational excellence in individual schools and throughout school systems

— avail themselves of existing human, material and financial resources to support program planning, development and operation.

— take advantage of the leadership and other specialized knowledge and skills possessed by members of the League (As consultants and technical assistants to each other, League members can help design and assess strategies for program planning and for staff, curriculum and school development.)

The League of Cities further intends to develop and disseminate a position paper defining what we mean by the arts in education. We also intend to produce a notebook describing and illustrating the components and strategies for the school and school district development process through the arts based on our experience. Further, the League will make available to its members and others pertinent documents and materials related to the arts in general, or basic, education and school development through the arts.

VIEWPOINT

"It is the first approach I have encountered that is truly comprehensive in its goal—all the arts, all the children, all the time. As such, it is an instructional framework based on psychological contracts that allows for a very broad and therefore very creative interpretation. It breaks the conventional educational mold."

(Chief administrator)

League Activities: Business Meetings and Site Visits

Most of the League's business meetings were held in Chicago for financial as well as geographical reasons. The general format was a day and a half of four sessions, the first of which was devoted to information-sharing about recent developments, new breakthroughs and setbacks. The balance of the meeting dealt with one or more issues and an agreed-upon task. Usually teams of two to four representatives (administrators, coordinators, principals and teachers), plus invited special guests (national authorities, interested observers and arts agency administrators) attended.

The issues discussed included: What does an arts in general education program look like and how do you do it in your locale? What are the strategies for school development through the arts? What are you doing about networking, curriculum and staff development, leadership training and community awareness and support? How do you define roles and functions, especially for arts specialists and artists? What about resources, especially money, and how are you getting the good word out? How do you expand without going bankrupt and without violating the integrity of the idea?

Site visits had a somewhat different purpose and focus. The idea was for the host district to showcase its program with as little artificiality as possible and for League members to observe, participate in and learn from the occasion. In addition to League members, local school folk, community leaders and state and national dignitaries joined the proceedings.

The impact on the local scene was incredible. School people, parents, volunteers and central staff, eager to plan each event carefully for maximum effect, made giant strides in their own understanding of the AGE concept and, in the process, got better acquainted with each other. The community became more aware of the existence of the program and of the positive role the arts could play in their schools. Administrators in the school system, especially the superintendent, the cabinet and the coordinator, got public recognition and credit for their accomplishments. Local teachers and principals were in the spotlight, center stage and had several opportunities to share thoughts, concerns and feelings with their counterparts from five different school districts. The students had a chance to perform, to express their pride in their art works and to boast about their schools and their hometown to a group of sometimes bewildering "foreigners."

There is no doubt that the benefits to the "host" site tended to outweigh those to the visitors, although the preparation, organization and sheer physical labor involved were staggering. Moreover, the visits were costly even though local expenses were more or less shared between the district and the Fund. But there is also no doubt that the experience helped to strengthen the bonds within the League by providing a first-hand glimpse of local conditions that no amount of talking or reading could ever begin to convey. And, though each visit revealed the idiosyncratic and unique nature of the six League programs, they inevitably produced some unexpected answers for the visitors to nagging questions that had sometimes been so stubbornly difficult to fathom at home. For me, each visit underscored the flexibility and adaptability of the AGE concept. I continued to marvel at the imaginative and frequently ingenious approach each city had devised while managing to remain faithful to the integrity of the basic idea.

AGE Proves to be Adaptable: Thumbnail Sketches of League Programs

When the Fund first established partnerships with League members, it was New York's experience and the New York City plan that proved instructive to the five other school systems. This is not to say that the New York City approach was taken on faith or followed blindly. Indeed, it was often difficult for some to imagine how anything that occurred in New York could apply to any other setting. However, where experience, processes and working papers could be generalized, members quickly adapted them to the local scene. Where they did not apply because of singular local conditions, they were set aside, sometimes for future reference.

A book of this kind cannot go into detail on each of the school district's programs. I will try to give the reader a glimpse of what happened in each place and cite a few examples as we go along. However, it may be helpful here to provide a thumbnail sketch of the origin and special aspects of each of the five programs not featured at length.[2]

HARTFORD   The Hartford AGE program began in the fall of 1976, several months after it became a charter member of the League of Cities for the Arts in Education. General plans for the program had been made before the League's formation, but no official steps had yet been taken. At one of the League's early business meetings, the Hartford team presented a draft of its plan for general review and comment by members—a first for the League and a bold step by the team. An intensive session produced ideas and suggestions for revision and soon six demonstration and eight cooperating schools were identified, a network had been set in motion and

---

[2] The New York City and Winston-Salem programs are covered in detailed case studies by Nancy Shuker and Charles Fowler in *An Arts Education Source Book: A View from the JDR 3rd Fund*. The Seattle program was evaluated by Junius Eddy in a document that received limited distribution and is no longer available.

a considerable amount of financial and in-kind support from the school, arts and business community had been generated. Hartford's AGE program became a reference point for a regional arts in education network in which the state arts council, the state education department, community arts agencies and concerned citizens played an important role.

LITTLE ROCK   The Little Rock Arts in Education Program began in January 1975 as a result of a joint effort by the Junior League, the Inglewood Foundation (a local philanthropy) and the school system. The venture was prompted by a district needs assessment that revealed deficiencies in arts education at the elementary level. After researching other national programs, including those in New York City and Seattle, a program coordinator was hired with modest grant funds from the Junior League and a $60,000 award from the Foundation for a three-year period. Five primary/elementary schools were identified, and an advisory committee was formed to provide direction and support for program participants. The program staff, funded by the district and supplemented by state and federal monies, grew from one person to five, and the arts in education schools ultimately numbered twenty-seven of the district's thirty-eight elementary and secondary schools. The Little Rock program attracted considerable state and national funds and attention and served as a beacon light to similar communities that had to invent ways to tap limited local "natural" resources and engender widespread community support.

MINNEAPOLIS   The Minneapolis AGE program began in the spring of 1975 because the superintendent, his cabinet and the school board felt it would be important to build upon and extend the experience gained from their Title III, ESEA-funded and nationally validated Urban Arts Program. This year-round program marshaled the arts resources in the Twin Cities area and provided learning opportunities in schools, cultural centers and studios for interested and/or talented junior and senior high school students who received academic credit for their work. It also provided artists-in-residence, performances, staff development workshops and curriculum materials. Urban Arts was funded as a line item in the school-system budget and provided significant support for AGE/Urban Arts staff and school development activities. Additional support for AGE was provided from the budgets of the Curriculum Office, the area superintendents, the State Arts Board (Council) and local businesses, corporations and philanthropies. An arts cluster team coordinated the program for sixteen schools from the central office.

SEATTLE   The Seattle program, originally known as Arts for Learning, began in January 1974 with the major impetus coming from the city's arts institutions, the District's Curriculum Department and the Junior League. The latter had conducted extensive research on national arts in education programs and approached the school district with a plan for a three-year pilot program. The program was launched in six demonstration schools with the Junior League providing a $40,000 planning and development grant. Following the pilot period, the original demonstration school network was reorganized and a number of new and larger arts-related networks were formed, representing thirty-one of the district's elementary and secondary schools. In addition to the steady support from the Junior League, the state education department, the state and local arts councils and the city's arts community, rapid expansion was largely due to the district's financial commitment of federal and local money and its voluntary decision to desegregate the schools, using the arts as a focus for much of this effort. Seattle ultimately formed the coordinating hub of a four-state regional pilot network, Arts Coalition Northwest, funded largely by the Department of Education and the Kennedy Center's Education Program.

WINSTON-SALEM The Winston-Salem Arts in the Basic Curriculum (ABC) program began primarily because of the efforts of its local arts council, the first in the nation. Beginning with two elementary schools in 1975, ABC systematically expanded into twenty-four elementary and most of the junior high schools (more than a third of the total system), using a "buddy" or pairing system that relied heavily on the support services from a multidisciplinary arts resource team, curriculum supervisors and the education staff of the arts council. The program was classroom teacher-oriented and focused on staff and curriculum development at the building level. It received strong leadership and financial support from the superintendent, his cabinet, the school board and the general community, which took pride in its long pro-arts history. It was also the recipient of an Education Department grant. The program served as a reference point for a statewide effort and helped start similar initiatives in several states and territories.

A Closer Look

SCHOOL DEVELOPMENT AND A RATIONALE FOR THE ARTS IN EDUCATION

SCHOOL DEVELOPMENT: THE ORIGINS OF THE CONCEPT

The term "school development" and the concept of networking presented by Edythe Gaines and her staff in "Design for Change" were partly inspired by two handbooks published by the Illinois Office of the Superintendent of Public Instruction in 1971 and 1973, respectively: *A Quality Schools Network for Illinois: A Report to Dr. Michael J. Bakalis, Superintendent*, by the Center for New Schools, and *It Works This Way for Some: Case Studies of 15 Schools*, also prepared by the Center and the Illinois Network for School Development. I often referred to these books as well as Edythe's doctoral and other scholarly papers when planning the Coop's Urban Resources Linkage Program in Lower Manhattan and later in designing the blueprint for the New York City arts in general education program.

I also spent hours discussing the subject with Kathy Bloom and studied and analyzed the project reports, evaluations and other occasional papers documenting the Fund's first six years of national experience with districts, schools and arts organizations. These early pilot projects provided vivid examples of ways in which the schools were (and were not) successful in introducing and integrating the arts into the general curriculum and the total school program.

But it was my introduction to and opportunity to work with Dr. John Goodlad and his impressive staff at the Institute for Development of Educational Activities (I/D/E/A) that provided me with an understanding of the theoretical foundations as well as some practical strategies for changing schools, in our case, through the arts. John and his associates were writing a prodigious number of accessible, readable books and materials based on their extensive field experience and empirical research into the nature and characteristics of effective schools. Their positive and negative experience and many of their warnings informed the theories and practice we were developing for individual school improvement through the arts.

The discussion that follows, therefore, owes an immeasurable debt to the work and experience of others around the country who preceded us or who were, without our knowing it—as is so often the case in education—toiling at the same time in different acres of the same vineyard.

SCHOOL DEVELOPMENT: A DISCUSSION OF THE CONCEPT

School development is a grassroots, self-help concept that assumes that the individual school is a definable cultural unit—a social microcosm—whose professional inhabitants are capable of organizing and governing themselves, analyzing their own needs and designing programs and services that deliver quality learning experiences to all of their students.

The article of faith implicit in the idea of school development is that school people, if given the proper motivation, resources, training and support, can chart their own destiny and manage the tricky process of change from within the school walls. The word "development" (which I use interchangeably with "improvement" and "renewal") is significant because it conveys the idea of flexibility and growth in human terms and suggests that school professionals can change the environment in which they work and improve their own performance.

School development does not have the harsher, more negative impact of a phrase like "school reform," which can sound evangelical, impersonal and punitive. The word "reform," moreover, carries a lot of negative bureaucratic baggage: it implies serious systemic dysfunction, if not downright failure, especially when used by dissatisfied outsiders who intervene in (or interfere with) the schools—theoretically "for their own good." Furthermore, reform movements tend to propose sweeping new social agendas with new laws, curriculum mandates and blueprints for governance and structure without providing the money or people resources to implement them. More often than not, the proposed changes either never filter down to the teachers, or they are simply ignored behind the classroom door.

The concept of school development is based on a fundamental, albeit paradoxical, assertion: change, though disconcerting, is a necesssary constant. Like it or not, there are no absolutes, no eternal verities, no definitive solutions to anything in a complex, technological world that keeps making or stumbling on discoveries that shake the very foundations of past and often sacred assumptions. Thus, schools must respond fluidly to new ideas; in fact, they should take the initiative in seeking out the latest and best information that will help them evolve.

The idea of school development casts the school in a new role. It is no longer regarded simply as an institutionalized baby-sitter, a surrogate family, a soup kitchen or a convenient mechanism for vocational training and acculturation. It is a new kind of social service center or, as John Goodlad has put it, a "pedagogical service station" that must somehow provide and integrate a broad array of educational, social and other supportive services to each member of every economic, racial and ethnic stripe in its community.

School development is a tall, abstract and daunting order in our impatient and cost-conscious society. It is neither a sexy idea nor a packaged deal that promises quick, flashy (and thus flash-in-the-pan) results. It is a process that, given time and the proper motivation, training, resources and support, can be translated, perhaps not all at once, but bit by bit, into daily reality.

School development programs can survive in spite (and sometimes, because) of changes in leadership, dramatic shifts in social or political policy, sudden and substantial reductions in education budgets and shifting or diminishing populations. However, it is unlikely that school systems threatened with near-bankruptcy or disruptive chaos would be able to initiate, let alone sustain, the process. A certain degree of stability and continuity is essential, though it will vary in nature and extent from place to place.

 IEWPOINT

"I think this effort of ours has restructured the classroom teachers in our system right back into the mainstream of the arts and education in general. I think that may be the ultimate significance of what we're doing because unless the teacher is excited and involved, education is going to be pretty boring."

(Superintendent)

The characteristics of the school development process and the conditions necessary for it to occur, shown in Exhibit 5, are ideals or perhaps utopian composites. I do not know of any one school to which I can point as a living, breathing embodiment of these traits. I suggest that you use this section as a sort of self-evaluation inventory to help you determine where you are and then keep track of your journey on your own continuum.

A RATIONALE FOR THE ARTS IN EDUCATION

During one of the early orientation and training seminars for central administrators and supervisors in the New York City AGE program, Edythe Gaines asked, "Why the arts as a focus for school development?" What do the arts offer schools in their search for self-improvement? What is the unique contribution the arts can make to the growth and development of the total school? How do the arts, the arts process and the artist in all of us affect:

— the school's sense of itself, its philosophical purpose and programmatic direction?
— the attitudes and behavior of everyone in the building, from the principal to the custodian?
— teachers teaching and learning from others?
— students learning and teaching others?
— the school's relationship with its immediate and larger community?
— the climate and environment of the school?

Kathy Bloom and I were struck by Edythe's question, and about a year later, while preparing material for the January/February arts and education issue of *Principal Magazine*, we hammered out a rationale for the arts in education (see Exhibit 6). The rationale, although still largely a theoretical and not a programmatic answer, has been widely used to substantiate a variety of claims for the importance of the arts to schooling.

THE CHARACTERISTICS OF SCHOOL DEVELOPMENT THROUGH THE ARTS

In October 1975, I put together a working paper entitled "A Definition of a Comprehensive Arts in General Education Program," in which I equated the program, the process and the distinguishing features of AGE with a comprehensive school-development effort. My reasoning was that when a school goes about planning and executing an approach that makes all the arts integral to the general, or basic, education of every student, it must by definition change. In other words, when a school establishes a structure and a climate in which to design and carry out activities to meet the five main objectives, new instructional programs, new methodologies and new patterns of behavior are bound to result. In addition, if a good portion of the school community is actively engaged in the process and the arts are used as content and instruments for change, the social climate and physical environment will also be transformed. Presumably these changes are for the better when quality as well as quantity is a criterion.

Put conversely, school development through the arts is a concept (all the arts for all the children) that is based on a change theory (the principal as leader of school based management teams, supported by networking and collaboration) that outlines the process by which individual schools design and carry out a truly comprehensive arts in general education program. When these programs have certain characteristics, they result in some identifiable and tangible outcomes that help to improve the quality of education. What follows is an updated version of the 1975 paper.

A Definition of School Development through the Arts

School development through the arts is a concept and a long-range process that is supported and accelerated by networking and collaboration. When schools have as their goal "all the arts for all the children" and plan and install comprehensive programs to achieve that purpose, fundamental and positive changes take place.

Characteristically, these programs view the arts as important areas of study in their own right, as tools for learning in all subjects, and as media for expression and self-discovery. They are also recognized as an impetus to staff, curriculum and leadership development.

A comprehensive arts in general education program is not simply a cultural enrichment program, an arts exposure project or a curriculum development effort. It is not just a series of performances, visits to a museum or encounters with artists for inspirational purposes. It is not a music appreciation or studio art course once or twice a week for thirty minutes or a few electives that are not required (and therefore not considered "basic") for graduation. It is not a set of curriculum materials or a special program affecting only a few children or one or two grades in a school.

When a program is truly comprehensive it affects and transforms the entire school. It includes significant study of , in, and about the visual, performing, literary, environmental, industrial, home and folk arts. It develops conceptual, thematic and functional relationships among the arts and

E X H I B I T   5

THE CHARACTERISTICS OF SCHOOLS ENGAGED IN THE DEVELOPMENT PROCESS

I. THE INTERNAL CONDITIONS NECESSARY FOR SCHOOLS THAT WISH TO DEVELOP AND FLOURISH

Schools engaged in the development process are orderly, lively, friendly, clean and attractive. They are dedicated workplaces for children as well as adults who can usually be found engaged in on-going dialogues, decisions, actions and self-assessment activities that produce:

— A well-defined philosophy and a commitment to quality education for all the children in the school.

— A comprehensive school-based plan that has been collaboratively designed on the basis of school needs and resources. This plan specifies aims for the school, defines roles and functions of all participants and integrates teaching and learning opportunities across program areas and subject disciplines.

— Regular schoolwide and small group meetings to discuss, decide upon and assess instructional and other programs that have been cooperatively planned and carried out within the established comprehensive framework.

— A schedule that is flexible enough to accommodate unexpected program opportunities, team teaching and resource and information-sharing.

— An on-going staff and curriculum development effort, in and out of school, that responds to needs identified by the participants.

— Linkages and partnerships with the community that tap into existing or create new learning opportunities in and out of school.

— An internal monitoring and evaluation system that keeps track of individual and collective progress, feeds information back immediately or in timely fashion to those who need it for diagnostic or prescriptive purposes and helps improve everyone's understanding of child development, the learning process and schoolwide change.

— An effective communication system that keeps the school community informed and up-to-date about current events and future opportunities and generates the respect and support of parents and the community.

II. THE PEOPLE ENGAGED IN THE DEVELOPMENT PROCESS

People in schools engaged in the process of governing and improving themselves have the following general roles, functions and characteristics:

— THE PRINCIPAL is an educational leader, a politician, a social engineer and a management expert with a point of view. He or she keeps order, sets high standards, takes risks and chances and knows when to lead, when to delegate or share power and when to follow. The principal is a presence and is visible in the classrooms and the corridors as well as in the office. The principal has respect for staff, parents and students, which is returned in kind. His or her administrative and support staff share responsibility, act as a management team and provide instructional and moral support to teachers, students, community volunteers and outside consultants.

- TEACHERS play a significant role in shaping the school's philosophy, planning school programs and making financial and programmatic decisions that affect the entire school. They work singly and in teams, during and after school on projects and activities that are often jointly planned and implemented. They exhibit a sense of pride, satisfaction and ownership in their work and in the control over their environment. They have high expectations for their students, whom they treat with respect and courtesy. As professionals, they are aware of each other's strengths and limitations and function accordingly. They recognize that learning can take place outside of as well as within the school building and seek out and use appropriate community resources regularly.

- STUDENTS are energetically engaged in the life of the school and help generate and formulate ideas for programs, events and the general curriculum. The extent of involvement varies according to age and maturity, but their pride in their school is manifest. They are courteous and friendly and show respect for their peers and their environment. They also laugh a lot.

- PARENTS, SCHOOL AIDES AND VOLUNTEERS are active on school committees, in the classrooms and as liaisons between the school and the larger community. They are advocates for the school and help secure resources for programs and events that they then help plan and carry out.

- TRAINED PROFESSIONALS of different ages, backgrounds and ethnicity act as resource personnel to the administration, staff and students. They participate in program planning and perform supplementary instructional and other supportive services.

— CUSTODIAL AND MAINTENANCE PERSONNEL are involved in plans and decisions that affect their job responsibilities and, when appropriate, help teach the skills of their craft or amateur interests.

III. THE EXTERNAL CONDITIONS NECESSARY FOR SCHOOL DEVELOPMENT

— Articulate, coordinated and sustained commitment and support—in words and deeds—from top and middle management in the community and the local school system and, if possible, state and federal agencies

— Availability of resources—human, material and financial; additional funds for planning, staff and curriculum development, research and program development

— Time and opportunity for planning, meeting, sharing, training and socializing

— The formation and support of a network of like-minded schools coordinated by a facilitating hub

— Partnerships or collaborative arrangements with public and private agencies and institutions at the local, state and federal level

— Specialized on-site technical and consulting assistance provided from the district and other designated sources in response to the school's perceived needs

— Community awareness, support and advocacy for public education

EXHIBIT 6 _____

A RATIONALE FOR THE ARTS IN EDUCATION

Many educators, as well as persons directly concerned with the arts, share the conviction that the arts are a means for expressing and interpreting human behavior and experience. It follows, therefore, that the education of children is incomplete if the arts are not part of the daily teaching and learning process. Arts in education programs are designed to make all of the arts integral to the general, or basic, education of every child in entire school systems.

Work with these programs demonstrates that changes take place in schools so that they become humane environments in which the arts are valued as tools for learning as well as for their own intrinsic sake. Experience further indicates that the arts are useful to educators in meeting some of their main goals—that is, providing a great variety of educational opportunities, distinguished by quality, for all children.

The following are specific ways that the arts can contribute to the general, or basic, education of every child:

1. The arts provide a medium for personal expression, a deep need experienced by children and adults alike. Children's involvement in the arts can be a strong motivating force for improved communication through speaking and writing as well as through drawing or singing.

2. The arts focus attention and energy on personal observation and self awareness. They can make children and adults more aware of their environment and help them develop a stronger sense of themselves and a greater confidence in their own abilities. Through increased self-knowledge, children are more likely to be able to command and integrate their mental, physical and emotional faculties and cope with the world around them.

3. The arts are a universal human phenomenon and means of communication. Involvement in them, both as participant and observer, can promote a deeper understanding and acceptance of the similarities and differences among races, religions and cultural traditions.

4. The arts involve the elements of sound, movement, color, mass, energy, space, line, shape and language. These elements, singly or in combination, are common to the concepts underlying many subjects in the curriculum. For example, exploring solutions to problems in mathematics and science through the arts can increase the understanding of the process and the value of both.

5. The arts embody and chronicle the cultural, aesthetic and social development of the world's people. Through the arts, children can become more aware of their own cultural heritage in a broad historical context. Arts institutions, cultural organizations and artists have a vital role to play in the education of children, both in schools and in the community.

6. The arts are a tangible expression of human creativity, and as such reflect man's perceptions of his world. Through the arts children and adults can become more aware of their own creative and human potential.

7. The various fields of the arts offer a wide range of career choices to young people. Arts in education programs provide opportunities for students to explore the possibility of becoming a professional actor, dancer, musician, painter, photographer, architect, filmmaker or teacher. There are also many lesser known opportunities in arts-related technical areas

such as lighting engineer, costumer in a theater or a specialist in designing and installing exhibitions in museums. Other opportunities lie in administrative and educational work in arts organizations such as museums, performing arts groups and arts councils.

8. The arts can contribute substantially to special education. Educational programs emphasizing the arts and the creative process are being developed for students with learning disabilities, such as the mentally retarded and physically handicapped. These programs are conceived as alternative approaches to learning for youngsters who may have problems in adjusting to more traditional classroom situations. The infusion of the arts into the general education of all children also encourages the identification of talented youngsters whose special abilities may otherwise go unnoticed or unrecognized.

9. The arts, as a means for personal and creative involvement by children and teachers, are a source of pleasure and mental stimulation. Learning as a pleasant, rewarding activity is a new experience for many young people and can be very important in encouraging positive attitudes toward schooling.

10. The arts are useful tools for everyday living. An understanding of the arts provides people with a broader range of choices about the environment in which they live, the life-style they develop and the way they spend their leisure time.

Kathryn Bloom and Jane Remer
November 1975

between the arts and all other subjects. It identifies and regularly uses all the appropriate arts and cultural resources in the school community in ways that increase an understanding of the arts and establish connections among the arts process, the creative process and the learning process. In addition, it uses the arts to meet the needs of special populations (including the gifted, talented, handicapped and bilingual) and to help reduce personal and racial isolation.

All participants, including chief administrators, principals, supervisors, teachers, artists, parents and other resource personnel, assist in program planning, execution and assessment. By engaging in the process, they develop a sense of pride and ownership in the program and the school and become effective advocates for the arts and public education.

Why the Arts Are Good for School Development

Why are the arts good for school development? Clues to the elusive, definitive answer lie in the rationale that makes a case for the arts and in the arts in general education goal: All the arts for all the children in entire schools. In other words, the daily and pervasive presence of the arts in a school and their integration into the teaching and learning process of all students can help effect total school reorganization and revitalization so that all children will benefit (see Exhibit 7).

I make no claim that basic skills and achievement rise solely because of the presence of the arts or that standardized test scores and minimum competency ratings improve because of an AGE program; variables influencing performance in these assessments have yet to be isolated, let alone controlled. It stands to reason, however, that if a school becomes a better workplace and the people in it are proud, satisfied and comfortable, productivity and general learning will improve. While both common sense and experience seem to support this inference, we have no reliable, statistically significant evidence to substantiate it. It is an important agenda item for the field of educational research and evaluation.

VIEWPOINT

"Arts in general education has been a key force in our desegregation plan, but it's much more than that. Good God, who in the world wants their kid to go through a so-called minimum competency program? So they can have a seventh-grade reading level and brag about it? Our building principals understand this, and they are the key to the success of this program."

(Superintendent)

E X H I B I T   7

SOME OUTCOMES TO ANTICIPATE

Following are some of the outcomes I have observed over the years in schools that are working toward change through the arts:

— Standardized test scores do not go down and learning in the "basics" is not jeopardized; it tends to be reinforced when certain arts techniques, concepts and processes are applied by skilled and experienced classroom teachers and specialists.

— Attitudes toward school and attendance improve among both students and teachers.

— Vandalism and violence diminish and a sense of personal pride in and ownership of the school develops.

— Morale climbs; people feel better about themselves and less isolated. They start to trust each other and work together to come up with creative solutions to traditionally difficult problems.

— New and improved programs, services and activities emerge. New instructional approaches and materials are developed and widely shared.

— Better and more varied programs in the arts and in arts-enlivened curricular areas tend to attract certain segments of the population who are wary of public education.

— Principals, teachers and parents behave in different ways individually and as a group. Roles and responsibilities change; new or hidden talents, abilities and interests are identified and tapped.

— Resource personnel from the community's arts and cultural organizations visit or become resident guest instructors and learn to work with teachers and students on mutually beneficial projects. The arts are a manifest presence in the school and artists become part of the extended school family.

— Students take a more active part in the life of the school. Their motivation for learning is increased, and as they find new avenues for self-expression and success, they relate more freely to their peers and "mentors."

— The climate of the school becomes livelier, more vital, more cheerful, and the environment changes from institutional drab to colorful and attractive. Space is used in more imaginative ways, and the school is often involved in restoration projects.

— Interest, support and involvement of the local and general community in its public schools is increased and vice versa. Parents become articulate advocates and active participants in school life. The school building serves as a community center for arts and cultural events.

— Support for public education has a broader base: existing financial, material and human resources are used in broader, more effective ways; new resources from the foundation, business and corporate communities are attracted as programs demonstrate their value.

School Development through the Arts and the Broader Aims of Education

When we examine school development through the arts in a larger context, it becomes apparent how arts in general education programs can help schools accomplish broad educational objectives.

John Goodlad describes four categories of goals for schooling in the U.S.:[1]

1. Academic (functional literacy)
2. Vocational (readiness for productive work and economic responsibility)
3. Social and civic (socialization for participation in a complex society)
4. Personal (self-fulfillment)

He breaks these broad categories into twelve goals based on an analysis and synthesis of statements by state and local boards of education:

1. Mastery of basic skills
2. Career and vocational education
3. Intellectual development
4. Acculturation
5. Interpersonal relations
6. Autonomy
7. Citizenship
8. Creativity and aesthetic perception
9. Self-concept
10. Emotional and physical well-being
11. Moral and ethical character
12. Self-realization

At first glance, goal number eight seems the only place where the arts have a direct and indisputable role to play. On closer inspection, it becomes obvious that the arts can help schools reach each of the twelve commonly agreed-upon educational purposes—directly or indirectly.

In the Fund's approach to arts in general education, the arts were not just for the gifted and talented or for the cultivation of the so-called finer or higher side of human nature. Rather, it was felt that they could help school superintendents and school board members, as chief administrators and

---

[1] *What Schools Are For*, John Goodlad, Phi Delta Kappa Educational Foundation, 1979, pp. 44; 46-52.

policy-makers, realize their overall instructional and social objectives, galvanize community support for the schools and add a touch of class, glamour and excitement to the process. When we were able to translate these rather global statements into specific examples of benefits for each child, resistance and skepticism generally softened.

Unfortunately, not enough hard research data exists to convince those—and there are many—who are dubious at best and hostile at worst toward the arts value of the arts for schooling. Recent clinical research in the synergistic relationship of the left and right brain hemisphere functions indicates the importance of the affective domain to balanced, holistic learning and intellectual as well as emotional development. As evidence mounts, the case for the arts in the schools and the role they can play in human development will be considerably strengthened. There are other studies under way that are investigating the positive effect of the arts on oral communication skills, self-concept, satisfaction on the job and the climate of the school. I suspect, however, that there are many who will not be satisfied until someone proves conclusively that the arts, alone, can guarantee greater academic (cognitive) achievement and higher standardized test scores in reading and math.

"THIS IS NOT A SANTA CLAUS PROJECT, BUT . . . ": AGE AND WHAT'S IN IT FOR YOU

On one of my first consulting trips to Hartford, Edythe Gaines (by then the new superintendent) asked me to help launch their AGE program, explain its purpose and describe its benefits. During the course of a meeting, her assistant superintendent for elementary instruction, Charles Senteio, said to a curious but still skeptical group of principals and staff, "This is not a Santa Claus project, but what it offers you and your schools is. . . ," and he went on to mention a long list of items.

The phrase was a good one, and I have used it ever since because it answers in part the first question asked by most newcomers to AGE: "What's in it for me?" They mean, of course, how much money and resources are available, and what will their share be?

It was always difficult for people to accept that a partnership with a Rockefeller did not automatically mean bushel barrels full of money. It also took a lot of talking to convince people that we did not have a prepackaged program designed to improve basic skills, the results of which we would measure in easily quantifiable and impressive numbers. Perhaps the most difficult task was to explain that arts in general education was a fairly well-defined although flexible concept that each school could put into daily practice in its own inimitable fashion. School people are not accustomed to being given ownership of an idea, let alone the encouragement, power and support to work it out in their own settings.

We finally convinced most people of the sincerity if not the total authenticity of our explanations. They simply refused to believe there would be no money and no additional resources. They usually proved to be right, but it was the kind of money that the program gradually attracted, in bits and pieces—not up-front, massive, incentive funds. The "hidden" resources were primarily those that already existed—largely untapped—in their own schools and community.

The inevitable question posed during discussions of this kind was if there wasn't any money, then what on earth was there to make the commitment of time and effort to the network and AGE worthwhile? When we began, our answers were "quality education for all children, personal and professional growth and fulfillment, strength and comfort in unity, consulting assistance" and a whole string of unassailable intangibles. It was probably not our rhetoric but our fervent and crusading spirit that persuaded many courageous principals and teachers all over the nation to join with us. I am sure they suspected all the while that we had both "the program" and the money up our sleeves.

AGE may or may not look like a Santa Claus project at the outset, but the programs did attract federal, state and private resources, and it would be naïve and misleading to leave the impression that participants committed to it solely for intrinsic rewards. Theodore Berger of the New York Foundation for the Arts, for example, estimated that over a ten-year period his organization was responsible for allocating about $1,000,000 in direct and indirect services to New York City, much of it earmarked for AGE. In the seventies, Little Rock, Seattle and Winston-Salem were also the beneficiaries of federal (arts in education, desegregation, gifted and talented), state (Title IV-C innovation, arts agencies, tax-levy) and local (agencies, Junior Leagues, tax-levy) arts and special project dollars. AGE did take money, but it was probably the multiplicity of sources it could tap and the purposes for which supplementary funds were used that helped distinguish it from the financing of other school improvement efforts.

How to Build Districtwide and School-based AGE Programs

GUIDELINES AND STRATEGIES

CONSIDERATIONS FOR SCHOOL SYSTEMS INTERESTED IN ARTS IN GENERAL EDUCATION PROGRAMS

The New York City AGE program began in 1973. By 1976—three short years later—five additional school districts had joined forces with the Fund and decided to form the League of Cities for the Arts in Education. The formation and operation of the League were examined in an earlier chapter. It might be helpful now to present an outline of the process by which League members set up, maintained and expanded their individual efforts.

News about the League had spread quickly, and the Fund was soon deluged with requests for information and participation. Although we were in no position financially to expand the League itself as an operating foundation, we felt we had an obligation to make information about the network available to others. If we couldn't enlarge the network or even provide from our own collective ranks all the consulting and technical assistance that was being demanded, we could at least try to put something in writing that would offer others a framework for planning and development. While written materials of this nature are no substitute for face-to-face, on-site encounters, a short, practical document might at least define a starting point for our growing and impatient audience.

What people wanted was a rationale for the arts in education, a definition of AGE and a plan of action for carrying it out. This chapter deals not so much with the "why" and the "what" as with the "how to." It is a composite series of steps based on the League's collective experience, a "model process" or "process model." It does not prescribe a categorical formula for program content nor a strictly linear and sequential approach to program design and development. Instead, it sets forth the concept, elements, strategies and some questions that any school or school system ought to consider before and after embarking on an AGE program.

The Concept and the Process

The basic conviction that underlies all League programs is that all the arts are integral to the education of all children because they can make an important contribution to the daily schooling process, kindergarten through high school, throughout entire school systems.

The hypothesis being tested is that the quality of education and equality of educational opportunity can improve when:

— quality programs in all the arts are available to all students
— the arts are related to each other and to other disciplines
— the community's artists and its arts and cultural resources are used regularly in and out of the school building
— special needs of special children (the gifted and talented, the handicapped, the bilingual) are met by the arts and through participation in creative activities
— the arts are used to create learning environments and activities that help reduce personal and racial isolation and increase self-esteem

This hypothesis is both fluid and flexible. The above five points often appeared as the main objectives or characteristics of League programs in proposals for funding or other descriptive materials.

The strategies devised to test this hypothesis are derived from a theory of educational change that regards the individual school as the most effective social unit for self-renewal because it is the smallest, yet most complete setting in which formal schooling takes place on a continuum. According to this theory, the principal can be both a creative educational leader and an effective social engineer when he or she works closely with staff, children, parents and community on programs that gradually and systematically translate the school's educational philosophy into daily reality. It is assumed that when those who have a stake in the consequences reach important decisions through a continuing round of dialogue, decision-making, action and evaluation of issues and problems, benefits can accrue to the total school community and especially the children.

Schools, however, cannot go it alone if they wish to make fundamental, comprehensive and enduring changes in their structure and operation. They need the support of other schools, the school district, the community and other local, state and national resourcesto help them to manage the change process. The means for securing this support is through collaborative action.

Thus, a network of schools committed to the same philosophical approach is formed. This network is supported by a "hub" (a person or a team of people) that coordinates its activities, seeks out and secures needed resources and provides technical and consulting assistance.

Under Certain Conditions

Experience with the League and with other comprehensive arts in education programs reveals the circumstances under which programs of this nature develop, thrive and survive. Following are a series of questions that might be asked before a school system decides to start a program. It is also useful to refer to them periodically during the planning, development and expansion process in order to determine the rate and nature of progress being made.

1. Are the school system and the community relatively stable and yet resilient enough to respond to change?
2. Is there (or is there likely to be) evidence of continuing top-level leadership and support for the concept of a comprehensive arts in general education program?
3. Can support be generated from parents, the arts and education communities, volunteer and civic groups, unions, professional associations, business and industry, local and state legislators?
4. Is the notion of partnerships—to plan, implement, fund— accepted by those who will be involved?
5. Have there been discussions with administrators, supervisors, principals, teachers, arts specialists, artists and heads of arts organizations and agencies, in order to make clear that the arts in general education concept provides a framework for a comprehensive educational approach and is not just a special arts program, an artists' residency, a cultural enrichment series or a remedial effort?

6. Have potential sources of planning and development funds been explored at the local, state and federal level? Is it clearly understood that "outside" funds are used mainly for special programmatic or developmental purposes and that the regular school budget will support the main cost of program administration and operation?

Getting Started

Getting started on an arts in general education program may (and probably should) take as long as a year or two, depending on the size and complexity of the school system, the configuration of the proposed network and the obstacles encountered.

Ideally, the initial impulse to start the program comes from the school district, but it can also come from a variety of other sources: a Junior League, a private foundation, a college or university, a state or community arts council, an arts institution, a group of concerned citizens. Regardless of its point of origin, community groups should understand from the beginning that the school system is legally responsible for the education of children and must have the final say in decisions that affect this process. While the school system must be committed and involved from the outset, the superintendent may choose to delegate some of the initial research and planning responsibilities to committees or task forces (see Exhibit 8).

BUILDING THE PROGRAM AT THE GRASSROOTS LEVEL: SCHOOL DEVELOPMENT THROUGH THE ARTS

School-based activity should begin as soon as the schools have been identified and the network and the hub are set up. Here are the components of the process and some strategies for carrying it out.

AGE School-based Planning Committees: Composition, Structure And Tasks

In arts in general education program networks, each school forms an AGE planning committee (or a schoolwide planning committee among whose priorities is the arts in general education program). Depending on the size and nature of the school, the planning committee, often led by the principal, can consist of the entire faculty or a representative core group (supervisors, generalists and specialists), all of whom volunteer for the task. Parents, artists and student leaders may also be represented.

EXHIBIT   8 _____

COMPREHENSIVE DISTRICTWIDE PLANNING STRATEGIES

Here is a synopsis of the strategies that were employed (sequentially or simultaneously) by League sites to place their comprehensive, districtwide AGE programs.

A. **FORM A PLANNING COMMITTEE CONSISTING OF KEY PROFESSIONALS AND PRACTITIONERS FROM THE SCHOOL SYSTEM, THE ARTS COMMUNITY, COLLEGES AND CIVIC ORGANIZATIONS.** The planning group's task is to design a comprehensive program. It should:

1. Examine the rationale, definition and concept of the arts in general education and their application to local conditions.

2. Study the local and national scene for promising programs and practices.

3. Conduct a needs assessment and identify existing and potential resources—human, material, financial— in and out of the school system; determine where the gaps are and suggest how to close them.

4. Prepare a proposed comprehensive plan with specific program objectives, activities, time line and outcomes, and include an evaluation design.

5. Suggest the size, composition and operational structure of a network and determine whether it should consist of one tier of "demonstration" schools or include additional tiers of "cooperating" or "satellite" schools.

6. Suggest the composition of a coordinating "hub" and define its administrative organization, role and responsibilities.

7. Check out all details of the proposed plan with potential participants and sponsors.

8. Report results to key decision-makers in the school system and the arts and business community.

9. Formalize acceptance of the plan and announce intentions publicly.

B. FORM AN ADVISORY COMMITTEE (OPTIONAL). The original planning committee can usually be converted into a consultative body. Responsibilities, roles and functions should be redefined.

C. IDENTIFY THE PERSONNEL FOR PROGRAM MANAGEMENT. Coordination may be provided by a single person working in consultation with others or by a multidisciplinary team. In most situations a team seems to work better than a single person since many diverse talents and abilities (not to mention time and energy) are required to coordinate a comprehensive, interdisciplinary program. The coordinators should be personable, capable administrators and have decision-making authority, power and political savvy. They should have practical knowledge of the arts, curriculum and instruction and understand how the schools and the system operate. They should be articulate on their feet and in writing.

D. INFORM ALL SCHOOLS IN THE SYSTEM OF THE OPPORTUNITY TO VOLUNTEER FOR THE PROGRAM (BY LETTER OF INVITATION, PUBLIC EVENT, THE MEDIA). Include the rationale, the need for and a description of the proposed program, the commitments of the district [and partner(s)] and guidelines and criteria for participation. Outline the time and task commitments required from the school and the benefits that can be anticipated. Request brief proposals for participation (declarations of commitment and intent signed by principals, parent association chairs and area superintendents and school board presidents, if appropriate).

E. FORM A TASK FORCE (OR ASK MEMBERS OF THE PLANNING/ADVISORY COMMITTEE) to screen proposals, visit the schools, talk with administrators, staff and parents and make recommendations for participation.

F. IDENTIFY SCHOOLS AND ANNOUNCE PARTICIPANTS. Describe the configuration of the network and the rationale for its formation. The original network should be small enough to manage and large enough to notice.

G. FORM THE NETWORK. Hold planning meetings to discuss and clarify the concept and the program. Chart an immediate, middle and long-range course of action based on needs and concerns as identified by coordinators, supervisors and network principals and their staffs. Teachers can also be included, providing numbers and space is not a problem, the tasks are appropriate and their role is an active not passive one.

H. REVIEW EXISTING AND SECURE ADDITIONAL FEDERAL, STATE AND LOCAL RESOURCES. Allocate or reallocate them based on the needs as identified. Decisions should be made in consultation with the schools.

I. VISIT THE SCHOOLS TO HELP THEM GET STARTED. The coordinator(s) should meet periodically with each principal and staff to discuss a schoolwide inventory, the school development process and how the arts can facilitate it. They should also help schools form a planning committee to identify and assess the needs and opportunities and strategies for implementation.

J. MEET WITH ARTISTS, ARTS AND CULTURAL RESOURCE ORGANIZATIONS AND ARTS AGENCIES TO DEFINE OVERALL PROGRAM PURPOSES AND NEEDS. The coordinator(s) should examine existing programs and services, suggest new approaches to be planned jointly with the schools and organize planning meetings.

The main purpose of the AGE planning committee is to provide inter-active school-based, articulate leadership for the idea of the arts in general education and the energy and brainpower for designing programs that make the arts available to every child in the building. The planning commit-tee also serves as liaison with the rest of the school faculty, the hub and the general public (see Exhibits 9-12).

Once the purpose and composition of the planning committee have been established, you should determine its structure and operation. You will need to decide:

— when, where and how often will you meet
— whether you should set up task-oriented committees, and by what criteria
— what is your timeline
— who is empowered to make recommendations, and to whom, when, where and how (verbally, in writing)
— what is the decision-making process (negotiation and con-sensus; majority vote; unilateral executive decision)
— what is the chain of command, and where does the buck stop

Strategies for Gathering Information: A School and Communitywide Arts Study

The AGE planning committee tasks outlined above suggest a process by which you can determine what you, as the school community, want to do, identify the resources you need to get the job done, find out what you have on hand and then figure out how to close the inevitable management, in-structional and resource gaps. The first order of business calls for a brief statement of the school's philosophy and its position regarding the place of the arts in the curriculum and the school program. Next, you need to deter-mine your immediate, middle and long-range objectives. (Do not spend end-less hours agonizing over the precise wording of the philosophy, rationale and goals and objectives. Arrive at a temporary consensus and move into action. The words will invariably change as you get more deeply involved in the reality of the process.)

This type of arts study calls for the design of simple questionnaires, some field research and then a series of rounds of Goodlad's DDAE process—discussions, decisions, actions and evaluations—through each phase of your investigation and information-gathering.

You will need to design a school staff inventory that consist of a series of friendly questions. These should be designed to ferret out everyone's outside professional and personal arts and cultural interests, hobbies and amateur pursuits—all of which you can tap for instructional or related purposes.

You will need another inventory to take stock of the physical and material resources—space, equipment, supplies, instruments, old costumes, material, scenery—that exist in your school and at your district office and those you will need to beg, borrow or scrounge from people in your immediate community. Be sure to scour the school building from top to bottom. Unlock all the closets, open all the dusty cartons, clean out idle desks. I have heard amazing stories of buried treasures uncovered.

Here are some practical ideas for using the information-gathering tasks as strategies for building awareness and interest in the arts in general education:

— The materials and equipment inventory gives you an opportunity to enlist your students and parents in a school (and perhaps community-wide) treasure hunt.

— The staff inventory is a wonderful strategy for alerting everyone to the school's current mission and building staff interest and morale.

— The community survey is an ideal mechanism for getting students, parents and other volunteers out into the neighborhood and by the same token enlisting the help of local business people in the school's arts in education program.

VIEWPOINT

"An arts in general education program helps a school change and broadens the decision-making base. It is also good politics because it's one of the few things everyone can support. It commands community attention and city and nationwide support."

(Chief administrator)

E X H I B I T   9 ⎯⎯⎯⎯⎯⎯⎯⎯⎯⎯⎯⎯⎯⎯⎯

TASKS OF THE AGE PLANNING COMMITTEE

1. Design and conduct a schoolwide needs assessment in the arts in order to develop a long-range plan of action that will reach every child in the school. Do a schoolwide study to determine what the faculty, students and parents need and want. Discover where the gaps are and then solicit ideas from the school community on how to fill them.

2. Design and administer a school staff and facilities inventory. Determine what exists in the way of space, materials and personnel. Include everyone in the school building—the administration, the office staff, guidance counselors, driver education, librarians, other specialists, the custodian. Identify "hidden" and "amateur" arts interests, talents and pursuits.

3. Draft a long-range plan for arts in general education (or a schoolwide plan that includes AGE) that will ultimately be discussed and ratified by the entire school community. Articulate the school's philosophy, naming the arts as a priority and indicating where and why the arts fit in. Describe immediate, middle and long-range goals, specific objectives and an overall budget for the AGE program. Solicit arts programming ideas from the entire faculty, parents, students (if appropriate) and community resource personnel.

4. Canvass the school and the community for actual or potential financial support (direct and indirect). Identify people (including volunteers), space, facilities, equipment, supplies and money for program design and implementation.

5. Research and identify community arts and cultural resources and establish and coordinate in-school arts
   programs and visits to community arts activities and events.

6. Act as school liaisons and public relations contacts with
   the hub, district staff and the general community.

7. Organize and budget money and time for staff and curriculum development workshops. Identify the school staff,
   community resource administrators and artists who will
   help plan, conduct and evaluate these support services.
   Make sure to budget funds for artist fees (and teacher
   compensation if activities take place after school or on
   their personal time). Publicize these activities and recruit
   participants.

8. Develop a communications system to disseminate information within the school and between the school, the
   community and other schools (through flyers, newsletters, faculty conferences, celebrations, retreats).

9. Participate in and make recommendations for management and financial decisions regarding AGE programs
   (especially artist services, staff and curriculum development activities, site visits to community cultural institutions) and priorities.

10. Organize and conduct on-going school-based research and
    evaluation studies on the arts and their impact on teach-
    ing, learning and school climate. Explore partnerships
    with the district office, colleges and universities and the
    business community.

11. Formulate a fundraising plan. Ask the district for assis-
    tance in designing it and carrying it out.

E X H I B I T   1 0 _____

THE SCHOOL-BASED LONG-RANGE PLANNING PROCESS:FIVE BASIC QUESTIONS FOR ARTS IN GENERAL EDUCATION SCHOOL PLANNING COMMITTEES

There are five basic questions that each arts in general education school-based planning committee needs to address so as to develop appropriate goals, objectives and a comprehensive long-range plan of action. Once schools have begun to answer these questions, it is extremely beneficial to share the process and results with other schools at network meetings and retreats.

1. How can our entire school plan for, develop and change through the arts?

2. How can the study of and about the arts and the creative process be integrated into the daily classroom experience of every child in this building?

3. How can the school meet the five main objectives outlined in the system's plan to which it has made a commitment: strengthen and expand study in and about each of the arts; promote interdisciplinary teaching and learning in the arts and between the arts and other subjects; use community arts and cultural resources more effectively; meet the special academic, social and cultural needs of special populations; reduce personal and racial isolation?

4. How will the school meet its own objectives, such as increased attendance, higher morale, reduced vandalism, better attitudes toward learning, greater community and parental involvement, maintaining racial and ethnic balance and better integration of staff and students?

5. How will the school relate to and communicate with the hub, the other schools in the district, the arts in general education network, the region, the country?

Making Mid-Course Corrections: Suggestions for AGE Networks

As programs move "off the page" and into operation, they develop a life of their own. Changes occur and, in domino fashion, precipitate others, of which some are desirable and some are not. Participants and decision-makers should be responsive to the flow of current events so as to make appropriate and timely adjustments. Here are some issues that surface and some guidance on how to proceed:

ESTABLISHING AND MAINTAINING BALANCE AMONG PROGRAM COMPONENTS. Frequently, the first year or so of operation will focus on some of the children, one or two art forms and one or two of the five main objectives. While obviously all aims cannot be realized simultaneously and immediately and you do have to start somewhere, you should be careful to keep programs from becoming "unbalanced," one-dimensional or for only a relatively few students.

REORGANIZING THE HUB.   The hub often changes as programs develop. A single coordinator may find that it is difficult if not impossible to manage all the complex aspects of a comprehensive program without additional help. If the hub is a team, its personnel may not adequately reflect the variety of talents and abilities required. Staff turnovers may result in leadership gaps. When these events occur, you should recognize them as a good opportunity to reorganize the hub and to redefine administrative roles and responsibilities.

REORGANIZING THE NETWORK.   Many networks in the League have remained relatively stable. Inevitably, however, principals retire, move to other schools or fail to follow through on their original commitments. Some may feel after a year or so that the program makes too heavy a demand on their time. Others may be disappointed in what they perceive as a lack of special recognition, extra resources or financial support.

In addition to network membership, other questions of an organizational or practical nature may arise:

— Was the original group of schools too small, just right, too large?

— Were the number of categories of membership and the number of schools in each manageable, and did they make programmatic sense?

— Has the concept of school development through the arts been internalized and given adequate time and support to flourish?

If the strength of the network appears to be in jeopardy, it may be wise and necessary to consider reorganization. You should review the

EXHIBIT 11

GUIDELINES FOR MANAGEMENT TEAM OR SCHOOL-WIDE DISCUSSIONS ABOUT THEIR ARTS IN GENERAL EDUCATION PROGRAMS

The first set of questions you should address is of a general and philosophical nature. Answers to them will provide you with a context for your program and a framework for further planning. Reminder: Do not spend too much time on the exact wording of a rationale or on the abstract goals and objectives; get on with the identification of specific resources and the concrete guts of the program.

As you work through these questions, keep in mind the following:

— What might classroom teachers, specialists and artists be doing to contribute as individuals, as a team?
— What kinds of staff and curriculum development activities will be required to support these activities?

QUESTION SET I: PHILOSOPHY AND RATIONALE— WHY AND TO WHOM DO WE TEACH THE ARTS

— who are our learners, what are their group and individual needs
— why are we teaching the arts; how will they meet our students' needs
— what populations do our children represent
— which cultures will be represented, which languages must we know
— which arts will we teach; where will we start
— are we teaching in, through, about, for the arts

QUESTION SET II: PROGRAM DESIGN—WHAT SHALL WE TEACH WHEN, WHERE AND HOW OFTEN

— what will we teach, by what methods
— what is the scope and sequence of study for all grades in our school; at what grades do we begin teaching what
— how frequent will classes be, how long
— when and where will instruction take place (preferably during regular school hours, but after school and on weekends to supplement your options)

QUESTION SET III

The third set of questions will start you thinking about how to define instructional qualifications. It also gets at the nature and quantity of resources you have at your disposal. When you have completed your inventories and have a first rough draft of your long-range plan, you will be in a better position to address the question of who shall teach the arts in your arts in general education program in light of the actual alternatives available to you. (Please refer to Chapter Seven, "Who Shall Teach the Arts," for a more detailed examination of this issue):

— what are the ideal skills, knowledge, information and experience the teachers of the arts must possess; what professional credentials are required by law or union contract

— who is available—on staff, in the community

— among those identified as available and affordable, who appears to be qualified by training, experience and temperament to meet our expectations; can they deliver a quality process to produce excellent products (achievement, skills, knowledge, etc.)

QUESTION SET IV

The fourth set of questions concerns your instructional support and program monitoring support systems:

— what kind of support services do we need, when and from whom for leadership training, staff development and curriculum development

— how will we keep track of progress and know whether and to what degree we have succeeded in our intentions and what measures of success will we use

— who will foot the bill and how will we satisfy them that we have used our resources wisely?

EXHIBIT 1 2 _____

> ### DISTRICT-WIDE STRATEGIES TO SUPPORT ARTS IN GENERAL EDUCATION PROGRAMS

The arts in general education networks in League sites and other locations have employed the following strategies to support school-based program and planning:

Monthly meetings of demonstration school principals and program coordinator(s) to discuss issues, meet with consultants in the arts and education, and define, redefine and evaluate plans and programs. These meetings may take place at a school, at the central office or elsewhere in the community. They should be mandatory (part of the commitment each principal makes when volunteering to join the network).

— Site visits by network principals (and staff) to network schools (and in the case of the League, to other sites) to observe what is happening, talk with administration and staff and explore a particular issue or problem in depth. These meetings are conducted by the host school principals (or site coordinators) and follow their agenda. The program coordinators, central administrators, partners and other resource personnel participate. When appropriate, local and national officials are also invited to these occasions.

— Half- or full-day schoolwide planning meetings in which the entire school staff assembles to define and

original guidelines and criteria for membership and update them, taking care not to make them so stringent that even the original network schools, if they had to reapply, would no longer pass muster. Give the original schools a fresh chance to declare their continuing commitment or to opt out. Add new schools and/or move schools from one tier to another. Form new and functionally related networks. In all cases, participation should continue to be voluntary but not necessarily cost-free: decide on a (scaled or flat) membership fee and other direct or in-kind financial contributions (release time for teachers, a percentage of a staff position, travel and transportation subsidy) you may feel are appropriate for full participation. You should be sure to formulate your new membership policy in cooperation with all the original principals, ideally at a network retreat or an all-day meeting.

solve issues and problems related to their arts in general education program.

— Network retreats or all-day planning and development conferences.

— School/community events, fund-raising affairs, showcases, festivals, performances, exhibits to which the media are invited.

— Staff and curriculum development activities, in and out of school (on school time, after school, for credit or not).

— Meetings with artists, arts and cultural organizations and other resource personnel to plan and develop programs, services and events.

— Artist residencies: short and long term, by individuals and resource teams.

— Research and evaluation efforts on the impact of the arts on classroom practice (questionnaires, reports, observations, interviews, home-made criterion-referenced tests, narrative histories, case studies, etc.).

— Documentation and dissemination activities (conferences, seminars, workshops, reports, portfolios, videotapes, film, exhibits, manuals, newsletter articles for school and local newspapers).

Extending the Concept,
Enlarging the Network—or Both

At some point, generally after about two years of school-based operation, the question of expansion is inevitably raised. Key decision-makers are encouraged by signs of the program's effectiveness and staying power and continue or increase their support. Other schools in the system are beginning to want "a piece of the action." The word is out, with some evidence to support it, that the arts in general education concept offers schools another way to reach some of their goals. You now have a substantial amount of experience that you can share with others verbally and in writing.

You can address the question of how to extend the concept to other schools in several ways. You can feed new schools into "open slots" in the original network, enlarge the network, set up new and related networks, or a combination of all three. Fundamentally, it means "going public."

Formal Strategies for Expansion[1]

Following are some of the ways that League and other sites have expanded their networks:

1. A school system, seeing the value and effectiveness of the idea in a few demonstration schools, declares the arts in general education a priority for all its elementary and secondary schools and encourages principals and teachers to join the program in a series of sub- or mini-networks, all coordinated by the central office. Increased staff and administrative time are allocated from central, and the original demonstration network provides consulting and training services for the new schools. Curriculum guides, administrator manuals and resource books based on actual experience are provided as references.

2. Programs begun in a few primary or elementary schools gradually and systematically expand to all elementary, middle and ultimately senior high schools. Technical and consulting assistance to facilitate this process is provided by curriculum supervisors from central, arts resource teams and a buddy system between original and new schools. Program, staff and curriculum development materials support this process. Schools are sometimes grouped in subnetworks according to grade level, program emphasis or location.

3. In systems that have districts or areas, "mini-" arts in general education networks are set up within geographical boundaries using the original demonstration schools as reference points and their staffs as resource personnel. The same planning process is undergone, and schools still volunteer and compete for participation. Main administrative support is provided by the district office with supplementary assistance coming from the central office, the hub and the community.

4. School systems under a desegregation mandate create magnet and special emphasis schools, some of which focus on the arts and the arts in general education. These schools form their own networks, are often staffed by former "demonstra-

---

[1] See Chapter 10 for a description of another set of network expansion strategies designed in 1989 by the New Orleans School District's Project Arts Connection.

tion school" principals and are served by the coordinator or arts resource team from the central board.

5. The central office sets up other networks using the arts in general education model process and interrelates the arts with the particular area of study, e.g. career, environmental, ethnic heritage and special education. Arts in general education principals, staff and management, plus central board or district supervisors, assist in this process through leadership, staff and curriculum development workshops and conferences. Manuals and other publications are used as references. These "new" networks have functional relationships with the arts in general education network.

6. Federal ESAA Special Arts Project Funds (Desegregation), Title IV-C and other state funds and grants are used to adapt and test out the arts in education concept in other schools and sites in those states that have declared the arts in general education a priority and eligible for funding. In this case the state education department, in concert with the state arts agency and local school districts, takes responsibility for coordination and servicing of a statewide network and, with the original demonstration sites, provides information and consulting expertise.

7. Regional networks involving a number of neighboring states are established with local, state and federal funds, using the original AGE district as hub and headquarters for dissemination activities, a source of technical and consulting assistance and staff and curriculum development materials.

8. State and local arts councils that have been closely involved as partners or sponsors of arts in general education programs spread the word to their constituency and to other schools and school systems.

9. National programs, such as the National Endowment for the Arts' Arts in Education Program, the National Endowment for the Humanities and the Department of Education/Kennedy Center's Alliance for Arts Education Program, help to initiate

VIEWPOINT

"AGE is a 'you' program. The principal is respected as an educational leader as well as a systems manager and encouraged to make innovations."

(Principal)

or support the concept of networks for the arts in education through competitive grants and categorical aid.

Informal Strategies for Expansion

The above are organized and formal ways to extend the arts in general education concept. Following are some that are informal, indirect or often accidental:

— Superintendents, chief administrators and principals move to new positions or places and take their philosophy and experience with them.

— Principals and staff from non-network schools meet principals and staff from demonstration schools sharing certain arts resources. Ideas and information are exchanged, and certain arts in general education practices are put into effect in non-network schools as a result of cross-fertilization.

— National volunteer organizations (such as the Junior League) and civic groups (such as the Urban Coalition) that have been involved with arts in general education programs share their experience with other schools and organizations through conferences, newsletters and other publications.

— Heads of schools in programs such as a principal-as-leader program or other school improvement initiatives that subscribe to an educational change theory similar to that upon which arts in general education programs are based pick up on the idea through formal and informal meetings, conferences and other means of communication.

5

Networking and Collaboration
A STRATEGIC DESIGN FOR CHANGE

"I DON'T MIND BEING LONELY IF YOU ARE LONELY, TOO": THE GOODLAD FACTOR

During my first year on staff at the Fund, when I was not walking the New York City beat, I was deliberately and systematically put through an orientation (more accurately, indoctrination) process by Kathy Bloom and her staff at the time: Jack Morrison, Gene Wenner and Jerry Hausman. I traveled the country with them, visiting most of the "earlier project" sites located, for example, in University City, Missouri; Jefferson County, Colorado; Oklahoma City, Oklahoma; Mineola, Long Island; and Portland, Oregon. I also attended an awe-inspiring spate of national and professional conferences and had the opportunity to meet with, listen to and learn from an impressive array of "elder statespeople" and current practitioners. The experience proved invaluable.

It was on one of those early trips that I had the good fortune to meet John Goodlad, then dean of the Graduate School of Education at the University of California, Los Angeles, and director of research for the Institute for the Development of Education Activities (I/D/E/A), the education arm of the Kettering Foundation. I had heard a great deal about John, and although I had not yet read any of his work, I was looking forward to meeting him. He had started on his ambitious, multi-year Study of Schooling, and the JDR 3rd Fund and the Rockefeller Foundation were supporting the arts component of this endeavor.

At our first meeting in his office at the University, I had an opportunity to mention the plans under way in New York City. John's eyes lit up. He told me that the school change theory, the principal-as-leader concept and our approach to networking bore a striking resemblance to much of his own field work and research, especially with the Lab School in Los Angeles and the study on the League of Cooperating Schools in Southern California. It was clear that although we were three thousand miles apart geographically, John and I were next-door neighbors philosophically. We struck an informal bargain to keep in touch.

As time went by, the grantor-grantee relationship between the Fund and John developed into a partnership. We invited him to work with us as a program advisor and to participate in our national dissemination conferences featuring the League, the Coalition of States and several of our earlier project sites. He also spent considerable time at the Fund's expense as a consultant to administrators, supervisors, principals and others in the New York City and Seattle programs. John was a friend and a colleague who also served as a mentor. He often had me join his I/D/E/A staff meetings, where they wrestled with some of the thorny but fascinating problems presented by the Study of Schooling.

In addition to reaping the benefits of his rich experience and practical counsel, I learned some valuable lessons about the field of educational research and the mercurial nature of the difficulties and frustrations that even experienced investigators encounter when trying to gather and interpret reliable data about schools and schooling.

Among John's many talents is his ability to capture a complex but important idea in a single homily. His oft-repeated statement, "I don't mind being lonely if you are lonely, too," neatly conveyed the notion that anyone embarked on the course of significant change in education is out on a limb. His message was: Take heart; strength and comfort can be found in the company of others with a common cause. Not totally original, perhaps, but certainly a pithy way to describe the value of networking to those principals and teachers struggling through the often solitary process of improving their schools.

As John spent more time with members of the League, he became convinced that AGE had more than a fair chance of success because it relied in so many ways on networking and collaboration. It is time to take a closer look at the phenomenon of networking and some of its manifestations.

A DEFINITION OF NETWORKING: BEYOND THE ROLODEX

Recently someone said to me somewhat facetiously that a network was nothing more or less than a good rolodex. The statement, like most wisecracks, has some truth to it, but it is too facile and misleading. A good rolodex is an important tool for matching people with the answers to those with the questions, but so is a computer if properly programmed. Networking is more than a mechanized computer dating game; it is an orchestrated, people-to-people process that requires a good deal of thought, patience and nurturing to make it work. Let me give you an updated version of a definition that I presented a few years ago at an "Arts and the Child" conference in Raleigh, North Carolina:

The Network: A Mechanism for Change

Networking is the regular and voluntary coming together of people with common or overlapping concerns to discuss issues, share solutions to problems and generate new ideas. It is an essential strategy in the planning and development of comprehensive arts in general education programs that have as their goal "all the arts for all the children."

Networking provides a nonthreatening, cost-effective mechanism for communication, mutual support and professional growth. It also furnishes a visible and sturdy platform for concerted action and attracts the attention and support of those who wish to effect change on a large scale. It helps promote the process of schoolwide change and improvement through the arts because it assumes that those who are working toward that end are each others' natural allies, best-equipped mentors and cost-free resources.

The Hub: A Coordinating Leader or a Team

To function effectively, all networks need a "hub," or organizing center. The hub usually consists of a team that provides leadership and on-site support services to its members.

VIEWPOINT

"It's the best device for leadership training that I know. You get immediate cost-free, expert technical assistance from on-the-job practitioners that you'd probably have to pay a fortune for otherwise, assuming, of course, you could find the right consultant to do the job."

The hub:

— coordinates and manages network activities
— helps maintain communication among program participants
— identifies, secures and "brokers" resources
— provides support, guidance and monitoring for program planning and development
— documents program activities and acts as a public relations liaison between the schools and the community
— champions the value of the arts in the education of the young

Membership, Size, Location

Arts in general education networks exist within and among individual schools and school systems, within and among state education departments and on a regional and national scale. Networks within school districts often link administrators, school principals, teachers, students, artists and arts organizations. They are large enough to notice and small enough to manage, depending on the size, structure and resources of the system and the community. Membership varies according to program needs and objectives, but it is always voluntary, not mandatory.

How the Process Works

An arts in general education network helps break down professional isolation; it operates laterally, peer-to-peer, as distinct from bureaucratically, from the top down. It relies on what John Goodlad has termed the DDAE process: a continuing, spiraling round of dialogue, decision-making, action and evaluation. The decision-making process rarely degenerates into a labor-management dispute. Network members and the hub arrive at solutions through negotiation and consensus rather than by unilateral fiat or external mandate.

The Value of Networking to Its Participants

The network's value is determined by the efficacy and efficiency of its service to its members. When individual needs conflict with the purposes of the larger group, decisions are reached by weighing the consequences for a particular member against the practical, political and financial realities that might affect the welfare or survival of the group.

The Value of Networking to Others in the Field

The network provides timely and useful technical and consulting assistance to the field. It can serve as an authentic forum for discussion of programs in progress. The hub and network members are a talent bank of experienced practitioners who can help others plan and execute their own arts in general education programs and help them form related coalitions. Since no one classroom, school, district or program is exactly like another, networks offer a wide but coherent choice of alternative models to study, choose from or adapt.

The Value of the Network to the National, State and Local Arts, Business and Funding Community

Arts in general education networks provide a tangible, organized and accessible field of operation that attracts the attention and support of those who wish to work as partners with the schools to effect broadscale change, conduct research or bring about specific improvements for a "critical mass" of students and teachers in, for example, curriculum and instruction. Rather than having to approach schools or districts one by one, potential arts, business and funding partners can contact and work through the network's hub or steering committee. This arrangement encourages community involvement in public education. It permits those unfamiliar with the schools and the school system to maxximize the impact of their resources and to make efficient use of their energy and ti me on purposes which are of concern to all participants.

HOW NETWORKING CAN BUILD, MAINTAIN AND EXPAND AGE PROGRAMS: TWO EXAMPLES FROM THE LEAGUE

AGE networks have served as political platforms for advocacy and survival as well as mechanisms for school desegregation. Following are two examples from League experience.

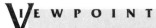

VIEWPOINT

"You can select solutions that suit you best from many different approaches."

"The Perils of Pauline" and the "Pedagogical Party Line": New York City Revisited

People in the New York City AGE program were no strangers to the art of surviving crises. They had managed to struggle through an impressive sequence of misfortunes, each of which seemed more severe than the last. "The walking wounded," as Kathy Bloom used to call them with affection and respect, bore their battle scars proudly. They felt that if they were able to prevail through several rounds of financial crises, teacher strikes and layoffs, changes in top administrative leadership and divisional reorganizations, there was virtually nothing left that was formidable enough to do them in.

In the fall of 1979, however, AGE suffered yet another brutal series of what threatened to be death-dealing blows. Our main champions and stalwart supporters at the Board of Education left for university jobs or were shifted to other positions. A severe budget cut led to one more reorganization of the Division of Curriculum and Instruction and, in the process, wiped out the line for the AGE coordinator. The formal partnership with the Fund, which served on several occasions as a bulwark against disaster, had dissolved when its program shut down. To this list add inflation, recession and declining enrollments, and the dismal picture is complete.

In a sequence of events reminiscent of film clips from "The Perils of Pauline," the force for survival that emerged and ultimately proved victorious was the unified clamor of thirteen AGE demonstration school principals who stubbornly refused to give up without a fight. They proceeded to:

— call emergency meetings, decide on a course of action and form committees to carry out designated tasks;

— demand hearings, send telegrams, write letters and generally "raise a ruckus" with the chancellor, his chief assistants, the acting head of curriculum and instruction and other decision makers; and

— contact congressmen and women, the media and any other influential voices they knew or could think of to bring attention to and pressure for their cause.

The results were astonishing. They manifested themselves in the following ways and roughly in the following order:

1. Money was "found" in a state-funded umbrella program to underwrite a half-year salary for an arts in general education coordinator with the proviso that membership in the network would increase by approximately 75 percent. (Participation had fluctuated over the years and the current rank of active network demonstration schools had dwindled to thirteen with another group of ten "cooperating schools.")

2. Sponsored by the Division of Curriculum and Instruction, a citywide "dissemination" conference was held at Central to announce the publication of the AGE Administrators Manual and Architecture Bulletin and to extend an official invitation to other schools to join the program. The conference hall was festooned with AGE displays. Chief administrators, a community superintendent, principals, teachers and artists made presentations and then broke into small groups to lead discussions and answer questions. A fact sheet and proposal forms were distributed. Raul Julia, noted actor and visiting artist in the program, struck a responsive chord in his keynote address when he said: "You are the artist in your own life. Be creative. Take a chance. Don't wait for money or resources to come to you. Make your own commitment first. The commitment will generate the resources because AGE is a good program. It celebrates the artist in all of us, and, frankly, I don't see the difference between being a good actor and an outstanding teacher."

3. In addition to regular and emergency principals' meetings, a day-and-a-half "retreat" (in the city, on school and personal time) was scheduled to make plans for expansion. A new organizational structure for the network was defined, roles and functions were spelled out and the agenda was set for an upcoming meeting with new schools. By that time, it was clear that AGE had made some new and important friends at Central who were supporting the program by their deeds as well as words.

4. A convocation was held at Central for all new (about thirty-five) school principals who had completed the response form. The *Administrators Manual, Architecture Bulletin,* and other materials were distributed. The terms and conditions of participation were spelled out along with the benefits to the school community. At this meeting (again chaired by the principals), the chancellor's senior assistant for instruction, Ron Edmonds, coined a wonderful phrase in the course of his introductory remarks to the group. He described the AGE philosophy and approach to school development as highly complementary to the theory underlying his newly launched School Improvement Program and to the Local School Development Program initiated by the New York Urban Coali-

V**IEW POINT**

"It means linking hands across school, department, district and other lines and joining in the search for solutions to the problems all of us share."

tion. He noted that AGE was very much in step with the current "pedagogical party line," which maintains that schools do make a difference, if not *the* difference in the education of children. He added that he was impressed with the voluntary principal-directed aspect of the effort and promised his full support and cooperation.

5. Meanwhile, word of continuing financial assistance from the umbrella program was received, and it was hoped that another Title IV-C state grant was forthcoming. Significantly, the proposal was written by Carol Fineberg, a former arts in general education coordinator, whose consultant services were paid for out of the demonstration school budgets. The principals had levied a program tax on themselves.

6. Finally, at an AGE party celebrating Charlotte Frank's appointment as director of the Division of Curriculum and Instruction, Chancellor Frank Macchiarola praised her leadership and assured us of his continued support.

These and many more events took place in the space of less than a school year, and while the story may not seem to have direct bearing on any other school district, it does point up the dramatic powers of networking. It also demonstrates how a diverse group of principals can work in concert with no financial compensation to save a program as well as enlarge it. What's more, the very struggle for survival not only strengthened the program internally but gave it more visibility and credibility citywide than it had had in a long time.

One sobering comment: AGE had begun over seven years earlier as a school change and development project, and "Design for Change" had been written three years before that. It took quite a while for the program to be recognized and pronounced "in step." It is an important lesson in patience and perseverance, though small comfort to those principals, for example, who must struggle every day to run their schools and at the same time fight to keep a program they believe in alive.[1]

A Study in Contrasts: The Seattle Story

In New York City, the AGE demonstration school principals not only saved the program but maintained their participation in it as a voluntary core group that would help expand the concept to new schools through a buddy

---

[1] How history repeats itself. The New York City AGE network is in exactly the same situation today (June 1990) as it was then—namely, cast adrift and leaderless at the Central Board of Education. The new schools chancellor is a strong proponent of school-based management teams, which has always been an essential AGE ingredient. Perhaps there is another rescue waiting in the wings.

system and other activities of a technical and consulting nature. The Seattle story, while not quite so melodramatic, provides a good illustration of how AGE can expand rapidly when a school system chooses to desegregate voluntarily and takes another approach to networking.

The Seattle program began in 1974 as the Arts for Learning (AFL) Project in six of the district's seventy-eight elementary schools. The major source of funds for planning and development originally came from the Junior League, which made a three-year grant of $40,000 that was stretched to cover a four-year period. As the program developed and gained steady and tangible support from the school district, local, state and federal funds, both public and private, were quickly attracted.

In 1977, to avoid a possible court order, the district embarked on a comprehensive plan to desegregate the school system, for which it received a substantial amount of federal assistance. On the basis of its experience with the AFL Project, the district felt that the arts were a natural vehicle for the social as well as curriculum integration process and proceeded to establish a number of arts in general education or arts-related networks for all grade levels. In contrast to New York City, the original AFL network was deliberately disbanded, and demonstration school principals were regrouped in several new consortia where they were asked to function as leaders and resource persons.

In 1980, there were thirty-one elementary and secondary arts in education schools in the district's 106 schools. State and federal financial support were considerable, and these monies were strengthened by a strong commitment from the superintendent, his cabinet and a general allocation of district staff, time and money.

In the beginning there were lean years, a small staff, a series of almost devastating tax-levy failures, changes in the superintendency, system reorganization and no full-fledged programs yet in evidence to provide tangible proof of AFL's value. Approximately six years later, the arts were fairly pervasive in about a third of the district's schools. In addition, Seattle became a reference point for a statewide arts in education effort and the headquarters for Arts Coalition Northwest, a regional program affecting three contiguous states: Alaska, Idaho and Oregon.

The desegregation effort certainly provided the major impetus for rapid expansion, but there were additional factors contributing to this "success" story: strong and articulate leadership at the top administrative levels, sustained support from the school board, parental and community satisfaction and pride, continued volunteer and professional assistance from the local arts community and the Junior League and a good working relationship with the state's Department of Public Instruction and the federal Education Department.

Not least important was the imaginative leadership provided by former Arts Supervisor Ray Thompson and a core of so-called middle managers who stubbornly breathed life and excitement into the day-to-day operation of the program and made sure that the various networks maintained functional connections with one another and with various curriculum and support areas.

Thus networking and collaboration were the keys to the growth of the program in Seattle.[2] The moral of this story may be found in something former Superintendent David Moberly once said:

> The arts are basic. They are a social, political and educational
> priority for Seattle. As superintendent, I've got to be personally in-
> volved in the fight to maintain not just standards but flexibility in
> this urban school system. The arts are a good weapon to have in my
> arsenal. Besides, they're good for our public image.

A FEW LAST WORDS ON THE SUBJECT

By now, the benefits of networking and collaboration as strategies for change should be clear. But the process has its share of problems, and in the interest of balance and candor, I will add a few last cautionary words on the subject.

Keep the Network Active; Idle Muscles Tend to Atrophy

Networking is at the very heart of the AGE school development process, and like any heart, it must beat regularly to keep the body of the program alive and vital. Too often, this notion is either misunderstood or not fully translated into action. There is a tendency to think that the job is done once a group of people, schools or school districts is identified and officially declared a network. The network exists—but on paper only.

Occasionally, administrators, principals, their staffs or artists show up at meetings or events to engage in some activity that has been planned for, not by, them, usually without their prior knowledge or consent. The results are boredom, impatience, disenchantment, secession—and in some cases, revolt.

---

[2] During the last decade, the Seattle school population declined dramatically by about 45 percent, several superintendents have come and gone, and only vestiges of the original AGE program remain. Judith Meltzer, a former JDR 3rd Fund administrative fellow, remains on the district staff and is the arts community's liaison with the schools.

Important Decisions for the Network are Made by Consensus of the Members

Networks operate laterally with group decisions reached through negotiation and consensus. The locus of power is in the group, not in any one individual. This power is elusive and has a tendency to shift and float, depending on the issue at hand and whose ox is being gored. Thus, decisions reached will almost always represent some sort of compromise in which everyone wins something and no one loses everything. This mode of operation makes some people uncomfortable and others downright impatient, and it certainly flies in the face of standard bureaucratic practice.

The Network's Needs Come First; The Hub Serves the Members

Networks cannot function without a hub, but the balancing act of power between the two is a delicate and difficult business. When networks are first formed, the hub often dominates the decision-making process. As time passes, network members get to know each other, become more secure in their understanding of program goals and objectives and more competent in carrying out their own individual responsibilities. As a result, they insist on a larger voice in policy and financial matters.

Unless it is understood that the hub's main function is to facilitate program planning and development and help members to help themselves, discussions can turn into labor-management disputes and collective action will be blunted.

Respect Individual Needs and Differences but the Group's Concerns Have Top Priority

The strength of the network is in its collective ownership and sharing of responsibilities. Although each member functions within a larger group, he or she can maintain his or her own identity and uniqueness while promoting the group's overall mission. But, unless the network serves primarily as a delivery system of assistance to its members and a reference point for others, it has no reason for being. If it is used or manipulated for other ends, its purpose will be subverted and its integrity destroyed.

Provide Assistance to Others to Counter the Charge of Elitism

Networks are often accused of being elitist, closed clubs. There is probably no definitive way to dispel the jealousy or even hostility sometimes directed at members. There are, however, some partial solutions: expand the network and eliminate distinguishing categories (or tiers) so that no one is a second-class citizen; help form and participate in related networks; provide technical and consulting assistance to other groups and individuals; circulate or distribute information and resource materials to a wide audience and hold conferences and meetings to which all interested parties are invited. In other words, go public and be on record as supportive of all schools committed to the AGE philosophy, whether officially AGE-designated or not.

You Will Need Money for Some Network Activities

Networking, though cost-effective, does require money for coordination, special resources, consultants, events, released time and, in the case of regional or national consortia, travel, food and lodging. In most cases, however, the value received by the large number of participants far outweighs the minimal per capita price tag. In 1978 for example, an average two-day League meeting in Chicago for twenty-five people cost the Fund about $6,000. School and district-wide events, on the other hand, can usually be subsidized for at most a few hundred dollars.

6

A Day in the Life of an AGE Demonstration School

P.S. 152 BROOKLYN

AT LEAST TWO GINKGO TREES AND A KIOSK GROW IN BROOKLYN

It was 9 A.M. on a cool, drizzly day in May. I arrived at Public School 152 in Brooklyn, a 72-year-old brick building surrounded by a wrought-iron fence and not just one but lots of budding trees, including two lovely ginkgoes and some ravishing azaleas. The community was mostly residential and the Brooklyn College campus was close by.

The first thing that caught my eye was an outdoor kiosk (actually a series of wooden display cases on the front lawn) presided over by a large painted figurehead whose abstract features reminded me of an Indian totem pole. I had come to visit my old friend and colleague, Dr. Herbert Shapiro, principal of one of the original AGE demonstration schools. I wanted to learn more about the story behind the construction of the kiosk, and I also hoped to get a close look at an AGE school that had spent over five years planning and developing a comprehensive program.

I was eager to experience the climate, environment, social atmosphere and human dynamics of this large elementary school that at the time housed over 1,300 predominantly black and Hispanic students in three separate buildings, two of which were on the Brooklyn College campus. I had arranged to spend the day with Herb to observe classes and activities and to talk with his staff, students and those volunteers and professionals who happened to be around on this particular occasion. My intention was to try to capture the often elusive kinds of things that happen in an AGE school.

I had selected Herb's school from among the more than 150 AGE schools in the League for several reasons. First, P.S. 152 was one of those with the longest experience in the program nationally, and it had had more than its fair share of urban traumas. My feeling was that if AGE could survive and thrive in a New York City school, it could survive anywhere. And while P.S. 152 was perhaps unlike any other school in some respects, its profile would probably be instructive to believers and skeptics alike.

Second, a one-hour subway ride to Brooklyn had obvious advantages over a long, expensive plane trip to other League sites. Considerations of time, money and geography always play a part in decisions of this sort.

Third, oddly enough, throughout all those years I had never visited the school for one reason or another. Having heard so many rave reviews about it for so long, I felt it was high time to see for myself what all the noise was about. Besides, my impressions would be fresh and uncolored by past experience.

Fourth, Herb was a thoughtful, analytic and deceptively low-keyed person who through the years had raised intelligent and often disturbing questions about AGE. He had expressed some reservations about taking a bunch of theories on sheer faith but had nonetheless kept working toward "the goal" deliberately and systematically. He was not a flashy man, but I had learned that Herb's still waters were not all that quiet and did indeed run deep. The father of three, he was also a sculptor and a photographer and a recent convert to disco dancing. On one of the League's first site visits (to Seattle), he got caught up in the spirit of the occasion and insisted that I teach him how to dance. I remember him literally dancing in the aisles on the plane ride back to New York, much to the amused astonishment of most of our fellow passengers. I wondered at the time what kind of a school a man such as this might run, and I was determined to find out sooner or later.

For these and other reasons, P.S. 152 seemed an appropriate school to study. Some day, I hoped, I would have the time and opportunity to do similar profiles of many more of the equally qualified AGE schools across the country.

PROFILE OF THE SCHOOL

Size and Staff

— Kindergarten through sixth grade (the latter housed in two "quonset huts" on the Brooklyn College campus)

— 1,330 students, approximately 80 percent black and Hispanic and the balance white or other

— Average class size: 30 students

— 50 classroom teachers (length of service in this school from 1 to 15 years)

— 11 cluster (specialist) teachers: 2 instrumental and 2 vocal music; visual arts; physical education; creative dramatics; science; language arts; English as a second language (E.S.L.); library

— 5 reading specialists

— 1 part-time guidance counselor

— 6 paraprofessionals

— 7 school aides

— 3 secretaries

— 3 custodians

— 1 security guard

— 2 assistant principals

— 1 principal

Total: 80 instructional, supervisory, and professional staff plus:

— Artists (visiting and in-residence): architecture, dance,

— photography, interdisciplinary team

— Parent and community volunteers

— Student teachers and observers (Brooklyn College)

Physical Facilities

— Three buildings: original, seventy-two years old; new wing, twenty-six years old; annex (two quonsets), five years old

— Three floors and basement in main building; one in quonsets

— Large playground, front yard, large auditorium with stage, gymnasium, library

School Patterns, Styles, and Designations

— "Open," "informal," "experiential" education
— Heterogeneous grouping in mostly self-contained classrooms
— Intellectually gifted children's (IGC) classes, mandated by the district
— Team teaching (three pairs of two teachers, plus artists and parent volunteers, "paras" and aides in various groupings) Title I (educationally disadvantaged compensatory funds); Beacon Light School (early 1970s); AGE School (1975 to the present)

District 22, Home of P.S. 152

— One of thirty-two in the city, located in the borough of Brooklyn
— Six AGE schools (two of which were "demonstrations") in a district of twenty-nine schools (twenty-five elementary, four intermediate and junior high)

WHEN IS A DAY A TYPICAL DAY?

There are dangers in observing a school on a so-called typical day, especially when there has been advance notice of the visit. School people, like the rest of us, can't resist putting their best feet forward and their nicest and cleanest clothes on "for company," and I have sometimes encountered marathon and dismayingly artificial show-and-tell productions. There is no way of completely eliminating this tendency, but it can be controlled. Herb and I discussed this several weeks before my arrival and agreed that apart from some special meetings, I would observe the school on a normally scheduled day picked at random, mostly for my convenience.

As it turned out, it was indeed a typical day—for New York City. One of the assistant principals had just been reassigned part-time to another school in the district, leaving Herb and the remaining assistant principal alone in charge during the busy and often hectic early morning hours. Ushering in over 1,330 students and overseeing a huge staff in a three-building, overcrowded school complex is a demanding job even for three able administrators; for two it was almost overwhelming.

The average citizen has literally no idea how many problems elementary-schoolage children can create: lost notes from home; lame but imaginative excuses for absences or tardiness; inexplicably lost brothers or sisters; sudden and suspicious stomach aches; unexpected quarrels or blows between schoolmates, each of whom naturally blames the other for starting the dispute—the list could go on endlessly. Most of these problems are quickly and skillfully resolved by experienced administrators who are wise to the ways of childhood, but some of them are complicated, often requiring a number of phone calls in the hope of reaching a nonworking parent or responsible adult. All this takes a great deal of time, not to mention patience and fortitude. I doubt whether the number of incidents was significantly greater than on any other "average" day; it just seemed that way to me because Herb was doing two jobs simultaneously.

In addition, quite a few classroom teachers were out ill and several had been "released" to participate in program-planning sessions or staff-development activities. This meant that most of the "cluster" (specialist) teachers were covering regular classes (thus canceling their usual schedules) and that a number of substitute teachers were coping as well as could be expected with unfamiliar children, inherited lesson plans and an altered school schedule. Add to this the usual but controlled frenzy of end-of-the-year testing, preparation for special community events, graduation exercises and the search for time to plan programs for the coming school year, and you begin to get the picture. Things were popping.

I am accustomed to these phenomena and so is Herb, who kept his balance and sense of humor throughout, never losing his head, even in the most difficult or potentially explosive situations. They are the all-too-familiar hallmarks of a large, crowded urban school, although they don't usually occur all at once, in a torrent. Despite everything, however, it was school business as usual. Classes ran smoothly, meetings took place, breakfasts and lunches were served and even eaten, corridors were quiet and clean, tempers were controlled, and a lot of people were smiling, laughing and intensely engaged in their work and play. On reflection, it certainly was a typical day, at least in New York—where if anything can go awry it will.

THE VISIT SCHEDULE

Once the early morning crush and crises were under control, Herb took me on a guided tour that was occasionally interrupted by a call for help from the office but that resumed quickly and lasted the entire day. Our schedule consisted of:

Morning: Visits to all classrooms in the main building and conversations with teachers, paras, aides, parent volunteers, student teachers and students

Noon: Two consecutive meetings with supervisors, teachers on the AGE planning committee, the PTA president and an artist (architect) in residence

Afternoon: Visits to classrooms in one of the sixth grade quonsets on the Brooklyn College campus and conversations with staff

Throughout the Day: A running dialogue between Herb and me about the school, the district, the New York City AGE program and the League of Cities.

SCHOOL CLIMATE AND ENVIRONMENT

There is an old bromide in education that asserts: You can tell the quality of a school the moment you set foot inside the front door. In the case of P.S. 152, I didn't even have to get that far; the kiosk, the azaleas and the ginkgo trees were the first clues. Once inside the door, I was greeted by an obviously permanent (not for show) display that proclaimed P.S. 152 as an AGE demonstration school, listed the arts resources in the building and projected a color slide-tape of school-based arts-related activities. The resources listed were an interdisciplinary arts team, an architect and a photographer "in residence." I later learned that these were only the tip of the iceberg.

As I proceeded to the office, I noticed photos, pictures, paintings and drawings everywhere. Once inside, I saw student-made copies of Impressionist and modern masters such as Van Gogh, Chagall, Klee, Cezanne, Modigliani, Dufy, Leger and Seurat. I have never been too keen on children copying "great" art, but Herb later explained that the purpose was to develop perceptual skills, promote an understanding of the artist's creative process and encourage teamwork, since several of the pictures were group efforts. The quality was unusually good and Herb was justifiably proud.

As I went from building to building, I was struck by the quantity, quality, variety and originality of visual art displays and by the amount of poetry and creative writing hung on bulletin boards in the corridors or on clotheslines in the classrooms. While not all classrooms were equally vivid or colorful and, of course, a few were virtually barren, I will list a sampling of what I saw, all of which was children's work:

— Masks, puppets, ceramics, sculpture
— Weaving, batik, macramé, woodworking
— Mosaic tile sculptures, cloth collages
— Islamic color designs based on algebraic equations
— Tin-can cameras, homemade darkrooms and photography displays
— Homemade wooden "lofts," paper sculptures
— Cardboard murals and musical instruments

I did not see any of the performing arts—music, creative dramatics, or dance—in action because the classes had either been canceled or were not scheduled at a time when I could observe them. I also missed seeing Sharon Sutton, the architect in residence, in action, although she was there that day and joined one of the noontime staff meetings.

The buildings were clean, the classrooms were airy, and the auditorium and the gymnasium were well-equipped. With few exceptions, there was a climate of warmth, respect and purposefulness. Large as it was, the school was obviously a community, a work space and a very safe and pleasant place to be.

EVIDENCE OF AGE IN THE TEACHING AND LEARNING PROCESS

There are five main objectives that provide the instructional framework for a comprehensive AGE program:

1. Quality instructional programs in all the arts for every student
2. Interdisciplinary teaching and learning in which the arts are related to each other and to all subject areas
3. Effective and extensive use of school and community arts and cultural resources
4. Special arts opportunities for special populations with particular needs
5. Use of the arts to help break down racial, cultural and personal isolation

While my purpose was to observe in order to portray, it is hard not to make an evaluative statement. It became quite clear from my observations, conversations and interviews that P.S. 152 had developed a well-rounded and exciting AGE program. While it did not (yet) include all the arts, all the students or all the teachers all the time (an impossible dream, but a worthy goal), a conscious effort had been made to build a fluid, comprehensive approach. I will use the most difficult "objective" to implement—interdisciplinary teaching and learning—to illustrate my point.

In the majority of classrooms I visited, I saw the arts process being used as content (end in itself) and as a concept (means to another end) for learning skills, knowledge and information in various curriculum areas. Some teachers were working at it consciously, others by instinct or natural inclination.

Example: In a fifth grade classroom the teacher, Eleanor Comins, was presiding unobtrusively over what amounted to a five-ring circus. Eleanor was a ceramist and considered herself an art for art's sake person. While she encouraged personal expression, she also stressed self-discipline and group harmony. When I walked in, three students were busy in the darkroom developing their tin-can films; another group was weaving place mats under the supervision of a parent volunteer; others were doing batik or clay sculpture. Still others were working on their own—reading, writing, painting, and so on. A few were composing imaginary music on a cardboard electric guitar, complete with "cord" and "amplifier."

Out of curiosity, I asked three of the students to explain the process of tin-can (pinhole) photography and to show me how to develop the film. A professional could not have been more articulate. Mathematics, creative thinking, problem-solving skills, manual dexterity, aesthetic judgments and teamwork were some of the more impressive components of this impromptu demonstration, which was carried off with pride and enthusiasm. After Eleanor showed me around, we sat down to chat. I asked her how she felt about the arts as aids to learning in other areas. She looked horrified.

"I'm really a purist, you know. I don't believe the arts should be used for anything except their own sake."

I persisted: "But you're a general classroom teacher and the arts are all over this place. Why?"

"Well," she said warily, thinking I might be trying to trap her, "what I'm trying to do is encourage my students to make their own discoveries and decisions, solve their own problems, feel more self-control and self-reliance, be creative, get along better with each other. What better way than through the arts?" She stopped short and we both burst out laughing.

"Case rests," I said.

Eleanor did not say she was using the arts to improve reading scores, nor did she say the only way to learn math was by using arts concepts or processes. What she did say, in effect, was that the arts are a powerful force in the three main domains of learning—cognitive, affective and social—and they seemed a natural ally in her daily teaching responsibilities.

Many teachers in Herb's school shared the same feeling. Several were very articulate about using the arts not only for their own value but for other ends. For example: Ida Arbital taught sixth grade algebra through the construction of fascinating geometric designs and beautiful tile mosaics. Fran Kaplan, a vivacious third grade teacher with a professional background in music, drama and dance, said she has been using the arts for years as a natural teaching tool "for just about everything." When I asked jokingly what on earth she was doing as a general classroom teacher, her shotgun retort was "sublimating"!

It was a funny but telling response. There are a lot of unofficial and often unidentified artists in our classrooms masquerading as "just" classroom teachers. In P.S. 152, these hidden talents are sought out, prized, encouraged and given recognition and reward.

Lack of time and space prevent me from going into detail on the manifestations of all five objectives. The reader will simply have to take my word for the fact that there were quality programs or activities in many art forms, special opportunities for students with particular needs and use of the arts (current and planned for) to improve social and human relations and to increase parent involvement in the life of the school. A special word, however, must be said about the use of community resources.

Artists and resource personnel had been visitors to or in residence at P.S. 152 for several years. Photographers, poets, visual artists, dancers and interdisciplinary teams were some examples. Some were practicing professionals, others were parents or volunteers. For example, the PTA president and member of the AGE committee, Diane Reiser, taught clay modeling; a father took a day off from work to conduct a science/environment tour of the school backyard; another mother taught weaving. Brooklyn College's School of Education supplied student teachers and observers and had planned a school-based cooperative program; it also made its library and other facilities available. The Brooklyn Academy of Music, the Brooklyn Museum and several arts organizations in Manhattan provided services on a regular and extensive basis.

One of the outstanding examples of the use of community resources was the architecture component of the then Artists in Education Program at the National Endowment for the Arts. Sharon Sutton, a professional architect who was also a born creative teacher, had been working with P.S. 152 (and other AGE schools) for two years, and plans were under way for her to continue. Funds for her services were supplied on a matching basis from three sources: the school (PTA and other money), the district and the New York Foundation for the Arts, which administered the program for New York State.

One year Sharon worked with several classes on architectural concepts, design and construction skills. The experiences culminated in a ceremony honoring the permanent installation of the kiosk in the school's front yard, a project that ultimately involved the entire school, the community and the district. The next year's activities culminated in the installation of a street museum that displayed artifacts and historical information about the immediate neighborhood.

The conception, design and construction of the kiosk was documented by a slide show with accompanying narrative. The process by which it was invented and shaped, and the incredible amount and diversity of skills developed and information learned, were preserved on charts and folding cardboard placards. On the day I was there, the kiosk's eight display cases contained student exhibits with themes such as "painting space," "drama and space," "world of creatures," "space and geometry" (with geodesic domes), leaf and paper collages and weaving.

Herb and many of his teachers agreed that the kiosk project probably did more to consolidate the school and its attempts to attract community support than any other single effort. Another important result was the development of an entire "core" curriculum inspired by and related to architectural and design concepts. The school planned to transcribe the information contained on the charts and the placards for wide distribution throughout the district and to other AGE and arts in education schools. The program, singled out for distinction, was described in some detail in an architecture bulletin available from the New York City Board of Education.

THE PRINCIPAL AS LEADER: "WE ARE SUCH STUFF AS DREAMS ARE MADE ON"

O God that madest this beautiful earth, when will it be ready to receive thy saints? How long, O Lord, how long?

George Bernard Shaw,
"Saint Joan"

. . . God is on the side of the big battalions.

George Bernard Shaw,
"Saint Joan"

I believe in Michelangelo.

George Bernard Shaw,
"The Doctor's Dilemma"

Amor vincit omnia [or] Love conquers all.

Chaucer; Virgil

Genius is patience.

Popular proverb

The answer, my friends, is blowin' in the wind.

Bob Dylan

To dream the impossible dream...

"Man of La Mancha"

In the epilogue to the Shaw play, Saint Joan, the former heretic, laments that the world is still not ready for the saints to come marchin' in. Her former comrade in arms, Dunois, is a pragmatist who states that God is on the side of power, raw and massed, and that battles are not won by sheer faith alone. Dr. Dubedat in "The Doctor's Dilemma" is something of a mountebank who nonetheless protests on his deathbed that his belief in great artists, science and the Life Force will ultimately redeem him. Chaucer and Virgil seemed to think that love will prevail over adversity. Someone knew that patience was more than a virtue. Bob Dylan lamented man's infinite capacity for destruction but saw hope for change. Don Quixote tilted at windmills to win his beloved Dulcinea and was oblivious to the world's scornful laughter.

What has all this got to do with the principal as leader? In my experience, everything. Rather than cite numerous references to the research literature on the subject of the principal as sparkplug and spearhead, I will give you my own list of characteristics. An effective principal is a Saint Joan, a Dunois, a Dubedat, a Chaucer, a Virgil, a survivor, a philosopher, and a Don Quixote all rolled up in one person. He or she is:

— an unofficial saint with a vision (not by calling but by necessity) whose job is often lonely and controversial
— a pragmatist
— a bit of a dissembler but a sincere humanist
— a caring individual whose love for children—all God's children—is often the only reasonable explanation for perseverance
— an optimistic risk taker who knows the hard questions and believes that an answer is indeed "blowin' (somewhere) in the wind," if he or she can just survive the current crisis to discover it
— a dreamer with a thick skin who does not let occasional setbacks or petty jealousies get in the way of larger purposes

In other words, a good principal is an able educational and administrative leader who knows how to organize the staff so it has ownership in the total school program and a certain amount of control and influence over decisions that affect it. He or she gives teachers the freedom and encouragement to do their jobs, has clear and reasonable expectations and knows how to balance an orderly structure with "happy abandon" to stimulate creativity and camaraderie. If a principal is not a skillful negotiator who can help the school community, including its parents, arrive at consensus on issues of consequence, chances of the school's ability to be responsive to the needs of its children are slim.

I know many principals who fit this description and, regardless of their personal style, they are all unorthodox. Herb is only one example of those men and women who are all to some degree mavericks with a vision. Herb is staunchly independent. He balks at arbitrary, autocratic behavior and believes unswervingly in what is known as informal, experiential education. He appreciates individual differences, dislikes tracking or labeling

(stigmatizing) groups of students and does his utmost to spread special opportunities around to as many people as possible. He is an iconoclast and,
in short, a leader.

Spending the entire day with him, I was able to observe his attitude
and behavior with staff, students and parents. He was alternately stern, af-
fectionate, funny, impatient with jargon or flabby thinking, suave, ambas-
sadorial and always sharp and clear-headed. He seemed never to be at a
loss in any situation and was always quick to come up with a solution (or
several) to a problem. A tall, attractive man in his early fifties, he was also
remarkably agile and fleet-footed when the occasion warranted.

He knew (or so it seemed) everyone by name, and they all knew him.
He was modest by nature but lavish with his praise of others. In addition to
all this, he was an educational thinker and philosopher and an adept administrator.

Interestingly enough, Herb admitted that he liked being "the boss." He
claimed, however, that AGE had enabled him to let go of the reins a bit and
to "broaden the decision-making base in the school." I was witness to the
truth of his contention during the course of the luncheon staff meetings
with the AGE committee. At issue were plans and preparations for a district
AGE conference; disposition of the street museum; the Brooklyn College/
P.S. 152 cooperative venture, Project Interaction and a grant to use the arts
for better integration of staff, students and parents; a schoolwide fundraising event to secure money for the architecture residency; and the school's
posture vis-à-vis the district, the citywide AGE network, the state and some
federal agencies.

As each item was discussed, everyone felt free to voice an opinion,
contribute ideas and suggest solutions. Several issues were joined and
resolved; others, such as a planning meeting to chart a course for the next
school year, were put off for future and larger group meetings. Responsibilities were voluntarily assumed and no one, including the United Federa-
tion of Teachers union representative, seemed to have any serious qualms
about spending some personal time on jobs that they agreed needed to be
done.

Make no mistake, Herb was still "the boss," and final decisions were
his. Where a discussion wandered off course, he steered it back into focus.
When time was running out, he moved rapidly through important items of
information. At the conclusion of each session, however, there was a tangible sense of accomplishment and satisfaction. What's more, the
dialogues, though serious, were peppered with jokes and humor.

In too many large schools, teachers feel isolated from each other and
especially from the principal. In P.S. 152, there was a growing community

spirit and a bonding of people engaged in a common effort. As Herb put it at a network principals' meeting, "AGE is a focus and a framework for making your dreams (of a better school) come true." The AGE Program at P.S. 152 was no pipe dream, and much of the credit had to go to its principal.

THE PROBLEMS

We have done so much for so long with so little we are now qualified to do anything with nothing.

From a printed card on Eleanor
Comin's bulletin board

P.S. 152 is a good example of how a city school can manage to survive budget cuts, teacher strikes, massive staff layoffs and turnover and the difficulties of serving a school population that is in constant flux. Its problems were severe, but they were apparently not insurmountable.

The teacher turnover rate was such that only about one third had been on staff for more than five years. New or reassigned teachers came in every September. Orientation to the school and "indoctrination" into the AGE philosophy required time for meetings, workshops and informal dialogue. Finding or making the time was a problem. One solution was teacher lunches with a prepared agenda; another was faculty conferences; a third was schoolwide "think tanks" where everyone concentrated on solving a few problems they had helped identify.

School-based staff and curriculum-development opportunities to build skills and learn methods for integrating the arts into daily instruction are key to an AGE program. The school day is crowded almost to "overload." Solutions at P.S. 152 were to build time for these activities into each program or artist residency, use sub days to release teachers, reschedule and make multiple use of staff for regular instructional services and, when necessary, hold after-school workshops, for credit if possible.

Formerly a mostly white middle-class school, P.S. 152 had rather suddenly and very rapidly become 80 percent black and Hispanic. The new parent population was largely unfamiliar with the school's educational philosophy and the reasons for its commitment to the arts. One solution was to promote parent and student interaction and involvement, using AGE as the vehicle. Parents were active on the AGE steering committee, in the classrooms as resource personnel and in the community as fundraisers for artists residencies.

Special planning and developmental funds for AGE are always hard to come by. Solutions were to join with other schools in writing state and federal proposals, hold PTA fundraising events, piggyback on categorical aid programs whose purposes were complementary to AGE (e.g., gifted and talented, ethnic heritage, Title I, ESAA desegregation monies, special and bilingual education), and share resources with other AGE and non-AGE schools.

While there were bits and pieces of money available from the district and a variety of sources for artists in residence and other special services, there was very little for materials and supplies. In an arts-oriented school—especially one so heavily engaged in the visual arts and architecture—this is a serious obstacle. Solutions at P.S. 152 included found and scrounged objects, teacher-bought, begged or "borrowed" supplies, PTA funds and a very heavy dose of creative imagination. Cardboard boxes, for example, were flattened and used for murals, and empty tin coffee cans became pinhole cameras.

Teachers can resent the fact that scarce money goes to pay for artists when supplies, materials and time for their own needs are in heavy demand. Partial solutions: patience, persuasion and many opportunities for teachers to discover the artist's value as an educational consultant and a good liaison with the general community. (This is one of the perennial problems that will undoubtedly never be totally resolved unless there is a pot of gold at the end of the arts and education rainbow.)

THE IMPOSSIBLE DREAM?

At the end of the day, Herb and I sat alone in his office and talked. I asked him what pleased him most and least about his school in terms of AGE. His answers to the first half of the question were that people were feeling the stimulation of "outsiders"—other adults—and responding more positively. The threatening aspect of "replacement by" as distinguished from "working with" new blood was diminishing slowly but noticeably, and the quantity, if not always the quality, of visual arts in all the buildings was satisfying.

His response to the second half was startling but indicative of the man: "Comprehensiveness," he said, "is hard to come by. I want to involve everyone and I want everything for everyone—all the arts for all the children. It's not an easy task. And I just can't seem to find enough time for total school planning, the kind of time—a day or so—that we AGE principals and others spend at our retreats. You know as well as I how important that is for progress, let alone for building the trust and confidence that lead to openness and cooperation."

Herb could have said that he lacked money to make so many of his dreams come true. Or he could have expressed reservations about some reluctant staff members. He could have said any number of things that pointed a finger elsewhere. But the essence of his displeasure was really a feeling of personal frustration that his vision had not yet fully materialized.

He might also have said something about the "basics," but as he stated vehemently at a meeting for new AGE principals: "This is not a program whose chief purpose is to use the arts to raise reading scores. This is a school development program that speaks to the whole child, the whole school and all the people in it."

I left P.S. 152 tired and a bit giddy. It was a long, exhilarating day that served to strengthen my faith in the power of an idea when in the hands of capable, creative people whose dreams make the impossible seem easy.

*   *   *

A lot of people commented favorably on this chapter. Many of them have said they would really like to meet Herb and/or work with him. He retired from the public school system a few years ago and is now the head of a yeshiva in Manhattan.

Perhaps the most telling reaction to this chapter is the experience I had after reading the section "The Principal as Leader" to the New Orleans principals at the end of a long day during their retreat in February 1989. Our discussion had centered on the solutions to the problems they faced as they tried to steer their schools through the difficult shoals of New Orleans contemporary reality. As I heard them alternate between dismay and optimism, helplessness and fortitude, it occurred to me that the passage might provide a soothing ending to the evening and a proper testimonial to the strength and courage of these men and women.

When I finished reading, there was heavy silence. Then, one by one, they told me they were amazed. They identified with my description of Herb, in New York City, and, apparently, the characteristics I defined for principal leadership ten years ago fit them—all of them—in New Orleans today.

For those who contend that the New York experience does not generalize or travel well, the Arts Connection people and the project seem to be demonstrating otherwise. (See Chapter 10 for a description and a sampling of their guidelines, criteria and other working papers.)

C H A P *7* T E R

Who Shall
Teach the Arts?

GUIDELINES AND CRITERIA FOR
ARTS SPECIALISTS, CLASSROOM TEACHERS,
ARTISTS AND ARTS ORGANIZATIONS

FRAMING THE ISSUE

The AGE Ideal and the Sobering Realities

In a prototypical AGE environment where the impossible dream has come true, all the children in a school are touched in some important way, every day, by the arts. As members of a temporary social order (school) and destined to spend twelve or more years within this institutional system, they spend their days in a workplace that is brightly painted, clean, orderly and filled with beauty. The arts are everywhere—in the classrooms, the corridors, the assembly halls, the lunchrooms, the teachers' lounge, the parents' room, the school yards and in the principal's office.

In this aesthetic paradise, students are respected as individuals, expected to achieve and held to high standards. As part of their well-balanced academic diet, they are exposed to the arts, involved in producing and creating them and actively engaged in learning about them in a historical and aesthetic context. They learn how to use, extend, and transfer arts concepts and processes to other subject matter, and they participate actively in individual and group activities that challenge and develop their problem-solving and critical-thinking skills.

In this educational Shangri-la, the arts curriculum is a disciplinary and interdisciplinary continuum designed and taught by resident arts specialists in the various art forms, classroom teachers and resident and visiting artists—singly and in disciplinary and interdisciplinary teams. Other members of the school staff such as librarians and paraprofessionals, as well as parents and other community volunteers, provide instructional assistance. Support services, supplies and money for leadership training and staff and curriculum development in the arts are abundant and regularly available from district staff specialists in music, visual arts, dance, theater, the literary arts, folk arts, media and architecture. These specialists spend the majority of their time as resource personnel for program, staff and curriculum development in the schools.

Individual and group instruction is offered before, during and after school because the arts are considered educational basics and a source of enrichment for the school's total program. The arts are never in jeopardy in this workplace because they reach and engage each and every young person in the school and pervade the school's social climate and built environment. They are integral to the structure and operation of the total school program, and the principal, the entire staff and parent body accept and value them as crucial elements in a holistic, multi-ethnic and multicultural instructional framework.

I have yet to set foot inside an elementary or secondary public school that exemplifies the paragon I have described. Most of the schools I know that are committed to the principles of AGE are working very slowly and unevenly toward this ideal, which calls for nothing less than fundamental changes in people's attitudes toward the aims of education in today's angry and contentious world and a strong belief in the place of the arts in that spectrum of competing educational priorities. Developing a full-blown AGE program requires a rethinking of the traditional nature of schooling, a restructuring of the conventional patterns of school governance and the equitable redistribution of adequate resources to include school system support for instruction in the arts for every child.

It has always been difficult for the arts to be assertive and to compete successfully for support when pitted against society's established needs for food, clothing and shelter. These days, especially in urban centers, the struggle for attention, let alone support, has become exhausting. As a concerned citizen, it is hard not to seem apologetic making the case for the arts in education when you stand side by side with advocates for crime and drop-out prevention and AIDS and drug education. It is hard not to appear frivolous—that is, until you remember that all of these causes are under-funded when compared with the dwarfing $120 billion dollars spent to date on a space station that hasn't a nut or bolt to show for it.

The AGE Dilemma: Arts Specialists or Artists for Instruction in the Schools

Not only do the arts have to compete for support with priorities external to the schools and with shifting educational priorities within the system, but they also must confront some skirmishes and power struggles within the arts in education community itself. AGE promotes strong ties with the community and encourages community participation and financial investment in school programs. Ironically, the concept of collaboration contains within it the seeds of potential conflict within the ranks of AGE. This conflict erupts when school decision-makers perceive artists as the all-purpose solution to education in the arts and hire them to teach what has been traditionally considered the province of the licensed arts specialists.

The AGE philosophy asserts that program planning, development and implementation should be primarily an inside job. It champions the licensed arts specialist and the classroom teacher and carefully casts the artist and arts organization as resources to the schools—as *supplements*, not substitutes for school personnel. But AGE also celebrates collaborations and partnerships with the community's arts and cultural resources, and the dilemma for AGE administrators occurs when there are few, if any, arts specialists available, no classroom teachers with sufficient training or skills in the arts and a plethora of artists ready and waiting in the wings.

The dilemma is compounded because current national, state and local government funding for the arts in education comes largely from arts endowments and agencies whose money is restricted for use by artists and arts organizations and may not be applied to basic teacher or school administrator salaries. Indeed, these days most of the money for the arts in the schools including instruction, curriculum development, teacher training and research and evaluation comes from the arts, not the education, agencies.

Thus, it should come as no great surprise that many schools following the AGE path have insisted they really have no choice but to turn to the artists and other "outside" sources for help. The danger is that some schools turn to artists for the "quick fix," which can serve to further antagonize, isolate and jeopardize the already tenuous position of existing arts specialists. In addition, while outside resources can address short-term needs, in the long run they serve to weaken the very fragile fabric inside the system that, if strengthened and reinforced, would help AGE programs become institutionalized. I shall have more to say about this issue at the conclusion of the chapter.

The Plight of the Arts in the Schools:
A Historical Context

The truth of the matter is that many of the comprehensive programs with which I am familiar have either chosen or been forced to rely on partnerships with artists and arts organizations to provide a great deal of student instruction and teacher training in the arts. Why should this be so? A very brief historical look at the state and status of arts instruction in the nation's schools may shed some light on the issue.

The arts and especially arts specialists are still in short supply and not taken seriously or for credit in most of the nation's elementary and secondary schools. When they do exist, art and music are generally the only disciplines represented and are usually reserved for those relatively few youngsters who can be identified as gifted and talented. Until very recently, programs for the academically or artistically gifted and talented have tended to overlook minority and other populations lacking the largely cognitive skills generally used to identify this special group. This has served to further segregate the arts from the mainstream of education and to preserve their image as elite fare for the privileged few.

In our country, education is considered a state and local responsibility, and there are no national standards or formal guidelines for instruction in the arts. Except at the secondary level, there is no generally accepted scope and sequence, no comprehensive curriculum framework and few state-mandated requirements for a significant number of arts credits for high school graduation. Very few colleges and universities demand either minimum competencies or arts credits for admission.

Since the sixties, the services of arts organizations and the community's cultural resources have gradually gained wide acceptance and public and private financial support for their enhancement or "enrichment" of school programs. Artists have been employed to provide a broad range of instructional and other services to students and their teachers in and out of school.

In the mid-seventies, a tidal wave of economic setbacks, education budget cuts and yet another frantic call for a return to the basics (which we have never managed to leave) succeeded in decimating the already thin and shaky ranks of arts specialists nationwide.

As a result, artists, arts organizations and the classroom teachers, especially at the elementary level, became more important than ever in the eyes of some educators and most of the community arts providers. They were promoted as safeguards for the continued presence of the arts in the schools and were expected to deliver school-based arts instruction, even though classroom teachers have little or no pre-service training in any of the arts disciplines, and few artists have an understanding of the schools, classroom management, instructional methodology or the various stages of learning and child development.

Continued outside subsidy for arts organizations and artists' services to schools has caused a number of professional arts educators to express serious concern about the "deschooling" of the arts. They maintain that artists are relatively cheap and uncertified substitutes for licensed arts specialists and that the school district's "matching" money that is being used for outside artists siphons off their sources of financial support. Some of these professional arts educators maintain that uncertified artists with little knowledge of pedagogy, classroom management and child development have no business teaching the arts to children within the school system. The protestations by the outside arts providers that they are tapping and marshaling community resources on behalf of the schools and only temporarily filling the pedagogical arts gap caused by forces beyond their control have not been altogether convincing.

Today, largely because adequate education dollars are still not forthcoming for the arts, the resolution of the dilemma is stalemated. The arts specialists, the classroom or subject area teachers and the artists each have their institutional partisans. There are skirmishes over the boundaries of instructional power and jurisdictional tiffs over what amounts to very small turf. There are arguments about the broad or narrow definition of art and culture, and everyone struggles for recognition, respect and adequate pay.

Examining the Options: The Definition of AGE Revisited

I do not subscribe to the notion that the artist should be the primary, let alone sole, source of instruction in an AGE program. Over the years, I made that position clear to my colleagues in the League of Cities and elsewhere, warning them that their comprehensive programs were in danger of becoming nothing more (nor less) than a glorified series of ephemeral artist residencies. I am convinced that the burden of teaching the arts, especially in a program whose definition is as comprehensive and complex as the one I use for the arts in general education, must be shared by specialists, classroom or subject area teachers and artists, all of whom are reinforced by trained and qualified paraprofessionals, parents and community volunteers.

My stock response to the complicated question of who should teach the arts is simple to state and hard to do: everyone who is available, motivated and qualified, under certain very rigorous conditions. The challenge, of course, is identifying, training, supervising and financing the appropriate personnel, and then figuring out who is best equipped to handle the various aspects of the instructional program in each school.

It might be useful to review my most recent operational definition of the modes of instruction native to an AGE program in order to set the stage for the balance of this chapter.

The Four Modes of Instruction in Comprehensive Arts in General Education Programs

— ARTS FOR ARTS' SAKE: study of, about and in the individual disciplines, including but not limited to music, visual arts, drama, dance, creative writing, poetry, film, video, architecture, etc.

— ARTS AT THE SERVICE OF OTHER STUDIES: arts concepts, ideas, themes, material, strategies and processes introduced or integrated into the study of other (primary focus) disciplines serving to illuminate other concepts, themes and ideas

— OTHER STUDIES AT THE SERVICE OF THE ARTS: educational concepts, ideas, material strategies and methodologies from other disciplines introduced or integrated into the study of one or several art forms

— ARTS AS AN EQUAL PARTNER IN A HOLISTIC, HUMANITIES/GLOBAL EDUCATION OR MULTICULTURAL APPROACH: the arts relate to, or correlate with the study of other topics, trends, movements in world history; as such they inform and are informed by this larger context

Assume for the moment that I had substituted "math" or "science" or "social studies" for the word "art" in the above taxonomy, and the point I am driving at should become obvious: no one person—no single source—can reasonably be expected to teach all there is to learn about any subject in today's fast-paced world. This is as true for the arts as any other discipline. It is especially true in an AGE program.

Looking for Solutions from Practice: The League's Experience

As much as I would like to present a balanced picture in this chapter, devoting equal time to arts specialists, classroom teachers and artists, I am unable to do so with integrity. This book is based on actual field experience in which, as I have said earlier, many of the AGE programs with which I am familiar characteristically rely, in the beginning years anyway, on the services of artists and arts organizations as the primary source of staff and curriculum development and instruction in the various arts disciplines. Consequently, I will offer only those thoughts and guidelines that spring from first-hand knowledge. While this means that treatment of the question "Who shall teach the arts" may appear unbalanced and heavily weighted (in terms of page space) toward the artist, that is a risk I shall have to take for the sake of authenticity. All it means, of course, is that to my knowledge the full-blown AGE ideal—the impossible dream, if you will—has not yet materialized, and it is important to start on the journey somewhere. Exhibit 13 may provide you with some initial direction.

ARTS SPECIALISTS:
SCOPE, SEQUENCE AND
QUALITY CONTROL

Arts specialists can provide regular and sustained study of the materials, processes, skills and production of the visual, performing and literary art forms. If they are adequately prepared and knowledgeable, they can be expected to teach the history of the arts, arts criticism, aesthetics and a multicultural approach. They can also provide excellent opportunities for staff and curriculum development when they are looked upon as experts and resources and when they are consciously integrated into (not isolated from) the total school program.

From time to time, AGE has been attacked as a conspiracy against the individual arts disciplines and arts specialists. Some have the impression that the program requires a complex and elaborate managerial infrastructure that "deschools" the arts and delegates or relegates their teaching to glamorous, fly-by-night artists. AGE and programs like it are frequently held responsible for contributing to the demise of arts specialists. However, the main institutional purpose of AGE is school development through the arts; its primary instructional goal is comprehensive and sustained programs in all the arts for all the children that teach the individual arts disciplines and attempt to relate them to each other and to other studies.

Unfortunately, expediency and necessity have conspired against those AGE programs in which artists and other outside resource personnel *have* served to fill a vacuum. In districts where specialists are rare or after they have been "riffed" or let go en masse, artists have been sent in to fill the pedagogical gap. In a few cases (such as Little Rock and Winston-Salem), however, as these programs grow strong and begin to make a

VIEWPOINT

"[AGE is]an interdisciplinary approach that helps put me in touch with the rest of the staff. Together we make conscious use of the arts for their own sake, but we have discovered that they tend to increase students' mastery of skills and concepts in other subject areas."

(Arts specialist)

E X H I B I T   1 3 _____

SOME TOOLS FOR DETERMINING WHO SHALL TEACH THE ARTS IN YOUR SCHOOL

When working with school-based planning teams, I have found it useful to rephrase the question "who shall teach the arts" as follows:

— Who on your building staff or in the community is available, affordable and the most qualified—the one(s) with the most professional (or equivalent) training and experience—for the job you have defined?

Here is a simplified list of the options that can be discussed. The first four apply only when the school boasts the appropriate resident arts specialist(s) or there are district arts supervisors with sufficient time to devote to the school:

OPTIONS FOR CHOOSING PEOPLE WHO CAN TEACH THE ARTS

1. Options Involving Arts Specialists

   — The licensed arts specialist(s)
   — The arts specialist(s) and classroom or subject area teachers who have volunteered for the job
   — The arts specialist(s) and the artist(s)
   — The arts specialist(s), the teachers and the artist(s), as a team

2. Options Involving Classroom or Subject Area Teachers

   — The classroom or subject area teacher(s) and the artist(s), as a team
   — The classroom or subject area teacher with other teacher(s), as a team
   — The classroom or subject area teacher, alone

3. Options Including Artists and Other School and Community Resource Personnel

   — The artist(s), in disciplinary and interdisciplinary teams or alone
   — Members of the school staff (as instructors or resources), including the school administration, the office staff, the librarian and other specialists,

the custodian—all those who love children and youth and who have the interest, skill and passion to share their expertise

— Community members, including representatives from cultural organizations (e.g. museum docents, curators), gifted students (peers and older), parents, paraprofessionals, civic volunteers, senior citizens

The preceding options can best be considered after the team has taken a talent and interest inventory of the entire school staff and conducted research into the community's arts and cultural resources. (See the section in Chapter Four, "Building the Program at the Grass Roots Level," for further details.)

SOME CRITERIA FOR SELECTING THOSE WHO SHALL TEACH THE ARTS TO YOUR CHILDREN AND STAFF

Assuming that the school planning team has spent time defining the context, objectives and desired outcomes for the task at hand, here are some of the questions team members should address when reviewing and selecting the appropriate instructional personnel.

Do these people have the necessary:

— arts knowledge, skills and information
— talent, energy, methodology and ability to communicate
— formal or other credentials, appropriate experience and motivation
— familiarity with schools, classroom management, stages of child development

To provide instruction that:

— is process and product-oriented, with a defined purpose
— is clear, compelling, substantive, relevant
— meets high standards of quality
— has significant scope and sequence
— whose breadth, depth and quality can be assessed in behavioral terms, by inventories, observations and other quantitative and qualitative measures?

compelling case to the community for the arts, the pressure on the districts increase, and specialists are rehired.

Also, in the early stages of some AGE programs, the first point of entry is through the use of community cultural resources. Some of these efforts begin to resemble large-scale artist-in-residence programs rather than comprehensive and balanced arts in education efforts. Nevertheless, it is critical to start somewhere, and in those localities where artists and community resources abound and where local private and public money can be marshaled to pay for their training and services, it is as good a place as any to begin.

Artists do get the community's attention quickly, even if they do not always gain the arts specialists' or classroom teachers' immediate trust and respect. Although their glamour-stock effect can be dangerous, if not counterproductive, where AGE programs have managed to get beyond the first splash, the result is often more, not fewer, courses in the discrete arts disciplines.

AGE programs have also been accused of diverting public education dollars as well as some private funds from the support of arts specialists and administrators to the purchase of artists' and arts organizations' services. I see no convincing evidence of this. First, educational resources are enormous, while money for the arts is relatively limited. Second, the amount of education dollars used to match or buy an array of arts services for a large number of children in any one program or district would normally not be enough to pay for even one teacher's yearly salary. And third, the sources of private funds that are tapped to support these services are almost always earmarked for the support of the arts and artists and rarely allocated for institutional management or curriculum and instruction; those areas are felt to be the province of an education budget.

Education decision-makers, especially principals, district supervisors and superintendents, need to recognize that arts specialists, itinerant or otherwise, are a resource for delivering better, more comprehensive and sustained instructional programs; they are not simply baby-sitters for uncovered classes or a once-a-week, fifty-minute cultural shot-in-the-arm. On the other hand, arts specialists need to reflect on whether some of the reasons for being ignored or dismissed when the budget crunch comes are among the following:

1. The arts are still regarded as peripheral, not basic.
2. Specialists, who mostly teach "electives," reach only a relatively small portion of the total student population.
3. Specialists have a reputation, deserved or not, of preferring to teach only the gifted and talented, not *all* the children.
4. Specialists are generally geographically, physically and systemically isolated from their peers (and the administration) because

there is no desire, no perceived need and thus no mechanism provided for them to connect with the rest of the school staff.

5. Specialists may actually prefer to remain apart, "in splendid isolation."

Arts specialists can strengthen their own political as well as pedagogical hand by endorsing the notion of all the arts for all the children and by joining forces with the rest of the school staff. They should continually seek ways to demonstrate, visibly and tangibly, how their instructional expertise, staff development skills and administrative services can benefit the population of an entire school and its community. They should sit on the schools' and the districts' AGE planning committees, help research and design interdisciplinary units of study and work on teaching teams with classroom teachers and artists. They can initiate proposals for funding their own special projects, and they can participate in training efforts that help the classroom teacher recognize and identify gifted and talented behavior or potential in all their students. These are only a few ways in which arts specialists can meet the needs of children by serving as resources to their colleagues, thereby increasing their visibility and the general perception of their value to the total school climate and organization.

CLASSROOM TEACHERS: THE HEART OF THE MATTER

While it is an educational axiom that teachers are the heart of the matter in all instructional efforts, the operational truth is that teachers are frequently bypassed or taken for granted in the research, planning and design phases of most innovative approaches, including those involving the arts. Teachers are expected to accept proposed innovations graciously, if not gratefully, and without question. It is almost assumed that they will flock eagerly to in-service workshops (on personal time) to learn how to carry out the new program or methods with understanding, skill and enthusiasm. Empirical evidence confirmed by research on school improvement efforts, however, is conclusive: when teachers are not involved in a purposeful way, they ignore or sabotage new programs and instructional methods "behind the classroom door."

In AGE programs, teachers are not regarded as mere pedagogues; they are considered indispensable to school governance, operation and the ongoing decision-making process. As a group, they are regularly informed and consulted about program development. As individual representatives on school-based AGE management teams, they are deeply involved in the planning, execution and assessment of all arts-related curricular and instructional programs and activities. And to make this power manifest, the principal often authorizes them to make important budgetary decisions.

In AGE programs, especially at the elementary level, classroom teachers are regarded as the linchpins of success for the program. They are frequently asked to fill a very tall order because it is they who have the most extensive, continuous contact with the children and because in many schools and districts there is insufficient access either to certified arts specialists—when they exist—and/or to appropriate professional artists. Thus, in many situations today, classroom teachers are expected to transform themselves (overnight) into the modern-day equivalent of the renaissance man or woman. Here is a partial list of expectations collected from principals, district supervisors and, more often, artists and arts administrators:

Partial List of Utopian Expectations for Classroom Teachers in AGE Programs

— Teach a little bit of music, dance, the visual arts, theater, creative writing and so on. "Teaching" includes knowledge, skills and information in the disciplines. It can mean that students will learn techniques for creating, performing and producing studio art works; gain ensemble performance experience and discipline; understand the history and philosophy of the art forms; and be familiar with various aesthetic doctrines and modes of critical thinking.

— Relate these arts disciplines to each other (thematically, by design concepts, functionally, historically).

— Infuse the form, content and concept embodied in these disciplines into the teaching of the basic skills (the three R's) as well as language arts, math, science, history and the like.

— Take their children on visits to museums and performing arts institutions, zoos and botanical gardens, libraries and historical societies, after preparing the class for the experience and armed with plans for appropriate follow-up and reinforcement activities.

— Attend after-school or summer in-service institutes with or without pay, and devote time to the research, development and design of arts-in-education courses of study, new thematic or topic-oriented units, specific lesson plans and other arts-related curriculum materials.

— Serve as school-based community liaisons with arts organizations that provide services to schools and perform administrative duties without a telephone, no access to a secretary and frequently no extra time to carry them out.

— Work on a teaching team with the school or district arts specialists and with professional artists in classroom or studio workshops and school residencies. In these collaborations, the partners rarely choose each other and the question of whether the "chemistry" is right for cooperation is often overlooked. Moreover, the roles, functions and expectations for each of the players is often fuzzy or downright confused since there is very little *common* planning time and no clear project agenda.

— Finally, the classroom teacher is expected to spend (personal) time learning how to identify and research the community's resources, contact appropriate "education" or public relations personnel and orchestrate events and services for the children in and out of school. If, as in some instances, the teacher is also made the exchequer, business skills in budgeting and accounting often come in handy.

This is not a tall order—it is an impossible job description for a full-time classroom teacher. And these lofty expectations are "only" for a super-teacher in an imaginary but prototypical arts-oriented *elementary* school. Secondary schools present the more difficult challenge of establishing a cohesive, interrelated program within a subject and department-oriented, turf-conscious, essentially conservative bureaucracy.

As I have said earlier, there is simply no way that the average or even the superstar classroom teacher can fill the comprehensive bill described above without collaborative help. In fact, no single instructor, regardless of whether it is a teacher, an arts specialist or an artist, can meet these expectations alone. The list above should be reviewed by the AGE planning team and factored into the roles and responsibilities of designated members or others on the school staff.

Classroom teachers must be treated professionally and made to feel comfortable with and in command of the arts they are expected to teach. They must be given the time and space (and frequently, additional compensation) to spend precious (personal) hours discovering how to use the arts in their own classrooms most effectively. They must be flanked by respon-

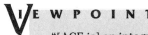

VIEWPOINT

"[AGE is] an integrative approach that builds and maintains morale, improves the school tone and ambience and helps staff relate better to each other and the kids."

(Teacher)

sive, qualified arts specialists; trained, experienced and respectful artists; and other authentic, cooperative "how-to-do-it" consultants.

The goal is not to convert classroom teachers into free-standing equivalents of professional artists. It is to help them understand how to use the arts, arts specialists and artists as resources to their regular instruction and perhaps to give them a grounding in a set of new techniques and skills to enliven their lessons. They, as well as arts specialists and artists, need to be shown how the arts relate to other art forms and where they connect with other subjects. AGE will not materialize otherwise. It will be a shell game—a network of principals and, as often as not, nothing more than a glorified but incoherent artist-in-schools program that leaves no trace of its existence or accomplishments once the artists and the outside money have gone. It should be remembered that designated teachers (who have volunteered for the job) must be given the released or compensated time and the support to coordinate in-school and community arts events and services.

ARTISTS: RESOURCES FOR CURRICULUM AND INSTRUCTION

Artists can perform many services for schools and their communities. They can work alone or in teams with the schools' arts specialist(s) and classroom or subject area teachers. Since most artists are not licensed, they should always supplement and enhance certified teachers, never substitute for or replace them. Exhibit 14 provides a checklist you can use to help define artists' roles in your program. Keep in mind that you will increase the artists' effectiveness the more you include them in your planning activities.

Arts Resource Teams: Flying Squads for Consulting and Technical Assistance

In League sites (New York City, Seattle, Winston-Salem) and many of the JDR 3rd Fund's arts in general education projects, Arts Resource Teams proved to be an effective mechanism for staff, curriculum and school development. The teams can coordinate the delivery of information and services between the schools and the community, pulling all the partners together in the teaching and learning process (see Exhibit 15). They have also emerged as an important strategy for program expansion and extension of the AGE concept to many schools within a district, state or region.

Profile of a One-Week Artists' Residency in an AGE School

Several books and pamphlets have been written about artists in the schools. The guidelines Gene Wenner wrote in the mid-seventies for the exemplary NEA Artist in Schools Dance Program are still applicable today. Tom Wolf's book, *The Arts Go To School* (New England Foundation for the Arts and American Council for the Arts, 1983), is outstanding. The New York Foundation for the Arts' Artists in Schools grant application booklet is a model of clarity. The manual I prepared for the Lincoln Center artist-in-residence program in the late sixties and early seventies remains surprisingly appropriate today.

While these and other materials are useful, they do not quite zero in on how to fit a residency into the context of an AGE program. The following are guidelines drawn from the collective experience of the League.

GUIDELINES FOR ARTISTS' RESIDENCY IN AN AGE SCHOOL

Phase I: Orientation and Planning (Assess School Needs and Meet the Artists)

The AGE planning committee, in consultation with the school staff, parents and students, decides which art form or forms would be most beneficial to the total school, considering the goals and objectives of its comprehensive plan. The planning group makes its decisions as a result of answers to questions such as:

1. How can the artists and the art forms they represent be used most effectively to help the school strengthen existing arts programs and/or expand into new areas; promote more interdisciplinary teaching and learning; meet the special needs of students; and reduce personal, racial or physical isolation?

2. How will every student and teacher in the school be involved or positively affected, directly and indirectly?

3. What strengths and resources now exist on the staff, in the school and in the community to support and extend the workshops (performances, residencies, other events) once the artists have gone?

4. What resources do we need, what do we have and what must we secure, do or change (scheduling, released time for orienting and training teachers, transportation, space, materials, books, supplies, money for teacher stipends, etc.)?

E X H I B I T   1 4 _____

THE ROLE OF ARTISTS IN AGE PROGRAMS

I. AS ARTISTS, THEY:

— demonstrate their art form as a process and a product
— stimulate curiosity about their professional trade and respect for the diligence and discipline required for excellence
— provide role models and open new options for professional or amateur pursuit
— help identify the artistically gifted and talented
— work effectively with special populations using the art form as the language and medium for communication
— bring normally isolated individuals together to work on group projects
— generate community interest in the arts and the schools

II. AS "RESOURCE TEACHERS," THEY:

— discuss, interpret and illuminate the origin, history and development of their field
— develop basic artistic abilities and problem-solving skills
— demonstrate how others can create their own activities or products using the arts
— orient and train other artists for school work

— make connections between the arts process and the learning process and help find ways to relate the arts to each other and to studies such as mathematics, science, social studies, language arts and so on

— help build curriculum frameworks, guides, units of study and other instructional and resource materials

III. AS TRAINERS, THEY:

— provide or participate in staff-development workshops and courses for entire or partial school faculties and community

— orient and train other artists for school work

IV. AS ADMINISTRATORS AND COORDINATORS, THEY:

— help schools establish linkages with arts organizations, community agencies and vice versa

— build bridges among schools and between a school and the central administration

— organize arts resource teams and schedule visits and services; document activities and evaluate progress

EXHIBIT 15 _____

ARTS RESOURCE TEAMS: THEIR DEFINITION AND FUNCTIONS

Arts Resource Teams are trained to act as "flying squads" of resource personnel. They are:

1. Multidisciplinary; members can work singly, in pairs or larger configurations. Orientation, training, (lesson) planning and sharing time is built into their schedule.

2. Hired by the district (or by a public arts agency on behalf of the district) and paid for by local tax levy funds; federal, state or community arts and/or education grants; foundation awards; private sources; or a combination of the above.

3. Employed for most of the academic year and often for the calendar year.

4. Generally comprised of professionally licensed and experienced arts teachers (at the precollegiate or collegiate/graduate level) but may include professional artists with strong teaching backgrounds and experience.

They can move as a group, from school to school, to:

1. Train teachers, other instructional personnel, visiting artists, parents and community volunteers.

2. Work collaboratively with visiting artists and arts specialists (itinerant or school-based).

3. Function as liaisons between the district and the schools.

4. Administer and coordinate certain aspects of the program and provide consulting and technical assistance to administrators, supervisors and staff.

5. Identify and secure resources (people, materials, space, time) for program development and support.

6. Document and share program information with the schools and the community.

7. Participate in assessment of program progress and make recommendations for improvement.

8. Act as parent and community liaisons and advocates for the arts in education at various community functions.

The AGE planning committee and the total staff meet with prospective artists to describe the school's overall philosophy and perceived needs. The artists respond with a description of how they prefer to work and state their goals, conditions and expectations. The AGE committee (and the total staff) select the artist(s) best suited to the purposes of this residency.

The AGE planning committee and selected artists agree on a schedule for planning meetings. Discussions at these meetings are frank, open and informal. The school and the artists agree on how they plan to work together. They negotiate and arrive at consensus about the goal, shape, content, schedule and number of participants in the residency. This agreement is put in writing.

Subsequent meetings explore programmatic issues in depth, spell out roles and functions and define the individual and mutual expectations of all participants. Minutes are taken at every meeting and copies distributed to everyone in a timely fashion. A schedule is drawn up, discussed, refined and then widely distributed. Plans for monitoring, evaluation and dissemination are discussed.

For a complete planning framework for AGE artist residencies, see Exhibit 16.

Phase II: Implementation (The Residency)

The schedule includes provision for:

1. An informal gathering and/or a formal orientation to introduce the artists to the school community and other interested or important people (sponsors, legislators, officials).
2. Training workshops, during and/or after school for all or part of the supervisory and instructional staff and parents. These workshops are open to other AGE network schools, and there is released time (or additional compensation) for teachers.
3. Weekly or daily planning time for artists, supervisors and teachers (separately and together) to assess progress, make adjustments and refine goals and expectations.
4. Class and room assignments and identification of artists' temporary headquarters in the school.
5. Descriptions of individual projects, activities and events (in newsletters, brochures, flyers, posters, etc.).
6. Performances, lecture-demonstrations and exhibitsfor the school community during the day and in the evening.
7. Social occasions and fund-raising events.

E X H I B I T   1 6

PLANNING FRAMEWORK FOR AGE ARTIST RESIDENCY PROGRAMS

The following can serve as a guide for AGE planning teams and others involved in and responsible for aspects of an artist residence.

ATTENDANCE: Key school personnel (district arts supervisor, principal, teachers, in-school coordinator, parents, artists, arts organization administrators, key community members)

NOTE: The following discussions assume that schools and teachers have volunteered or been identified according to criteria agreed upon by both the arts and the school personnel.

A. DISCUSS THE SCHOOL'S EDUCATIONAL PHILOSOPHY AND GOALS AND DETERMINE WHERE, HOW AND WHY THE ARTS FIT IN

B. DISCUSS THE OVERALL PROJECT GOAL. FOR EXAMPLE: TO BRING TEACHERS AND THEIR STUDENTS TOGETHER WITH PROFESSIONAL ARTISTS, ARTS EDUCATORS, EXHIBITS AND PERFORMANCES SO THEY CAN GAIN

1. Knowledge, understanding and appreciation of the art form(s) (both students and teachers)
2. Increased oral and nonverbal communication (students)
3. Increased self-esteem (students)
4. Information, experiences and skills to infuse the arts into other instructional activities and integrate basic skills and concepts into the teaching of the arts (teachers)
5. Increased self-confidence and ability to deal with the arts in an instructional setting (teachers)

C. DECIDE WHICH ART FORM(S) WILL RECEIVE FOCUS OF ATTENTION AND STUDY

1. Opera (all the arts)
2. Dance
3. Drama
4. Music (vocal, instrumental)
5. Visual Arts
6. Creative writing, poetry
7. Media, architecture and other

D. DETERMINE THE SPECIFIC INSTRUCTIONAL OR CURRICULAR OBJECTIVES (IN BEHAVIORAL TERMS) FOR:

1. Students (whole school; target classes)
2. Classroom teachers (whole school; target classes)
3. School arts specialists
4. Other school special project personnel
5. District arts and other personnel
6. Teaching artists
7. Performing artists
8. Arts organization
9. College or university
10. Community organization
11. Parents/volunteers

E. DETERMINE THE EXPECTATIONS OF AND DESIRED OUTCOMES FOR EACH OF THE ABOVE

F. CURRICULUM AND INSTRUCTION DESIGN (FORM AND CONTENT)

1. Decide number of planning meetings, student events (classroom workshops, other), teacher training workshops, student performances, student exhibits,

visits to community sites (including concert halls, studios)

2. Decide the specific content of each of the above and the need for and collaborative design of lesson plans
3. What will be taught (scope and sequence) and by whom (role of artist, teacher, other instructors)
4. What will be learned and by whom
5. By what means will it be taught, i.e. strategies, methodology

G. SUPPORT SYSTEMS

1. What orientation and training workshops and other opportunities will be provided for all supervisory and instructional participants including artists, arts educator, parents, community volunteers?
2. Who will conduct them (staff, outside consultants)?
3. When, where, how often and for what purpose?
4. Who will document and evaluate them?

H. SCHEDULE (MASTER CALENDAR AND CALENDAR FOR EACH COMPONENT)

1. Timeline and grand design
2. Where will instruction take place (in-school, elsewhere, location)?
3. When will instruction take place (time of day)?
4. Length of each session
5. Who will participate?
6. Who will observe?
7. Discussion of kinds of support and resource materials needed for

   — students
   — teachers
   — artists
   — other instructors

I. PROJECT ADMINISTRATION: ROLES AND FUNCTIONS

1. Coordination (staff)
2. Supervision and monitoring
3. Contact person in each organization
4. Management Team—to include parents, community representatives and students, where appropriate
5. Community Advisory Board

J. RESEARCH AND EVALUATION (FORMATIVE/ON-GOING AND SUMMATIVE/PRODUCT)

1. Who will be involved, how, when (staff, consultants)?
2. What are we tracking or measuring (refer to goals and objectives)? What are our claims? What audience do we need to gather to support them?

   — At the school
   — At the concert halls, studios, community venues
   — How will we know; what empirical evidence will we have; who is "we"?
   — Techniques: Interviews, observations, critiques, written test instruments, opinionnaires, question-naires
3. Who is our "audience"; to whom are we reporting and who are we persuading (for moral support, volunteer assistance, money)?

K. BUDGET AND FINANCING

1. Fees (for artists, consultants and other professionals)
2. Honoraria or regular compensation for teachers
3. Space rental, supplies, materials, transportation
4. Overhead and administration

8. A final meeting for assessment and recommendations for the future.
9. Unexpected and unforeseen opportunities.
10. Breathing space—a little R&R (critical for artists and teachers).

The residency begins. The principal and other supervisors (and consultants) participate in and monitor all program activities, providing immediate feedback for mid-course corrections. Formal or informal evaluation and documentation continues.

Phase III: Follow-up (After the Artists Leave)

1. The normal school schedule, which has been pretty much disrupted, is reinstated and all participants take (or are given) time to digest, analyze and savor the residency experience.
2. Core teachers and supervisors continue to offer staff and curriculum development workshops before and after school, at faculty meetings, in AGE network meetings and during holiday and summer conferences. They also work with curriculum supervisors (often in tandem with artists) at central headquarters to develop guidelines and manuals based on their own experience for distribution to all AGE and other interested schools.
3. Core students form committees, write newspapers, broadcast over the public address system and share their new knowledge and skills with other students. These activities can occur during the residency as well as after it.
4. Parents and community volunteers work more often in the school(s), raise funds and publicly advocate the value of AGE to the school's overall instructional program.

VIEWPOINT

"Working as an artist in the schools, especially the classrooms, is difficult. But what a difference it makes when you're in an AGE school! In some respects, you work twice as hard, but the rewards are also twice as great. This is true, of course, in any school with a deep commitment to the arts and to all the kids."

(Artist)

5. The principal and the AGE committee (and the artists, if appropriate) review their comprehensive plan, determine the effects of the residency in advancing their purposes and decide on the next developmental steps.

ARTS AND CULTURAL ORGANIZATIONS: PARTNERS FOR LEARNING

The Question from Kathryn Bloom

Alice B. Toklas: "What is the answer?"

Gertrude Stein: "What is the question?"

Kathryn Bloom: "The question is not what the schools should do for the artist, but what the artist and arts organizations can do for the culture and climate of the school."

In the sixties and early seventies, I worked in and with several of New York City's arts and cultural organizations designing and administering programs and services for elementary and secondary school students and teachers. At Young Audiences, for example, I coordinated a variety of in-school chamber and vocal music performances for elementary-age students and designed a pilot program for modern dance that, though not immediately implemented, helped lay the groundwork for subsequent approaches adopted by that organization.

At Lincoln Center, I managed the New York City portion of the student program consisting of group visits to performances at the center and a series of in-school performances and lecture-demonstrations in vocal and instrumental music, theater, dance, opera and film. I also designed and coordinated the so-called R.P. program (short for resource personnel—a term we inherited from the federal program that supplied the money). In this program, we identified and trained over one hundred young professional artists to work individually and in teams in a series of in-school workshops with junior and senior high school students and their teachers. The purpose of the workshops was to provide a series of participatory experiences that would cultivate an understanding of each of the art forms, develop insights into the creative process and enhance and illuminate the students' response to and appreciation of the performances.

The R.P. program represented one of Lincoln Center's attempts to make the arts more accessible and more "relevant" to young people in and around New York City. Assembly hall performances, program notes and teachers' guides were making little lasting impression on the schools. Audiences were often restless or downright rowdy; some resented their lot as captives for "just another assembly program" that had no apparent connection to their lives. On the assumption that interest and attention would increase, we decided to offer students and teachers more direct and personal exposure to the art forms and extended classroom contact with professional artists. Our assumption proved correct, but only for those students in the few classes to which the artists were assigned. Furthermore, even the most ardent principals and teachers tended to regard our program as cultural enrichment: a pleasant encounter for students, exposure to the "finer arts," a brief diversion in the day's routine, but nothing to be taken too seriously. In other words, it was nice to have us but not necessary.

Over a five-year period, we expanded and intensified our artist training sessions, changed the scope and sequence of our classroom workshops and treated the performances as illustrations of concepts and themes rather than subjects for intensive preparation and study. We doubled our efforts to identify outstanding artists of both genders and many ethnicities. We veered between the abstract, conservatory methodology and the practical, contemporary, "hands-on" improvisatory approaches. We had our successes and our setbacks—mostly the former, according to our school friends—but we were disturbed by nagging doubts.

Despite our efforts, the arts were not making significant headway up the ladder of the schools' educational priorities, nor had they established a firm beachhead behind the classroom door. Ironically, while our state and local financial support base broadened, we never affected the life or climate of an entire school. The numerous consultations and planning conferences we scheduled with central board of education, district and local school personnel did very little to improve the impact of the program on the schools' administrative or instructional staff, not to mention all the students.

Working first with Edythe Gaines at the Learning Cooperative and then Kathy Bloom at the JDR 3rd Fund gave me a fresh perspective on the role of the arts and artists in the schools. Thanks to them, I began to understand the nature of the problems that confront "outside" organizations and schools when they try to work together. I thought I knew and understood the culture of the schools; I was certainly sympathetic to their difficulty of adjusting complex schedules to accommodate our artist workshops and often technically complex production requirements, but I was mystified by the superficiality of our impact. If we were earnestly trying to do so much for and with them, why wasn't the response more positive? Certainly quality wasn't a problem, and in those days money wasn't either. Most of the performances and services were underwritten by private and public funds; the schools paid only a fraction of the total cost.

I eventually came to realize that I had been seeking the right answers to the wrong question. At issue was not what the schools could do for the arts but rather what outside arts agencies and artists could do for the entire school—in other words, what services they could provide as instructional resources to all the children and their teachers. Improving the status of and respect for the arts and artists in schools was important—a probable outcome, in fact—but only if the arts services supplemented, extended and enhanced the existing curriculum and the total school program.

With few exceptions, the compelling reason for the arts community's acceptance of this rhetoric and its decision to "play the schools" was philanthropic or practical, not educational. Cultural institutions and arts agencies were quick to realize that they, along with the artists and the schools, stood to benefit in the short and long run. They had found a new arena in which to hawk their wares and provide employment for many underemployed, deserving professional artists. They were "reaching out" into all of the city's neighborhoods, beyond their intimidating bastions to the "less fortunate" (economically deprived and culturally isolated). And they were sensibly investing in their own future by introducing their product to a larger, more diverse audience. Parenthetically, these arguments were then and still are used to good effect by public and private arts institutions in their fundraising campaigns.

LESSONS LEARNED ABOUT THE NATURE OF THE PARTNERSHIPS BETWEEN COMMUNITY ARTS PROVIDERS AND THE SCHOOLS

The relationship among arts organizations, artists and schools trying to build a structure for systemic change through the arts is complex. But while it is often harder for outside cultural organizations and personnel to fit into an AGE school development effort at first, invariably, over time, the partnership works well for all concerned. The school people develop respect and trust for the artists, who become important allies in the search for new dimensions in curriculum content and fresh instructional methods. The artists develop admiration for and reliance on their teacher partners to lead the way and provide a proper context for their arts instruction and activities.

Other important lessons I have learned include:

The institutional philosophies, purposes and operating modes of schools and arts organizations rarely synchronize. When you are lucky, they overlap to a small degree or converge tenuously. Areas of compatibility must be identified and a level of trust established. The resulting partnership must be constantly worked on and nurtured. This takes a seemingly endless and frequently agonizing series of continuing rounds of negotiation and consensus, a frustrating process given the barriers of time, terminology and primary institutional mission.

Regardless of the relevance or merits of an outside arts program, the abundance or quality of services offered or the thoroughness of artist preparation, schools and school systems will not absorb them into the fabric of schooling unless they feel they are equal and in some respects senior partners in the venture from start to finish. Responsible for the health, welfare and formal education of children, schools must be convinced of the inherent as well as potential value of a program. They must have the final say about its general conduct though not necessarily its artistic content.

Artists can act as role models, live illustrators and catalysts for school projects. They can extend and enrich routine curriculum offerings in the arts and other subjects. However, unless a significant core of the school staff and the principal are actively committed to the arts as basic education and to artists as instructional resources to teachers, the arts will continue to remain on the fringes of school life. Unless programs and services are jointly planned and implemented, no enduring changes of any consequence can occur.

Visitors to schools, whether artists, consultants or volunteers, are just that—visitors. Unless their credibility is established and their roles are mutually defined and widely understood, their potential contribution will be blunted against a wall of silence, indifference, suspicion or even outright hostility. Many teachers resent the fact that artists are often paid more money for working fewer hours with small groups of children under better conditions than are normally available to the regular staff. In stringent financial times when teachers, particularly arts specialists, are being laid off, this is an especially bitter pill to swallow, even when teachers recognize the value of the artist's contribution to their own professional growth or to the children in their charge. This issue must be met head on, openly and honestly.

Artists must be seen as resources and supplements, not substitutes or permanent replacements for specialists and other licensed teachers. It is a thorny problem considering that in so many situations artists are, in fact, expected to fill the pedagogical arts gap. Unfortunately, the arts are still among the first to go in budget cuts, and we can only hope that artists will understand that they can help to "hold the line" and alter the prevailing negative attitude about the value of the arts to general education.

Artists have worked with schools for many decades, primarily as performers and guest instructors for a limited number of students. In traditional programs, the artist's presence and the work produced tend to be physically and philosophically isolated from the main business of schooling.

Thus, when the artist leaves, the excitement generated by new blood and fresh ideas disappears without a trace. There is no one left with the interest, skills or training to carry on the momentum. In AGE programs, artists are trained to function as a means to larger and more comprehensive ends: the improvement of school climate and environment and the upgrading of the quality and variety of its instructional offerings for all students. They also function as liaisons to the community and help generate local support for the arts and the schools.

Many artists-in-the-schools programs founder as a result of inadequate preparation of artists who have no pedagogical training, are new to the culture of schools and politics of education and are unfamiliar with the various stages of child development. Some artists are born teachers; most are not, and life in the schools bears little or no resemblance to life in the studio or on the stage. There is no longer any excuse for artists to be sent into unfamiliar settings and allowed to "sink or swim" at the expense of the students. Orientation and training are essential, and experienced artists and educators should be responsible for formal sessions and hands-on workshops that provide practical information, tips on the do's and don't's and a forum for the exchange of ideas that work. It is unthinkable that teachers would be allowed to work in schools without adequate preparation; the same holds true for artists.

Unless there is a pot of gold at the end of the arts or the education rainbow, there will never be enough money from one single arts or education source to cover the full costs of artists' services to schools. The name of the game is, and will be for some time to come, collaborative funding.

JOINT PLANNING:
SOME QUESTIONS TO RAISE

"Who's Program Is It, Anyway?"

1. The main institutional purpose of arts organizations and school systems differs significantly. Where do interests and capabilities converge or coincide? Two linked rings provide a convenient metaphor for this concept if you shade in the overlap and agree to collaborate in that area.

2. Is this to be a partnership where both parties discuss and agree on mutual and limited goals, objectives, activities and responsibilities in light of existing realities (resources, time, structure, organization), or will one side attempt to dictate all terms and conditions to the other?

E X H I B I T   1 7 ─────────

GUIDELINES AND CRITERIA FOR EVALUATING PARTNERSHIPS AMONG ARTS ORGANIZATIONS, ARTISTS AND THE SCHOOLS

One set of criteria developed for use with members of the League, the Coalition and other projects seems as relevant today as when we first wrote it in the mid-seventies. It has been widely circulated and found useful, so I include it here for your reference:

CRITERIA: "COMMUNITY ARTS PROGRAMS AND EDUCATIONAL EFFECTIVENESS IN THE SCHOOLS"

A. HIGHEST LEVEL OF EDUCATIONAL EFFECTIVENESS

1. The form, content and structure of the program grow out of a cooperative effort by school personnel (teachers, curriculum specialists, administrators), artists and arts organization representatives and are related to and supportive of the content of teaching and learning in the schools.

2. Programs are planned as an on-going series of related educational events.

3. The program includes the participation of artists who serve as resources to teachers and students in a variety of direct teaching and learning activities. These include creative experiences or demonstrations of the techniques, skills and talents indigenous to their particular profession.

4. Preparatory and follow-up curriculum materials planned specifically for the program are provided to the schools. These materials result from work done jointly by school representatives, artists and arts organization educational staff. Related visual and written materials and resources such as slides, recordings, tapes, films, reproductions and teacher's guides are available in the schools and used by teachers in classrooms.

5. In-service training is available to teachers to promote general understanding of the arts organization, its purposes, its resources and the nature of its services in terms of curriculum development.

6. Orientation and training are available to artists and arts organization educators so that they have an understanding of the nature of schools, the content of the educational program and the learning characteristics of students at different age levels.

7. As a result of the foregoing, the arts event becomes part of the process of teaching and learning, not just a "field trip," time off from school work or another assembly program.

B. MIDDLE LEVEL OF EDUCATIONAL EFFECTIVENESS

1. The content of the program is planned by arts organization educators with some help from school personnel, but is not focused on the content of school studies.

2. Programs are isolated and sporadic events.

3. Contact with artists is limited.

4. Some preparatory materials are provided to the schools for the arts events. Few related materials are available in the schools.

5. No in-service training is available to teachers. Often they have no more information about the arts event or organization than the children they accompany.

6. No training is available to artists or arts organization educators. They assume an automatic interest or curiosity on the part of teachers and children. Capability to work with different age groups is learned on the job by trial and error.

7. The arts event is of some value to children and teachers but remains separate from the larger educational program of the schools.

C. LOW LEVEL OF EDUCATIONAL EFFECTIVENESS

1. The content of the program is accidentally determined by the fact that the arts organization has a special event it feels has some significance for the schools, and the schools decide to send all fifth grade classes and their teachers to it.

2. Programs are single, isolated, unrelated events or activities.

3. Artists are not involved as resources to teachers and students in the program.

4. No preparatory or follow-up materials are available.

5. No in-service training is available for teachers.

6. Arts organization representatives do not work with teachers and students since their regular responsibilities make very heavy demands on their time or the schools have not made appointments for their classes in advance.

7. Educationally, the arts event is of dubious value to students and teachers.

3. Will the process used be one of negotiation and consensus to assure the best possible accommodation and compromise, or will one or each party make unilateral, arbitrary decisions without consulting the other?

4. Are the participants ready, able and willing to spend the considerable time and energy necessary to plan, review, adjust and assess mutual efforts? (For sample assessment criteria, see Exhibit 17.)

5. If an effort falters or fails, who gets the blame, and if it succeeds, who gets the credit?

6. Who pays for what, directly or indirectly, and who seeks additional outside support from whom? Will support be secured by pooling and reallocating scarce resources and collaborative fundraising?

7. Will a letter of agreement or some form of contract containing the terms and conditions of the collaboration help or hinder continuing efforts? If the former, who should draft, review and sign it?

INSTITUTIONALIZING
THE ARTS IN THE SCHOOL PROGRAM:
PROBLEMS AND PROSPECTS

"Let me not to the marriage of true minds admit impediments"

William Shakespeare, Sonnet 116

A Paradox for AGE:
Artists as Partners or Perils

In the ideal, comprehensive AGE program, there is harmony and balance among three basic elements: intensive and sequential study of the individual arts disciplines; schoolwide multi-arts and interdisciplinary activities; and the creation of partnerships to ensure regular use of the community's cultural resources in and out of school. In these programs, instructional responsibility is placed on arts specialists, classroom teachers and artists—in that order. Since most of this chapter has dealt with the role of artists and arts and cultural organizations, it suggests that many of the League of Cities' programs were off-center, or perhaps even topsy-turvy, depending on your priority order of AGE components. With the possible exception of the programs in Little Rock and Winston-Salem that revolved around the classroom teacher from the beginning, the lopsided impression is probably a fair one.

In most League programs, especially those located in large urban centers rich in the arts, the schools usually turned to the cultural resources first because there were existing mechanisms and funds to facilitate these partnerships, no specialists at the elementary school level (where most of the programs were initiated) and too few at the district level with enough training, skill or time to respond to the broad and urgent needs of the network schools. Thus, artists became the immediate, all-purpose solutions to instructional problems in most of the AGE schools in the League. In some cases they came to dominate the program, giving AGE the unfortunate appearance of an *artists* in education, rather than a comprehensive *arts* in education, effort.

Educational Equity and Long-Term
Stability

The overwhelming lack of arts specialists at the school and district level in AGE and other sites ultimately produced a Catch-22 with serious consequences and even more critical implications for the future of the field: reliance by the schools on the community's artists and cultural organizations may help to plug the pedagogical arts gap, temporarily, and the fact that many schools are willing to chip in to pay for a portion of these outside services is an important indication of their commitment to the arts. However, in the long run an exclusive dependence on outside services will only serve to weaken the cause for institutionalizing the arts in the schools.

Artists and arts organizations have, in fact, "come to the rescue" when arts specialists were dismissed en masse. In many cases, without artists in the schools, there would be no arts at all in the education of many of our children. Furthermore, partnerships with the community generally strengthen school programs and build important bridges and mutually beneficial alliances between the schools and these outside, often underutilized resources.

Unfortunately, the supreme irony of these much-desired partnerships is that they have inadvertently served to numb the consciences of school decision-makers who, having set aside some "matching" money for arts services, believe that the artists and the arts organizations are "taking care of the arts." Never mind that only a small fraction of the children for whom they are responsible receive any consistently high-quality arts instruction, and never mind that most of the instruction they do receive is of short duration, low intensity, with no scope or sequence and relatively little opportunity for developmental articulation between elementary and secondary schools within any given district.

Even where arts resources are abundant, and even if artists are sufficiently trained and experienced to be considered as viable substitutes for the school's regular instructional staff, there will never be enough artists or enough money for outside arts services to ensure educational parity, equity and access to the arts for each and every student in a school or district. In other words, in the short and long run, *exclusive reliance* on artists for instructional services not only defers the attainment of the AGE programmatic ideal of balance and harmony, it also succeeds in stalling the school district's acceptance of financial responsibility and moral obligation to provide all the arts for all the children.

There are those who contend that the presence of artists in the schools is tantamount to the arts in education. I dispute this position because it is contrary to the AGE philosophy, but more importantly because it is misleading and dangerous to the case for the arts in the basic curriculum. It renders arts specialists superfluous and unnecessary, weakening an important part of the constituency within the schools needed to fight the uphill battle for the institutionalization of the arts in the school program. Furthermore, while their contribution to the schools can be powerful, artists and arts organizations are outside resources, paid for largely by outside funds. For those who are interested in promoting and producing the conditions necessary for enduring institutional renewal through the arts, it is important to remember that artists are valuable as potential catalysts for and resources to school improvement, not the native agents on whom pervasive and lasting change depends.

The Promise of AGE: Building a Constituency for the Arts

This analysis puts arts in general education partisans squarely on the horns of an uncomfortable dilemma. Change takes time, arts specialists will not materialize nor be reinstalled overnight and classroom teachers need extensive immersion and training in the arts. Since I maintain that these days we had better get the arts in the schools any which way we can, what do we do on Monday?

I do not have a quick-fix answer to this question, but I am convinced that apart from strong advocacy efforts directed at parents, school board members, community power-brokers and the general public, arts and school people must unite to identify and build a "bipartisan" constituent army inside and outside the schools. I am convinced that we need the passionate words of school administrators, arts specialists and classroom teachers in the vanguard of the troops to make the case compelling and authentic.

Meanwhile, let me conclude this discussion with another paradox. If we want to accomplish that "bloodless [educational] revolution" to which Edythe Gaines alluded in "Design for Change," we had better identify and marshal all our resources—all the pieces of puzzle—and shore up and build on the status quo together.

Pieces of the Puzzle
POTENTIAL SOURCES OF
LEADERSHIP, ADVOCACY AND SUPPORT

A wide variety of people, organizations, agencies and institutions can fit snugly into the three-dimensional jigsaw puzzle known as a comprehensive AGE program design. I will attempt to make some general observations about the roles they can play and the contributions they can make as potential leaders, advocates and supporters.

PARENTS AND COMMUNITY VOLUNTEERS:
AN INVALUABLE RESOURCE

Without parents, Junior League members and other community volunteers, AGE programs would undeniably suffer. They are a source of free and conscientious support and can be both persistent and persuasive advocates of the benefits of the arts to schooling, especially when they are talking about their own children. They can provide vocal and articulate leadership in the state and local corridors of power; galvanize and orchestrate any number of fundraising events; run conferences; write newsletters; organize and operate arts resource centers; teach special arts skills; and research and develop curriculum materials for arts resource kits.

The local chapters of Junior Leagues were key forces and instigators in the early formulation and implementation of plans for the League of Cities programs in Little Rock and Seattle. They also played a major role in developing arts education programs in Birmingham, Alabama; Memphis, Tennessee; and Oklahoma City, Oklahoma.

One illustration of how parent and volunteer power can be harnessed to generate support for AGE took place at two schools in the Minneapolis West Area that were consolidated because of declining enrollments. Parents and teachers from each school thought that the arts would be a unifying force, so they formed an AGE committee and submitted a proposal to the central office to become an AGE school. The request was granted, and the school was given a $500 allocation of "seed" money to help it on its way. In short order this modest sum, amplified by contributions from the PTA treasury, generated funds from local corporations and foundations, the state and local arts councils and the area superintendent's budget. To this coffer were added the proceeds from a schoolwide car-wash event, a roller-skating party and the principal's commitment of $1 per child for AGE purposes. Thus, $500 generated more than $5,000 of discretionary money, the most difficult to come by and over which the AGE committee had total jurisdiction.

The prime movers in this effort were the parents who volunteered many hours to write proposals, solicit funds and organize the fundraisers so that their "new" school could purchase services, supplies and the time of a program coordinator. This example not only illustrates parent power but gives you an inkling of how a school can play the seed-money matching game. It also indicates the potential influence parents might exert on their entire school district if only they, too, would consider forming a network across school lines to lobby for the arts in general education.

Parents, Junior League and civic volunteers can be invaluable resources, but it should be kept in mind that as with most volunteers, personal responsibilities often and unexpectedly take precedence over their program assignments. Remember that volunteers need guidance; be sure that a key member of the AGE management team is responsible for liaison with and coordination of all volunteer efforts.

CONSULTANTS AND AUTHORITIES IN THE FIELD:THE ANSWER DEPENDS ON THE QUESTION

The growing need for "on-site technical assistance" in the arts and education field is being recognized by an increasing number of agencies and organizations, although, at this writing, no one has quite defined what is meant by the term, who is to provide the services and how they will be funded. My personal bias is to look for help from the practitioners, people at the national, state and local levels who have credibility and can speak from current experience with schools, arts organizations, community groups and the like.

Probably the most important thing to remember about consultants is that if you have not identified the general problem area, they cannot help you define the nature of the difficulty or resolve it. Consultants are catalysts, facilitators and analysts; they are not witch doctors or soothsayers with the magic answer.

In the mid-eighties, the New York Foundation for the Arts (NYFA) created a statewide technical assistance grant program (TAP) for schools and arts organizations in need of professional help in the planning and implementation of their arts in education efforts. With basic funding from the New York State Council on the Arts, TAP provides assistance for short term or extended services in areas such as long-range planning, institutional development, staff and curriculum development, identification and use of community cultural resources, artist training, fundraising, marketing and public relations and evaluation.

Applicants submit simple proposals that are reviewed year round and, if eligible for support, are funded on a first-come, first-served basis. They describe their program and identify the problems or tasks on which they need help. NYFA recommends several appropriate consultants drawn from a large roster representing a wide range of experience and art forms to the applicants who select their own consultants based on written biographies and telephone interviews. In some cases, the organizations ap-

VIEWPOINT

"AGE is one of the programs we point to with pride. We've always believed the arts are basic, and we know they're not controversial. The program here helps us defend the arts when it comes time to strip the budget. We always have to fight, but the fight's getting easier in spite of what you read in the papers."

(School board member)

peal to the foundation for support of a local expert whom they have already identified and who meets NYFA's guidelines. Applicants contribute a modest, sliding-scale percentage towards the service fees and travel. Consultants have attended orientation and training sessions and participate in yearly evaluations of program structure and operation.

The TAP program should be studied for replication at the national, state and local levels. I was involved in its initial design and operation and now serve on its roster, so I can attest to its potential as a model for a regional or national clearinghouse of information and a consultant referral service. It would be an excellent pilot project for the National Endowment for the Arts.

COLLEGES AND UNIVERSITIES: SLOW BUT SURE

Colleges and universities are gradually becoming more deeply involved in AGE programs. They are providing student interns and practice teachers, in-service training for generalist and specialist teachers, leadership training for administrators and supervisors and management training for arts administrators with course offerings in the arts in education. They are starting to develop AGE-related curriculum materials, conduct field research and evaluation and open their campuses to high school students who wish to take specialized arts courses.

The main lament I hear from public school people, particularly in urban centers, is that the "academics" prefer their more orderly, insulated environment to the rough and tumble of everyday school life. Many of them rarely venture out into the classroom and are sometimes unsympathetic to the problems of schooling.

School people also feel that partnerships between schools and institutions of higher education too often end up with the latter telling the former what to do and how and when to do it. Gradual progress is being made on this front, however, and, increasingly, efforts are being collaboratively planned and carried out in the schools, on school time and on school terms.

There is an interesting new development in this area that merits study and replication. Seattle Pacific University, under the leadership of Professors Carol Scott, chair of the Music Education Department, and Ray Thompson, former director of Visual and Performing Arts in the Seattle Public Schools, has developed an innovative, one-year, 45-credit masters degree program requiring fifteen credits in AGE. The program, which is limited to fifteen students per year, has enrolled over ninety teachers since its inception in 1983. The main focus is on the AGE projects that all students are required to develop. These projects must meet identified needs in their school, school district or community, and they must have the tangible support of key administrators and decision-makers. Both Scott and Thompson work individually with each of the students and closely monitor their progress in the field.

The course content at the university includes intensive study of the basic principles and practices of AGE, using this book and a number of other texts that suggest alternative approaches. Students are also informed about the most current research in arts in education and related areas and learn the basic principles of research. They spend about fifty hours in hands-on workshops and other experiences with art, music, dance, drama and the literary arts that are conducted by experienced artist master teachers and coordinated by Ann G. Gilbert, an acknowledged dance education authority. The workshops focus on the elements of the arts, their commonalities and their differences.

According to Ray Thompson, students emerging from this program have become curriculum leaders in the concept of AGE throughout western Washington State. One recent graduate with twenty-two years of teaching experience said, "This program has opened new doors of understanding for me. I have never been so excited about my teaching." Seattle Pacific University requires all undergraduate students to take ten credits in the category "The Individual in the Aesthetic World," which includes courses in the integrated arts. Education majors who complete all their courses at the university are required to take twenty-five credits in the arts, which includes courses in the individual arts and integrated offerings dealing with the concepts of AGE.

The University of Montana in Missoula plans to begin an AGE masters program modeled on the Seattle Pacific University approach in the fall of 1990. The chair of Montana's Theater and Dance Department in the School of Fine Arts visited Seattle last summer and was convinced of the validity of the approach.

Undoubtedly, there are similar examples of which I am unaware that should be cited here. That is all the more reason for a national clearinghouse of information and a teacher center dedicated to the arts in education so that this type of precious information can be collected, catalogued and shared with a wider audience.

PROFESSIONAL ARTS AND EDUCATION ASSOCIATIONS: POTENTIAL ADVOCATES FOR AGE

There are literally hundreds of national and state professional arts and educational associations, alliances, councils, guilds, assemblies and leagues. Most of them exist to provide professional visibility, a forum for exchange of information and the delivery of a variety of services to their dues-paying membership. Several of them publish newsletters, journals and occasional books and monographs and many hold an annual conference focusing on particular topical issues. Since these organizations rarely design, operate or participate in programs in the schools, their potential power lies in their individual and collective ability to articulate and advocate the idea of the arts in general education to their constituencies who presumably, as individuals, will work for change within the power structure of their own localities.

Unfortunately the field remains adversarial and competitive, rather than collegial and collaborative. There is still a lack of agreement as to what, both in theory and practice, the AGE program means and how it is complementary to, not in conflict with, certain professional and organizational aims and interests. I actually believe that the concept of AGE would provide a fertile common ground for discussion. As a comprehensive approach, it provides lots of room for the active participation of everyone who wants to help make the arts a presence in the education of the young and who is willing to make a concrete contribution (of deeds, not just words) to the endeavor.

TEACHER UNIONS AND SUPERVISORY ASSOCIATIONS: UNTAPPED RESOURCES

Teacher unions and supervisory associations vary in their prominence, power and influence throughout the country. Although their main purpose is to lobby for, bargain for and protect the rights of their members, they too hold conferences and workshops, cosponsor educational events and programs, provide consultant services and publish newsletters and journals. In localities where these groups are strong and vocal, they are still a largely untapped resource and potentially powerful advocates for AGE.

SCHOOL BOARDS:
FINANCIAL AND POLITICAL ADVOCATES

School boards can be extremely influential in supporting AGE programs. They have the power to make educational policy and financial decisions as well as to formulate requests and make recommendations to state and local legislatures. League of Cities sites used various techniques to attract and capture attention. Some of them included securing a place on the monthly agenda to make formal presentations; extending personal invitations to members to visit AGE schools and participate in special cultural events for the community; and persuading them to serve on arts in education advisory committees.

What we tend to forget is that board members are often parents, too, and therefore have a personal interest in the quality of their own children's education. Time and again in the Minneapolis program, two board members were instrumental in defending the Urban Resources Program (of which AGE became an integral part) and championing the arts at budget time. Their passion and conviction was infectious, and backed up by the concrete evidence of the area superintendents, threatened cuts were restored; in a few cases, allocations were even increased.

ADVISORY COMMITTEES:
MARSHALING THE COMMUNITY

Not all AGE programs establish permanent advisory committees. In those that do, these consultative bodies are a potent force for advocacy, steady guidance and local political influence. Representation on them includes chief school administrators, board members, arts administrators, civic volunteers, higher education officials, foundation officers, PTA council presidents and other community-action people. Meetings are generally held monthly or quarterly in a central location where simple refreshments can be served. The agenda is generally set by project leadership with input from representatives. Meetings address issues that affect every aspect of program planning, development, assessment and financing. They provide an excellent forum for open communication, networking and collaborative community action. In Little Rock, for example, the program owed much of its success to a strong and active advisory group in which Arkansas Arts Center Director Townsend Wolfe and the Inglewood Foundation's Polly Keller and Frank Mackey played a prominent leadership role.

PRIVATE FOUNDATIONS, CORPORATIONS AND THE BUSINESS COMMUNITY: SEED-MONEY SOURCES

These entities, next to the federal and state education departments, are the most important sources of outside financial support for program planning and development. Frequently, however, business and corporate giving officers prefer to invest in "tangibles," such as artists' services, student tickets to performances, sponsorship of art exhibitions, school art displays, national conferences and documentary publications.

Foundation and corporate administrators rarely make site visits to observe the activities of their school or arts in education grantees. They prefer to engage in a safer practice that I call "program paper monitoring." I wish that these capable men and women would re-examine their armslength posture and somewhat arbitrary one-to-three-year funding-cycle policies because:

1. Firsthand experience over time, especially at the staff level, promotes a deeper understanding of complex situations and a greater satisfaction on the job when you can provide sound technical and consulting support.
2. Field experience generates useful knowledge for determining enlightened and responsive grant-making and program policies. It also puts you in touch with the pulse of the enterprise, the texture of the process and the dynamics of the political and other social interactions.
3. Profitable lessons learned from authentic experience can and should be shared with a larger audience, especially your constituency and your institutional peers.
4. Educational innovations need time and patient nurturing to take hold. Five to ten years is considered about average for the institutionalization of new practices and procedures.

STATE EDUCATION DEPARTMENTS: NATURAL MECHANISMS FOR LEADERSHIP AND EXPANSION

State education departments can declare the arts a priority in the education of every child in the state and design comprehensive plans that assure adequate technical and consulting assistance, coordination, and funding for programs at the local district and school level. They can play a major role in disseminating information about, and championing the idea of, the arts in general education on a statewide basis. They can make the arts a requirement for high school graduation, mandate arts specialist services for every school building in their jurisdiction and design interdisciplinary curriculum frameworks.

Through statewide and local networks, leadership-training institutes, staff and curriculum development workshops, teacher certification procedures, legal and fiscal mandates, publications, conferences and the department's technical resource people, state education departments can provide guidance and inspiration to a very broad audience. They can earmark categorical, competitive and block grant funds from a variety of state and federally funded programs and make them available to arts education programs and activities. And they can assist in the difficult task of research and evaluation.

Information about the Coalition of States for the Arts in Education and two case studies on the Oklahoma and Pennsylvania arts in education programs are contained in *An Arts in Education Source Book: A View from the JDR 3rd Fund*, available from the American Council for the Arts.

ARTS AND HUMANITIES ENDOWMENTS, AGENCIES AND COUNCILS

These national, state and local agencies are natural partners for all AGE efforts. They supply money for teacher training, curriculum development, and research and evaluation. They support artist residencies, arts programs and exhibits in the schools, performances and visits to cultural sites and centers, special festivals and celebration events and the production and publication of documentary and other dissemination materials. Grants are either outright or on a matching formula basis.

There are many national, regional, state and local councils, commissions and federally-assisted programs around today. Some of them have long and impressive track records in the arts in education and many of them are operative in League cities. I urge you to study the archival records of the artists in education dance component of the National Endowment for the Arts; the Technical Assistance Program and Artists in Residence efforts

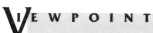

VIEWPOINT

"AGE has helped me attract and keep middle-class parents of all races and backgrounds. It is a force for integrating my school population as well as the instructional program."

(Principal)

of the New York Foundation for the Arts; and the Arts in Education programs of the Minnesota State Arts Board, the New York State Council on the Arts and the New Jersey State Council on the Arts. These programs offer comprehensive process models that have been tested and tempered in the field and widely acclaimed by both artists and educators.

Under former Chairman Frank Hodsoll, arts education moved closer to the top of the National Endowment for the Arts' agenda in the early eighties, and two programs have become national flagships of support for the arts in education. In 1987, the Artists in Education Program was renamed and the thrust of the new Arts in Education (AIE) Program was shifted from funding state arts agencies' artists-in-residence programs to basic planning and implementation grants meant to encourage collaboration between state arts agencies and state education departments. Over five-and-a-half-million dollars—as much or more than the amount allocated to certain discipline areas—is now budgeted for these and other AIE program efforts, including the two national arts in education research centers funded jointly with the federal Department of Education. And, beginning in 1987, the NEA's Challenge Grant program has targeted substantial matching-funds assistance to arts in education projects that can provide greater access and/or "deeper and broader education in and appreciation of the arts."

In the fall of 1989, the New York State Council on the Arts released a set of revised guidelines for its Arts in Education Program. Written by the program's former director, Andrew Ackerman, the guidelines incorporate the basic principles of AGE —comprehensive planning, networking and collaboration, a broad operational definition of the arts and the arts in education, staff and curriculum development, and research and evaluation. I believe they constitute a model for the field and they are included in the Appendix for your study and reference.

THE U.S. DEPARTMENT OF EDUCATION AND THE EDUCATION PROGRAM OF THE JOHN F. KENNEDY CENTER FOR THE PERFORMING ARTS

The Department of Education (formerly the Office of Education and the National Institute for Education) was heavily involved with the arts in education beginning in the early 1960s (see the Interpretive Chronology of Major Events in the Arts in Education in the Appendix, as well as my article expanding on this subject, "Arts Policy and Public Education," in *The Journal of Arts Management and the Law*, Spring 1983). Currently, the U.S. Department of Education continues to provide the major source of funding for the Kennedy Center's Education Program, established in 1972, and for a few cooperative ventures with the NEA focusing on national arts in education research centers and an instructional television project.

In the past, the Education Department has made competitive grants for comprehensive arts in education programs and provided categorical title money for compensatory and other special efforts such as desegregation. Arts in education programs were able to piggy-back onto these funds by maintaining that the arts were justifiable and legitimate means for achieving the primarily social and remedial purposes of the various pieces of legislation.

The Kennedy Center Education Program coordinates a national Alliance for Arts Education network, administers a program for local schools, provides funds for certain developmental projects and has issued a first-rate newsletter, *Interchange*, about the arts in education. The Kennedy Center, the Department of Education and the two national endowments collaborate from time to time on national and regional conferences, investigative studies and reports and certain programmatic efforts.

While there are recent indications of greater intra- and interagency communication and cooperation at the national level, there is still much room for improvement, especially in the areas of leadership training, technical assistance and research and evaluation.

Support Systems
WHAT WE HAVE AND
WHAT WE NEED

LEADERSHIP TRAINING

Whether you are a chief administrator, supervisor, coordinator, principal, teacher or artist in an AGE program, there is no real substitute for learning the ropes on the job. There are, however, ways of speeding up and fortifying the professional development process. One method is through networking, where practitioners engaged in common pursuit meet regularly to address the problems they have identified and work together to create solutions they can apply and test out immediately. This strategy produces a cost-effective, floating academy run by and for its members, who become their own best resources and resident experts.

I have often remarked in meetings of network principals or teachers that if each of them were paid for their participation at their daily salary rate, the total cash outlay would represent a staggering fee, one that no single arts in education consultant could legitimately command. Furthermore, no single consultant, regardless of the fee, could possibly match the diversity of styles or equal the cumulative wisdom and wealth of experience of the group. Once networking becomes the *modus operandi*, controversial guest speakers and provocative outside experts are useful, on occasion, to stir up the dust of complacency and stimulate fresh thinking.

Other methods for professional development include institutes, workshops, seminars and college courses in which national and local leaders and authorities in the field address specific conceptual, instructional and administrative topics. They use current material such as source books, case studies, administrators' manuals, curriculum guides, instructional frameworks and occasional papers as references and points of departure. The most effective approach combines task-oriented study with supervised field work and observation of exemplary programs in action. Many of them are offered to a broad audience for professional or service credit.

Another approach to professional development involves fellowship programs, in which fledgling administrators with a background in both the arts and education are introduced to all aspects of AGE and assigned specific tasks and responsibilities for which they are paid a modest stipend.

THE ADMINISTRATIVE FELLOWSHIP TRAINING PROGRAM

After I had spent a couple of years working with the Coalition of States and League networks, one fact became clear: state education departments and school districts rarely had the resources to administer, supervise and monitor their existing arts programs. When a dedicated but already overburdened staff was asked to assume additional arts in education responsibilities, the groans became audible. What both networks needed most was people. As a result, Kathy Bloom asked me to prepare a fellowship program design that was distributed for comment and feedback to network members. The response was universally enthusiastic.

The Fund provided $1,000 a month plus travel and expenses toward a stipend for the fellows. While we deliberately left the selection, supervision and training to each site, the grants included general guidelines and criteria for job descriptions, periodic progress reports and final evaluations. Fellows participated in an orientation conference, all network meetings, site visits and a group evaluation discussion. League and Coalition members and the fellows hailed the program as a success, and many of the fellows have continued in their newly-created positions as program coordinators, researchers and evaluators. Some were assigned to other departmental roles and responsibilities, all at city or state expense. In Seattle, for example, the fellow, Judith Meltzer, moved from a position on the school district's arts resource team to the position of arts in education coordinator.

The success of the program was not unqualified. There were some supervisors who virtually ignored their charges and other who threw their unprepared and overwhelmed trainees "into the lion's den," as one of the fellows plaintively put it. Some were used as only slightly glorified "gofers" and given mostly clerical or drudge work.

In balance, the Fund's fellowship program has left a blueprint for a larger national effort in which seed money can be used to encourage people at the local level to identify the personnel they need and the incentive to provide the matching money to hire and train them.

What we need is a national arts in education academy or institute that addresses a broad audience of current and potential practitioners. Staffed by past and current personnel in the field, it would combine on-the-job administrative training in the form of fellowships and internships with structured, in-depth study of the arts and education. It would offer work-study opportunities for leadership, staff and curriculum development. It would be school-practice oriented and deal with the theoretical as well as experiential aspects of designing and carrying out an AGE program from the perspective of administrators, teachers, artists, parents and community volunteers. If such a pilot venture were to prove successful, it would offer another model process for regional and local replication.

STAFF AND CURRICULUM DEVELOPMENT

It is difficult to convey to classroom teachers and arts specialists that AGE is not a course of study. I try to assure them that AGE is really a framework composed of several interrelated instructional parts. Much of the content is probably within their grasp, and they need only to tap their experience, imagination, and ingenuity. "But where's the curriculum?" they ask. "What's the scope and sequence? What should I be doing and my children be learning so I know I'm teaching AGE? And, where do I begin?"

My stock answer has become:

You cannot teach AGE as such. It is not a subject and it is not a new curriculum with its own separate scope and sequence. It is a holistic way of thinking about teaching and learning. It allows you to look at your school and your classroom, to see where and how the arts can fit in as independent studies, as interdependent, companion studies and as bridges to learning other material.

Your challenge, and it is not an easy one, is to determine what pieces of the AGE instructional matrix interest you, which parts of the process you feel most comfortable with and equipped to handle. A lot depends on whether you have a broad, inclusive definition of the arts, formal or informal arts background and training and especially a willingness to take the time to break new ground and take some risks.

Perhaps the best place to start is with a personal inventory of your arts interests and abilities...don't be modest. Then you might want to look at your lesson plans for the next several months to see if there is a theme or topic that provides you with an opportunity to introduce the arts. Check the school's calendar of events for more ideas. Consider the children's background and needs and poll them for their ideas and interests. Then, if you need it, don't be afraid to ask for help—from your principal and your colleagues, from the school's or district's specialists, from artists. Remember, everyone needs help, and no one person can be expected to teach all the dimensions of AGE anyway, no matter how we define it.

You can imagine the sighs of impatience and frustration that greet this response. There are not too many teachers who are willing to spend the kind of time and energy implicit in this approach without a safety net and some assurance of payoff for the children and themselves.

An AGE "curriculum" is a composite; it is the sum of what classroom teachers (kindergarten through high school) and arts specialists (when and where available) make it—supported, augmented and reinforced by trained professional artists and other qualified resource personnel. Although there is no single AGE textbook, there are a number of instructional resources to which teachers can turn for guidance and inspiration. However, the commercially-produced materials tend to be too expensive and the homemade teacher products, apart from being scattered all over the country, are too generally site-specific for general application.

Currently-employed classroom teachers agree they need structured exposure to, and immersion and training in, the arts. They need regular access to professionals with field-tested, "school-wise" knowledge and skills who will make them feel more comfortable with the processes. They require support from each other and the principal to explore, take chances, make mistakes without fear of retribution or ridicule. They must be assured that they don't have to be bona fide professional artists or arts specialists to be able to teach certain aspects of the arts or relate the arts to general or subject-area learning. They do need to be shown by the specialist and the artist where these connections exist and how to make them without damaging the integrity of the art form.

Ideally, of course, these opportunities should have begun long ago in their own school days and the teacher training institutions, and they ought to continue throughout the teachers' active careers. But we cannot afford to wait for these major changes in practice and in pre-service requirements for the arts. We need to begin now, in the schools, by helping the teachers on the scene.

By and large arts specialists agree they need to fill some important gaps in their own pre-service training and experience. They want intensive schooling in aesthetics, art history, criticism; some of them feel they need more training to improve and diversify their studio and performance skills. Perhaps they might benefit from extended workshops in which they could explore new ways to use their current knowledge and skills so as to improve their visibility and usefulness to every school that they serve.

Most of the artists I know, even the best of them, need to learn about the culture of the school. They should study child development, pedagogy, learning theories and classroom management. They need to understand the value and purpose of making their own lesson plans. They should be taught how to identify clear and simple objectives. They need to learn how to make the subtle as well as the obvious connections among the various arts disciplines and between the arts processes they teach and the content of the classroom teacher's lesson plans. They need to understand the role of the arts specialists and be sure to seek them out and spend significant time with them (as well as the classroom teachers) when planning their school programs.

Artists need to ask themselves, each and every time they leave a classroom, "What skills, knowledge and information has the classroom teacher or other instructional resource person learned from me today? What have I left behind that has value for teachers and some chance of permanence in the school?" If these questions cannot be answered positively, no matter how wonderful the experience for children, the artists will have failed to meet one of the most important criteria for any program's success. If there are *no* answers to these questions, then the program's structure and operation are seriously flawed and need to be overhauled.

We need a campaign to ferret out, collect and organize—in one place—information about the best procedures and the most effective materials

V̵IEWPOINT

"Many collaborations between artists and schools are superficial. This is generally not the case in AGE. Artists usually function differently in AGE schools. They fulfill the needs of that situation according to how the staff defines it, and residencies often result in new courses that are teacher-designed and taught. In addition, working in AGE schools has opened new professional vistas and new creative possibilities for artists; it is also a very fulfilling personal experience."

(Arts agency administrator)

that exist all over the country. We must mine these nuggets of informational gold and share them with those who are clamoring for concrete help. We need an information clearinghouse to make these approaches and ma-terials easily and quickly accessible and a directory of where they can be obtained or studied. The current educational information systems such as ERIC are woefully inadequate for the task of providing practical counsel on AGE.

We also need national, regional and local AGE teacher-artist networks run for and by teachers and artists as equal partners. These mechanisms would probably do more to strengthen the delivery of curriculum and staff development services to practitioners in AGE programs than any other single effort.

These teacher-artist networks might become part of the various teacher centers that exist nationwide. This project should appeal to the teacher unions, the National Endowment for the Arts and the Department of Education.

RESEARCH AND EVALUATION

I discovered some years ago that in the field of educational research and evaluation of the arts in education, simplicity was considered a dangerous idea. When I suggested that the researchers and evaluators put their designs into plainer English, they frowned. When I ventured that some of their theoretical hypotheses would benefit from a strong dose of school-wise common sense, they scowled. When I stated that a combination ap-proach uniting quantitative and qualitative inquiry might be more sensitive to our mercurial and highly subjective field, they shrugged impatiently. Many of them refused to entertain the notion that the standard approach could be tempered by a more sensitive, "responsive" mode that might reveal a more comprehensive and comprehensible picture. Others simply declared that these methods were incompatible.

While there are a few refreshing exceptions—John Goodlad, Robert Stake and Elliot Eisner come immediately to my mind—most of the educa-tional researchers and evaluators that I know continue to prefer elaborate matrices and insist upon a jargon that is so abstract, so arcane, so intimidating that I arrived at a perhaps hasty and certainly nasty conclusion. The smoke screen was deliberate. It was meant to camouflage a sad fact: research and evaluation of arts in general education programs is in a primitive state.

This sounds like a broadside against all educational research and evaluation. It also makes no distinction between the purposes and modes of operation of the two related but different fields. To oversimplify, one is primarily investigative—testing out a hypothesis, and descriptive—of the findings and their implications. The other assesses worth and tries to make sound judgments about program value and performance effectiveness. In this discussion, I will deal with them together.

My plea to the professionals in both fields is to be more direct and to provide greater public access to digestible information in sources other than obscure scholarly journals or expensive information-retrieval systems. I especially ask for more collaborative action in the planning and execution of efforts so statisticians, educational psychologists, researchers and evaluators can begin to tell practitioners what they need to know, in language they can understand, as soon as they need the information, not what the computers spit out, three years too late.

I know, as do others in the field, that under certain conditions arts in education programs work. They are good for students, teachers and artists. They benefit the school and the community. I know, for example, that the arts can have a positive impact on children's ability to express themselves verbally and in writing. I also know that over time certain arts experiences such as creating an original opera will build a "can-do" attitude and positive self-concepts in children. I know that the introduction of theater games and improvisations can make a significant difference to social studies teachers, for example, because they help bring otherwise dry and abstract historical and political ideas vividly alive. And I know that the presence of the arts can contribute to a warmer school climate that nurtures teacher satisfaction, fellowship, open communication, mutual respect and relaxed, unpressured learning. I know all this, but I can't prove it using standardized measurements and other no-nonsense quantifying tools of the trade. In fact, I can't prove it at all.

I have a lot of empirical knowledge and general hunches about why these statements are true and how they happen, but I am handicapped by a serious lack of incontestible, air-tight evidence to brandish at the dubious policy and decision-makers. I am forced to base my testimony on evidence gathered largely by several pairs of practiced eyes and corroborated by logical inferences from repeated patterns of observable behavior. I can be quite persuasive, but eloquence can quickly degenerate into speculative rhetoric. I desperately need more comprehensive evidence defining causes and effects, isolating variables and providing more facts and fewer reasoned deductions. Perhaps the field is not susceptible to this kind of precise examination. There are those who contend that it is not worth the time, money and effort, but I think we owe it to ourselves to try. But, to do the job, we need a new atmosphere, a new set of conditions. If only I could persuade my colleagues in the research and evaluation communities to rely far less exclusively on culturally biased, gender-specific and badly worded pre- and post-tests; elaborate instruments that cost a fortune to develop, administer and decode; and a whole set of "scientific" formulae that treat schools and the people in them as if they were so many dots on a graph or robots in an airplane factory.

We need a more responsive approach to research and evaluation in schools so we can better understand the elusive but precious phenomenon of the arts in education. I want the investigators to balance and integrate the hard data, pre-post approach with another softer but no less accurate dimension: the well-disciplined and boundary-defined case study approach. I want them to rely far less on abstract conjecture and more on what is. I want them to acknowledge and understand that schools, as Edythe Gaines used to say, are messy places and that schooling is not a neat and tidy business.

For this new attitude, this new set of conditions to occur, all the full professors and their graduate assistants need to go back to school. They should visit school yards, hang out in the lunch rooms, wander the corridors, observe classrooms. They should speak with the people involved (especially principals, teachers and parents) and examine the program and the dynamics of the process in its native habitat. If they cannot shanghai the building principal for the occasion, I suggest they make the first of these regular safaris in the company of another guide who knows the territory.

When a team of investigators gets to know the schools, talks with the children and works with arts and education professionals in the process, it should be possible to design a battery of imaginative, age-appropriate inventories, checklists and a set of pre- and post-test instruments that, when taken together, capture the affective, social and cognitive aspects of teaching and learning in the arts. The team should be composed of professionals in the arts, education, psychological measurement and statistice. They should be able to collect, analyze and interpret data from a multitude of sources: the students, the teachers, the artists, the parents, the administrators.

They should be able to look at the hard and soft data together, comparing results, seeking patterns and trying to account for consistencies, corroboration or discrepancies. And they should be better able to compare what is with what someone said (or thought they said) they set out to do. Information resulting from an approach such as this is bound to help policymakers and other practitioners take informed action based on solidly grounded recommendations for program improvement.

Let me be even more specific. Throughout this book there are enough goals, objectives, criteria, strategies, processes and outcomes (actual and anticipated) to provide a framework for a comprehensive set of research and evaluation designs that would speak to what we, our sponsors, clients, parents and especially the skeptics and doubters need to know—now. Drawing on some of these as examples, I would propose that we need balanced teams of researchers and evaluators who will thoroughly explore the following propositions. Under certain conditions:

— The program, operation and climate of schools change, develop and improve when the arts are significantly present in the formal and informal curriculum.

— The five main points of AGE programs (interdisciplinary teaching and learning, increased arts offerings, greater use of artists and community resources, etc.), when in sufficient evidence, collectively characterize a quality arts in education program.

— The quality of teaching and learning improves significantly for all children in a school when the arts become an integral part of their daily experience.

— The presence of the arts and artists in the schools increases community involvement and public support.

— Networking and collaboration are effective strategies for staff, curriculum and school development through the arts.

— AGE programs provide a new dimension in the formal education of children and help schools meet the broader aims of education.

— It takes five to ten years for a new theoretical concept to become an accepted and established educational practice.

As my colleague, Jack Morrison, once eloquently put it:

Questions like the above can be answered in a common sense, systematic manner and presented to all concerned in clear, simple and persuasive ways. Honest reporting of these answers in effective modes that touch the consumer's sense of caring about children is in the realm of the possible. But it takes imagination and insightful interpretation with great integrity. It means the use and respect of subjective data carefully collected and ordered. It means demystifying objective data in the subjective realm of feeling.[1]

Although we still need to develop the techniques and the instruments that provide hard evidence, as well as the considerable sums of money to support the developmental process, there is progress in the field. The NEA's 1988 report on arts education to Congress, "Toward Civilization," calls for "more sustained support [money] for arts education research . . . [that] should be focused on improving classroom instruction."

The American Council for the Arts, in a research seminar, examined the nature and dimensions of the problems as well as the opportunities facing researchers in arts education. Its monograph, *The Challenge to*

---

[1] Stake et al., *Evaluating the Arts in Education: A Responsive Approach* [Columbus, Ohio: Merrill, 1975]. The quotation is from the chapter entitled "A Consumer's Concern."

Reform Arts Education: What Role Can Research Play? (ACA Books, 1989), edited by David B. Pankratz and Kevin V. Mulcahy, presents a useful analysis of the contemporary scene. The book incorporates the presentations delivered at a meeting entitled "After Interlochen: Research for a New Era in Arts Education," held in Philadelphia in February 1988.

About a year earlier, the ACA and the Music Educators National Conference had sponsored the Interlochen Symposium "Toward a New Era in Arts Education," which issued a proposal urging the development of better research and information dissemination in the arts education field. A few national coalitions and working groups have included research and evaluation on their agendas, so at least some people are willing to talk about the issue.

There is another ray of hope. In 1987, the U.S. Department of Education and the National Endowment for the Arts jointly established a National Arts Education Research Center in two sites: the University of Illinois at Urbana-Champaign and New York University in New York City. Both centers are exploring issues that have concerned the field for years. Of particular interest, New York University is proceeding on the premise that useful research derives theory from practice (not the other way around); it supports the AGE philosophy of teacher ownership in the business of schooling and promises some practical results for the field—based on the experience of the practitioners.

The Center at NYU "is studying modes of response to the arts with the intent of applying research findings to the development of teaching strategies and curricula in arts education . . . . In addition, since the Center is interested in exploring arts education [at all grade levels and] in all contexts, it is centering its research efforts in urban, suburban and rural classroom settings." [It is currently working with secondary teachers from over twenty-five sites around the country on projects in art, music, theater and creative writing.][2]

The NYU Center has also embarked on a study examining the impact of the arts and community arts services on the improvement of oral expression and self-concept in elementary school children. Federal funds for the research centers were authorized for only three years and hearings are now under way regarding reauthorization and continued support. Each of the current centers has supplemented its federal funding with money from the local public and private sectors.

---

[2] National Arts Education Research Center, Information Bulletin, New York, 11/28/88.

DOCUMENTATION AND DISSEMINATION

Over the years, I have collected many books, reports, monographs and reference materials about the arts and education. Only one quarter of one shelf deals specifically with arts in general education programs, much of it published or financially assisted by the JDR 3rd Fund. Given that the notion has been around for quite a while and now seems to be gaining, or at least maintaining, momentum, one quarter of one shelf does not an AGE reference library make.

I know for a fact that literally hundreds of reports, documents, case studies and other sources of useful information are scattered far and wide, not just among the League sites. The pity of it is that most of it is lying around on dusty shelves, buried in storerooms under piles of paper, forgotten in crammed file cabinets or simply out-of-print. The rest of it is still unwritten. AGE people, like most pioneers, have been so busy "doing it" that they have sadly neglected to keep written or visual track of their work. Much of our legacy depends on oral history and a sound memory, and those are not, as we know, entirely reliable sources.

There is a need for a thorough search, cataloging and collection—in one place—of all existing information and a conscious and sustained effort to document all aspects of current and future programs so information about the field is comprehensive, fresh and easily accessible. We must get organized now, before our collective memories fade.

My bookshelf of hardcover or serious softcover titles that make general reference to the arts and education has recently grown by about a foot. It includes Goodlad's Study of Schooling, the NEA's arts education evaluation reports of the seventies and eighties, the full version of "Toward Civilization," and all the Getty materials. One foot in ten years? I guess that's progress. It certainly makes for a more interesting bibliography. A casual glance at the titles and the publishers also reveals that the old McGraw-Hill hegemony on the arts has been successfully broken up by the American Council for the Arts, Book Division. ACA is also in the process of organizing a much-needed national arts resource and reference library.

FINANCING

Funding for AGE programs comes from a variety of public or private sources, but local tax-levy money is always used for basic operating expenses. The trick is to learn how to supplement these bedrock funds. One way is to identify potential resources from existing budget items using a piggybacking technique that might be called "creative plundering"). The object of this game is to reallocate a portion of these funds earmarked for seemingly unrelated purposes to arts in education activities that support the intentions of the budget item. An obvious example would be the use of funds set aside for teacher training or curriculum development.

Other not so obvious examples would include use of allocations for purposes such as school integration, drop-out prevention, health and drug education, the gifted and talented, special education and, more recently, multicultural education. With a little imagination, audacious administrators can claim that a lot of categorical and competitive money can be used to good advantage by AGE, since the program's objectives are clearly complementary to or in direct support of many broad educational and social goals.

The funding game is a very intricate and complicated one. It is also in constant flux, especially at the federal level. Rather than provide a laundry list that, without considerable annotation, would be meaningless to the casual reader, I will mention a few of the generic sources of public and private funds for AGE programs.

FEDERAL: the Department of Education (see especially the Elementary and Secondary Education Act, as amended, for direct or piggybacking funds; practically every title can be used to support the components of AGE programs . . . and see the Emergency School Aid Act/Special Arts Project); the National Endowments for the Arts and Humanities; the Kennedy Center Education Program; the National Parks Service; Law Enforcement Agencies (Drug Addiction, Juvenile Delinquency)

STATE: education departments; arts councils, commissions, boards; cultural enrichment programs; governor's discretionary budget; special legislation for heritage funds

LOCAL: school districts; city and county agencies; arts councils, cultural commissions; foundations, community trusts, businesses and corporations; banks and insurance companies; parents associations ; civic groups and volunteer organizations (especially Junior Leagues); merchants; professional associations; individual benefactors

What we need is obvious: increased and more sustained financing. Given the current state of the economy and the national inclination toward greater state and local responsibility for educational innovation, large sums earmarked for the arts in education will probably not be forthcoming from federal agencies. The days of sudden abundance so characteristic of the sixties are probably gone forever, and even the modest but significant seed-money sources of the early seventies are under scrutiny or threatened with extinction. Basic support for AGE has always come from state and local budgets, supplemented by corporate and philanthropic funds. The handwriting is on the wall: a grassroots program needs grassroots support. Now, more than ever, we need to cultivate the gardens in our own backyard.

One thought continues to trouble me. When pursuing money for AGE programs, I always face a philosophical and, in the end, practical problem. Do I ask for "arts" money or "education" money? AGE tries to wed the arts and education. The JDR 3rd Fund was, to my knowledge, the only philanthropy that looked at the two fields together. What is the best tack to take with foundations and corporations that usually keep their arts and education areas of jurisdiction separate, if not isolated? AGE always falls between the cracks or gets shunted back and forth because no one will acknowledge responsibility for it.

It is probably wisest to continue to hedge the bets and work both sides of the street. I persist in hoping that donors partial to the arts will recognize their importance to the AGE concept of schooling and that those concerned with school improvement and educational change will be willing to take a chance on programs that focus on the arts as content and vehicles for the process. These days, we need both "camps" to see and understand the value of concerted action and collaborative financial support. This takes a united front and a far more vocally consistent constituency.

ADVOCACY

In the preceding sections, I have identified a series of needs that, when taken together, form an interesting agenda for the formal and informal groups of advocates in the field. To summarize, here is what we need in the areas of:

LEADERSHIP TRAINING: We need a national arts in education academy or institute that addresses a broad audience of current and potential decision-makers and practitioners so as to identify the trailblazers of this and the next generations. We also need an administrative fellowship training program to support this process.

STAFF AND CURRICULUM DEVELOPMENT: The content of current pre- and in-service training opportunities for classroom teachers, arts specialists and artists needs to be overhauled. We also need to develop an organized campaign to ferret out and collect the best field-tested procedures and the most effective materials that exist throughout the country, as well as national, regional and local AGE teacher-artist networks run for and by teachers and artists as equal partners.

RESEARCH AND EVALUATION: We need a more responsive approach to research and evaluation in schools to understand better the mercurial phenomenon of the arts in education; a new atmosphere in which more collaborative action in the planning and execution of efforts can flourish; and an investigation of the AGE approach.

DOCUMENTATION AND DISSEMINATION: We need more information gathered in regional clearinghouses that easily can be shared with a wider audience.

FINANCING: We need increased and more sustained financing from a broader funding base that includes the U.S. Department of Education and all state education agencies, as well as funding that is collaborative and concentrates on local programs stressing the value of concerted action.

If those agencies and organizations that believe advocacy for the arts in education to be a top priority will call upon those whom I have identified as teachers of the arts—specialists, artists, classroom teachers—and band together with those whom I have referred to in the previous chapter as actual or potential pieces of the solution to the puzzle—parents and volunteers, professional associations, unions, school boards, advisory committees—just think of the campaign we could mount!

To paraphrase Teddy Roosevelt, we have a plan and we have identified the waterways (but not the shortcuts) to support. All we need is the man or woman—or group of them—who will lead the charge, who will steer the ship through the narrow straits to the promise of the open seas.

Any volunteers?

In Conclusion

IN RETROSPECT:
THE AGE IDEA PROVES POWERFUL

Seventeen years ago, when Edythe Gaines, Kathryn Bloom and I formed our partnership, we had no grand design for changing schools through the arts. We simply liked and trusted each other and thought that by joining forces, we might do something for the schools, the arts and the children. We never dreamed we would end up claiming that under certain conditions the arts could qualify as a motivating force, an organizing principle and the instructional content for institutional renewal.

As I look back, I realize that the idea was actually born out of a combination of need and serendipity. We began with the need to marry two different institutional imperatives. It was the common link—children—that forged the alliance between Kathy's mission for the JDR 3rd Fund, "all the arts for all the children in entire schools," and Edythe's passion, a "Beacon Light" network dedicated to comprehensive school development under the creative management and instructional leadership of the principal. Our sustained opportunity to work closely with John Goodlad cinched the deal, and in a matter of a few years, a program that was conceived in New York was taken over and elaborated upon by a national network. What a marvelous and unlooked-for bonus for all of us.

In this final chapter, I will offer my views on the significance of the League model, discuss a recent project it has spawned in New Orleans and then recount some of the lessons I have learned in the field over the years. My last words will be a call for action.

THE SIGNIFICANCE OF THE LEAGUE: A NETWORK MAKES A DIFFERENCE

The model for school change through the arts, the formation of the League of Cities and its refinement of the AGE concept constitute an interesting chapter in American educational history. Here are some of the reasons:

1. **WORKING WITH A PRIVATE FOUNDATION, SIX SCHOOL DISTRICTS FORMED A NATIONAL NETWORK FOR THE ARTS IN GENERAL EDUCATION.** Six urban school systems of widely different size, geographical location and structure agreed to form individual partnerships with a private foundation and decided that it would be helpful to set up a national network. This network met regularly and worked together in common cause with the understanding that differences were to be both respected and cherished. The network served the field and its members well.

2. **A PLAN DEVELOPED IN ONE CITY BECAME THE BLUEPRINT FOR ALL LEAGUE OF CITIES PROGRAMS AND FOR A NEW VARIATION ON THE THEME IN NEW ORLEANS.** League members and other school districts used the blueprint of the model process developed in New York City to plan and develop their own unique efforts for change and development through the arts. While the basic goal and general approach remained intact, collective ownership and experience led to gradual refinement and often gave more practical meaning to theoretical ideas. The basic principles of networking and collaboration that the Learning Cooperative's "Design for Change" spelled out almost twenty years ago have proved viable for individual schools and for many school districts nationally.

3. **THE LEAGUE'S PROCESS MODEL IS FLEXIBLE AND ADAPTABLE.** It does not propose a single rigid formula with a set of unalterable strategies to be followed, obediently, in lockstep fashion. The process encourages divergent rather than convergent thinking and behavior. It was quickly orchestrated into six idiosyncratic variations on a theme, and a decade later, a seventh

adaptation has emerged. Each program reflected local needs, conditions and opportunities. Program content and emphases, approaches to leadership, staff and curriculum development, schemes for management and coordination and the means for expanding the program were highly individual.

4. **THE POWER OF THE IDEA—ALL THE ARTS FOR ALL THE CHILDREN— SPEAKS TO A BROAD AUDIENCE.** The power of an idea that speaks to the improvement of the quality of education and equality of educational opportunity for every child regardless of race, national origin, religion, social background, gender, aptitude or special ability is one that has caught the attention of a broad audience. The slogan "all the arts for all the children" is compelling; no art and no child is left out. Even in the face of social stress, shrinking budgets, systemwide overhauls, declining enrollments and a reduced teacher force, the idea is appealing to decision-makers. It promises solutions to broad educational, economic, political and social questions. It also helps to build or restore faith in public education.

5. **THE EXECUTION OF THE IDEA DOES NOT DEPEND ON AN INFUSION OF MASSIVE SUMS OF SOFT, "OUTSIDE" MONEY TO MAKE IT WORK.** Many of the resources—people, places, things—required for basic program operation exist at the local, state and federal levels. Additional funding, or often the reallocation of existing money to match or leverage new dollars, is needed for artists' services, teacher training, curriculum development, planning and developmental activities, documentation, research, evaluation and dissemination. Most programs have been able to attract new resources. "Matching," "piggybacking," "parlaying" and "pooling" are key strategies for solving the funding problem.

6. **THE PROGRAMS FOCUS ON THE BROAD EDUCATIONAL NEEDS OF ALL CHILDREN AND BUILD THE ARTS INTO THE FABRIC OF SCHOOLING.** The proposition is what the arts can do for the schools and the general education of every youngster. Special programs and cultural-enrichment efforts for a few students are no longer regarded as cost-effective or politically wise. If the arts are woven into the very fabric of schooling, there is hope that when the budget axes fall, these programs won't be cut because there will be no way of extricating the arts from the basic curriculum and regular school practice.

7. **SCHOOL-BASED PLANNING TEAMS MANAGE AGE PROGRAMS, WHICH GENERATES OWNERSHIP AND ACCOUNTABILITY AT THE GRASSROOTS LEVEL.** School change and development through the arts is a notion that is gaining acceptance by an increasing number of educational leaders. These people agree that the key to progressive and lasting change in schooling will happen only when the individual school takes charge and shapes its own destiny.

The programs developed by the League proceed from a deceptively simple notion: those held accountable for results must actively participate in the decision-making process. They must be given the opportunity to exert control over the conditions that produce the results by which they are judged. In other words, the motivation for those in schools to invest their professional time and emotional energy is the belief that they have a stake in the action. A sense of real power comes from deciding what will be taught and learned and how money should be spent.

8. **AGE PROGRAMS DEMONSTRATE THE INTRINSIC VALUE OF THE ARTS AND THEIR USEFULNESS FOR ACHIEVING BROADER EDUCATIONAL GOALS.** The League and similar programs have been able to illustrate ways in which the arts, artists and the arts process are valuable for children. They show how the arts are in themselves rewarding and how they can be personally, socially and politically useful. They also indicate how the arts can help schools meet the broader aims of education.

9. **LEAGUE OF CITIES MEMBERS BECAME IMPORTANT ADVOCATES FOR AGE AND INFLUENCED NATIONAL OPINION AND THE DEVELOPMENT OF OTHER ARTS IN EDUCATION EFFORTS.** The League of Cities provided moral support and leadership training for its members, a forum for debate and a tangible field for inspection. It also provided resource materials, manuals and direct technical and consulting assistance to the Department of Education and its predecessor, the Office of Education, the two national endowments, private foundations, professional arts and education associations, state education departments, school districts and arts agencies and organizations.

10. **LEAGUE OF CITIES PROGRAMS FORGED STRONG LINKAGES WITH THE COMMUNITY AND HELPED CREATE A MORE FAVORABLE CLIMATE OF OPINION FOR PUBLIC EDUCATION AND THE ARTS.** Its programs have strengthened the scant testimony on what is right with education and particularly what is good and successful in urban public schooling when the arts are a presence in the curriculum. League of Cities programs have also helped develop positive attitudes toward the arts and the beneficial effect they can have on school life.

THE NETWORK COLLAPSES
BUT THE MELODY LINGERS ON

In 1979, a year after John D. Rockefeller 3rd's death, the trustees of the JDR 3rd Fund closed down the Arts in Education Program, leaving the League in a "holding pattern." We were, as my colleague Arnold Webb so aptly put it, "much like six cities in search of a coordinating hub—with apologies to Pirandello." We kept in touch by phone and by mail. We knew we needed to find another institutional base whose mission complemented our own or to form an independent organization whose purpose would be to:

— Continue to support and expand the League of Cities and help form or participate in other arts and education networks at the local, state and national levels

— Provide technical and consulting assistance to the growing number of people who seek advice in the planning, development and execution of their own programs

— Welcome others to League of Cities schools and districts to study and learn from on-going programs

— Participate in research, evaluation and dissemination efforts about the arts in general education

The group was determined to stay together and was ready to seek alternative sources of support. Members came to New York at their own expense, and we spent two intensive days planning our strategies and meeting with prospective sponsors. We drew up a formal prospectus and a budget and submitted them for review. The (now-defunct) organizations that had expressed interest turned us down for lack of funding resources or board support. We considered incorporation as a nonprofit organization, and I made the rounds of several foundation offices looking for start-up operating money. Many of my colleagues welcomed me with warmth and ushered me out with mumbled regrets. No one wanted to inherit a project—especially a mature one—with the name of Rockefeller stamped all over it.

The League of Cities for the Arts in Education no longer exists. As time passed, people in key positions in the school districts and the community began to move on, retire or die. Losing colleagues, we lost continuity and momentum, and without an administrative hub, we lost the ability to galvanize and maintain interest and commitment. Ironically, while I was unable to attract long-term support for League activities, I was successful in attracting a major publisher and securing sizeable foundation and corporate grants for a book documenting its efforts.

Gradually, one by one, the programs in each of the six sites began to fold, in almost the reverse order of their creation. Even the phoenix-like AGE program in New York City that has been going strong for many years is threatened with extinction unless, once again, a group of committed network principals can persuade a new chancellor who subscribes to the theory of school-based management that AGE translates that theory into action. The rest of the original League sites still boast individual schools keeping the AGE faith. They maintain arts programs and services, and some districts even have vestiges of their original AGE efforts. But as far as I can determine, their district-based, comprehensive, school-development-through-the-arts programs have disappeared.

The fact that the League is gone and that most of its local arts-in-education programs are splintered is a sad but not uncommon commentary on the fate of educational innovations, especially those that had their philosophical and financial roots in the optimistic, progressive and abundant days of the sixties' "Great Society." Actually, it is surprising that the network and the individual city programs survived as long as they did considering the demise of the Fund and the federal, state and local retrenchment from "innovative and exemplary education programs" generally and the arts in education in particular.

In effect, the League suffered almost the same fate as most of the earlier federally-sponsored and JDR 3rd Fund demonstration programs. I say "almost" because it gives me pleasure to be able to recount a Louisiana story that shows how a powerful idea can travel, take root and grow in fresh soil when there is a receptive climate, strong leadership and a field-tested blueprint available for study, encouragement and validation.

NEW ORLEANS' PROJECT ARTS CONNECTION: THE LATEST VARIATION ON THE AGE THEME

The New Orleans School District has been active in the arts in education since the 1960s. It was one of the three sites for the Educational Laboratory Theater Project, a research and development effort by the Arts and Humanities Program of the U.S. Office of Education, directed at the time by Kathryn Bloom. Since then, District Supervisor Shirley Trusty Corey has created and managed an Arts in Education Program that offers extended artist-in-schools services, in-school workshops and performances, staff and curriculum development opportunities and a variety of school-community cultural partnerships. She oversees a Cultural Resources Performing Arts Series that offers 500 programs to elementary and secondary school students. And she helped found the nationally-recognized specialized high school, the New Orleans Center for the Creative Arts.

Shirley is a theater artist, a dedicated educator and a consummate politician. Over the years, she has successfully weathered numerous program-threatening storms. She has served on many national arts in education panels and is now a member of the Louisiana Arts Council and chair of the superintendent's task force for a statewide comprehensive plan for the arts in education. People turn to Shirley to get things done.

We first met in New Orleans during an American Educational Research Association Conference in the early seventies. The JDR 3rd Fund had organized a pre-conference seminar on the relatively pristine subject of evaluation in the arts in education, and the entire JDR 3rd Fund staff was in town for the occasion. I was still working with Edythe Gaines and the New York City Board of Education at the time, but I was able to accept Kathy Bloom's invitation to join the proceedings as her guest.

As it turned out, Shirley's program was under another budgetary siege, and she asked Kathy to make a personal pitch to key district administrators, including the superintendent. It was the first time I saw Shirley in action, and it was unforgettable. Since then, we have been together at national conferences and worked as teammates on Young Audiences' chapter certification site visits. On one of those visits, Shirley casually mentioned Arts Connection, a new project she was developing using the first edition of my book as a guide. Somehow, the significance of that piece of information did not register at that time.

In February 1988, Shirley engaged me as a consultant for Project Arts Connection. She asked me to help draw up an agenda and facilitate work sessions at a two-day principal's retreat held in a lovely home in the Bayou just outside New Orleans. In preparation for the event with Shirley and Project Coordinator Kimberlye Hunicke, I asked for background information and materials. Imagine my surprise and quick delight when I read the opening paragraph of the minutes dated November 19, 1982:

"The first meeting for Project Arts Connection was held in Room 215, 4100 Touro Street. The purpose of this meeting was to give an overview of the National Arts Model upon which this network was established, the J.D. Rockefeller III Comprehensive Arts in Education Program [sic], and to establish guidelines for the program."

Reading through the materials, I discovered that Project Arts Connection bore, at least on paper, all the earmarks of an AGE program. Their invitation to participate to all elementary schools described the rationale, the objectives, the school change theory, the structural concept of networking and collaboration and the school selection process using language taken almost verbatim from the first edition of this book. Joint funding sources listed were the Louisiana State Arts Council and the National Endowment for the Arts' Artists in Education Program.

I have selected materials and working papers from Project Arts Connection for inclusion in this book because they provide a dramatic illustration of how a model process is adapted for local use (see Exhibits 17-23). In New Orleans, they picked, chose and spliced together large chunks of copy from my original book and then, in the spirit of the League of Cities, added quite a few nice twists and emphases of their own. It is equally if not more important to share the techniques they used to install the program at the individual school level—techniques designed to cultivate broad-based ownership by teachers and building administrators alike. If the nuggets of gold contained in the New Orleans approach inspire others to take heart and encourage them to follow Project Arts Connection's lead, then the influence of the League of Cities may spread even further.

Project Arts Connection has expanded on the League's concept of school-based planning and teacher ownership of the program. It has also concentrated on staff and curriculum development, self-evaluation and accountability and documentation. It has given new meaning to the notion of principal commitment in its imaginative—and expensive—criteria for individual school membership. It has also provided some interesting guidelines for the effective use of professional artists in residence as teacher trainers and teaching partners.

In New Orleans, members of the Arts in Education office and project staff hire, train and supervise some twenty local men and women. The artists teach their art forms to the children and, in a well-planned partnership with the classroom teachers, provide support for staff and curriculum development. In this respect, the program resembles the model developed about ten years earlier by Winston-Salem.

Project Arts Connection began in 1982 in a network of eight elementary schools with three artists who spent three weeks with thirty-two teachers. The network has grown to twenty-eight schools; twenty-one local artists spend two to three days a week in each school for the full school year working with four teachers each semester.

In addition to Shirley Trusty Corey, the network's hub consists of dynamic Project Director (and former dance arts specialist) Kim Hunicke. Kim is assisted by two seasoned members of the Arts in Education office staff, art specialist Judy Burks and drama specialist Linda Cook, both of whom are qualified to select and train local artists and work with teachers in staff and curriculum development. Rounding out the team is Barbara Warnie, who coordinates the Cultural Resources Performing Arts Series and acts as the program's community relations liaison.

For the first four years, funding came from public and private sources outside the district. Beginning in the fifth year, the program became a line item in the district's budget. Today, the funding base is local tax levy money supplemented by federal Chapter I funds. The district covers the costs for a resident artist in each of twenty-two schools; schools new to the network are required to pay either half a staff position or $9,000 in cash for a year-round resident artist. Any school wishing more than one artist (and there are several) must pay for services out of their own budgets. Additional program support comes from arts agency, business and private sources.

Shirley has described Project Arts Connection as a strong, school-based staff development model, not as "just another artists-in-schools program." This year, in addition to their on-site training, the 130 network teachers spend two days of release time together working in depth in the art forms of dance, theater and the visual arts. Shirley maintains that to be able to integrate the arts with other subjects "teachers need immersion in the content of the art form in order to develop the skills and understandings that are a prerequisite for making connections in the classroom." Plans are now under way for summer institutes, during which the teachers will be paid to continue their professional development in the arts.

Shirley says that she is indebted to the League approach because it provided her with the philosophy, concept and structure to build on and the encouragement and affirmation to continue despite the inevitable logjams and bureaucratic resistance. She sees a staff development model building gradually, comprehensively and systemically.

Project Arts Connection is a promising version of the comprehensive school-development-through-the-arts model because of its emphasis on artist and teacher partnerships for staff and curriculum development. In addition, there is a leadership development component and an active principal's network of diverse, energetic and articulate men and women. This group meets formally four times a year and at annual retreats to share information and solutions to their common instructional, management and operational problems. At their latest retreat the principals immersed themselves in a variety of arts exercises, during which they made their own art objects, analyzed the process and critiqued their own products. The experience gave them, as instructional leaders, a better understanding of the content of the arts.

I urge those of you who are interested to spend some time in that glorious town of New Orleans. Visit the schools and speak with those who are making this singular Governor's Award program work.

VIEWPOINT

"I never knew I could dance. It makes me feel good. I like to know I can reach for the stars."

(Student)

E X H I B I T   1 8 _____

NEW ORLEANS PROJECT ARTS CONNECTION

THE BASIC COMPONENTS OF A SCHOOL-BASED ARTS PLAN

— Arts education instruction in the specific arts disciplines by qualified arts specialists
— Arts in basic education—infusion of the arts into the total curriculum
— Utilization of cultural resources—all appropriate arts learning resources in both the school and community

WHO IS INVOLVED IN AN ARTS IN EDUCATION PROGRAM AND THEIR DUTIES

TEACHERS AND ADMINISTRATORS:

— plan a comprehensive arts program that is unique to the school
— work with the arts, artists and students
— support and attend staff development experiences in the arts

[SCHOOL-BASED] ARTS PLANNING TEAM CHAIR:

— provides leadership and assists teachers and administrators in planning a comprehensive arts program

STUDENTS:

— a variety of students with a variety of needs and skills work with teachers and artists

RESOURCES:

— individual and group artists including arts specialists (music teachers, talented in the arts, and art teachers)
— large arts organizations (such as the Philharmonic, Ballet, Art Museums) print and non-print materials

DEVELOPMENTAL COMPONENTS OF
A COMPREHENSIVE ARTS IN EDUCATION PROGRAM

The sequence of development for an arts in education program seem to be the following:

— AWARENESS
— ASSESSMENT
— PLANNING
— IMPLEMENTATION
— EVALUATION

The following questions may help you begin "futures" planning (long term) as well as focus on areas of development for effective arts in education programming.

AWARENESS:

— Has your entire teaching staff been introduced to the Arts in Education, Arts Connection Project concept?
— Do they have access to information and materials published by the Arts in Education staff?
— Do they understand the program expectations and their role in these expectations?

ASSESSMENT:

— Is there a strong nucleus of administrator/teacher commitment to the development of the Arts in Education, Arts Connection Project?
— Is there evidence of student needs for arts experience?
— Is your community receptive to the idea of Arts in Education?
— Are there community arts resources available to your school?

PLANNING:

— Are you developing a long-range plan for an Arts in Education Program in your school?
— Are all members involved in the planning?
— Does the plan make use of community art resouces?
— Does the plan provide appropriate experiences for all students?
— Is there cooperative planning between the arts specialists, classroom teachers and artists?

IMPLEMENTATION:

— Does your Arts in Education program reach all students in the school with a variety of arts experiences?
— Are interested and gifted students developing arts skills?
— Are students with special needs involved in arts experiences?
— Is your plan providing for the continual expansion of the program into other arts and basic skills areas?
— Does your program utilize available community arts resources?
— Does your plan provide for continual in-service for teachers?

EVALUATION:

— Are you collecting data that can be used to show the impact of the Arts in Education Program?
— Is the data related to the purpose of the program as stated in your plan?
— Is the data used to show if student change has occurred?

E X H I B I T   1 9 ———————————

EXPECTATIONS FOR ARTS IN EDUCATION SITES

1. Commitment to the basic philosophy of the Arts in Education, Arts Connection Project as outlined in Arts Connection guidelines

2. Commitment from principals and district-level administrators who recognize the value that the arts have for the education of all students

3. Principals who share with other administrators on a regular basis as part of the networking activities

4. Staff commitment to interdisciplinary teaching and learning situations where the arts are related to each other and to other areas of the curriculum.

5. Quality programs in all the arts available to students

6. Effective use of the community's artists and its arts and cultural resources used regularly in and out of the school building

7. Special programs in the arts for children with special needs, e.g., the disadvantaged, the multilingual

8. Use of the arts, artists and arts organizations, services to create learning situations that help to reduce personal and cultural isolation and increase self-esteem

9. Arts planning team who meets regularly and establishes an effective communication system with the total staff

10. Active participation by administrators and teachers in sponsoring and attending AIE staff development activities

11. Willingness to demonstrate program in various ways: presentations, speeches, workshops, on-site visits, planning meetings; provide technical assistance to other schools in the district who are planning for Arts in Education programming

12. Willingness of school staff to engage in documentation/evaluation activities that "tell the story" of the AIE program in the school

E X H I B I T   2 0

RESPONSIBILITIES OF THE ARTS PLANNING TEAM

DUTIES OF THE PLANNING TEAM:

1. Meet regularly to develop and implement the school's Arts Connection Project for the year. This generally includes:
   - determining the major focus for the year
   - selecting arts resources to be used in carrying out the focus
   - planning both to sponsor and attend staff development opportunities throughout the year
   - planning specific advocacy efforts to expand the program
   - assisting in determining the budget for the year
2. Develop a system for total staff input
3. Develop a system to keep the total staff informed of team decisions

DUTIES OF THE TEAM CHAIR:

1. Become knowledgeable in all areas of the arts
2. Understand learning patterns and the physical capabilities of various age levels
3. Assist in identifying, securing and managing a variety of appropriate arts resources
4. Become acquainted with existing education programs in the school site and make appropriate linkages for the arts programs
5. Arrange for and encourage participation in appropriate in-service programs on a regular basis
6. Serve as the site coordinator for the Project Arts Connection for the New Orleans Public Schools
7. Participate in called meetings throughout the year and report back to the principals and arts planning team
8. Participate on the district arts planning team
9. Provide leadership in long-range planning of arts programs

E X H I B I T   2 1

CRITERIA FOR PARTICIPATION : 1989-1990

1. A commitment of principal and faculty to the philosophy of developing a comprehensive arts in education program for your school is essential. This commitment should be reflected in your school accountability plan.

2. A comprehensive arts in education plan includes programming experiences in art, drama, dance, music, creative writing and other allied art forms. A comprehensive arts-in-education plan addresses:

    ARTS EDUCATION: An in-depth study of each art form. It ensures the integrity of strong programs in the individual arts and encompasses the role of arts specialists and professionals trained in the arts.

    ARTS IN BASIC EDUCATION: The integration of the arts to enhance and expand concepts in all curriculum areas.

    UTILIZATION OF CULTURAL RESOURCES: The use of artists, arts institutions and community resources for educational effectiveness.

3. All Project Arts Connection sites are required to pay an annual participation fee of $600. This fee covers expenses of staff development, special projects and networking activities. (An additional $150 is collected for arts materials and supplies.)

E X H I B I T   2 2 _____

| CHECKLIST FOR PARTICIPATING SCHOOLS |

ASSESSMENT INVENTORY: Schools wishing to participate in the project should meet the following criteria:

1. Ongoing networking of existing arts programs as evidenced by visual art exhibits and/or programs that share processes and end results in the performance arts

2. Staff commitment to interdisciplinary teaching and learning situations in which the arts are related to each other and to other areas of the curriculum as evidenced by the scheduling of school in-service time for teachers and appropriate planning/evaluation time

3. Evidence of interdisciplinary teaching reflected in teacher lesson plans as influenced by arts specialists

4. Arts planning team that regularly shares arts programming opportunities, in-house resources and activities

5. Identification and use of community resources to extend current programming

6. Active participation by principal and staff in arts-in-education activities, including staff development as scheduled through the Arts in Education office

7. Willingness to demonstrate the program within the school district and community

8. Evidence of arts programming as reflected in school accountability plan, job descriptions and documentation/evaluation that state recommendations for refinement and expansion

SCHOOLS MUST REVIEW AND RENEW THEIR PARTICIPATION IN PROJECT ARTS CONNECTION ANNUALLY BY SIGNING A PROJECT ARTS CONNECTION CONTRACT. Contracts must be submitted to the Arts in Education office no later than [date] at the end of each calendar year. Contracts will be reviewed by the Arts in Education office. Individual schools will be scheduled for review and renewal appointments on [dates]. These sessions will replace the Principal Meeting scheduled for [date].

CONTRACT REVIEW AND RENEWAL WILL BE BASED ON:

1. School accountability plan

2. Payment of annual participation fee

3. Documentation of participation activities of the previous school year

4. Plans requesting arts discipline for the upcoming year

5. Attendance at the review and renewal session

ALL CONTRACTS SHALL BE SIGNED BY THE ARTS IN EDUCATION OFFICE, THE PRINCIPAL AND MEMBERS OF THE ARTS PLANNING TEAM.

E X H I B I T   2 3 ─────────────────────

CHECKLIST FOR NEW SCHOOLS ENTERING PROJECT ARTS CONNECTION

New schools entering Project Arts Connection shall agree to adhere to the above guidelines and comply with those listed below:

1. A letter of intent/proposal from school principal must be submitted by the interested school to the Arts in Education office by the close of the academic school year.

2. A .5 staffing point released to the Arts in Education office from your school staffing formula or Chapter I is necessary to provide for an artist/teacher. It is recommended that this be addressed during your spring staffing session.

— Funds of $9,000 allocated by business partner(s) may be used in lieu of the .5 staffing position.

— Funds of $9000 allocated by Chapter I may also be available in lieu of the .5 staffing position.

[Author's note: All new Project schools make a financial commitment of the .5 or equivalent staffing point, the $600 participation fee and the $150 budget for supplies. The latter funds are generally raised from the PTA or other school "discretionary" coffers.]

E X H I B I T   2 4

TECHNICAL ASSISTANCE PROGRAM FOR NEW EXPLORATORY SITES

Schools interested in exploring Project Arts Connection for potential participation are defined as "Exploratory Sites." Exploratory Sites are schools that have expressed interest in the Project but as a result of lack of funding, staffing or faculty commitment are unable to join. It is hoped that as a result of this technical assistance program, schools will both comprehend the underlying philosophy and be in a stronger position to identify and implement needed resources and staffing.

Each site must propose such requests in writing to the Arts in Education office and agree to the following criteria:

1. School Principal(s) will attend two of the four regularly scheduled [network] Principal meetings.

2. Identified staff will participate in a minimum of three site visitations to schools with existing programs in dance, drama and visual art respectively.

3. Schools will identify a core of teachers to participate in and report back to faculty and administrators, information received from two of the four regularly scheduled Teacher Curriculum Council meetings, one of the two all-day staff development workshops for classroom teachers and the annual end of the year celebration.

4. Schools will be provided the services of a Resource Artists Team [from the district's Arts in Education office staff] for one-half day for the purposes of staff development.

5. Schools will agree to pay a participation fee of $100 to assist in covering the costs of staff development and networking.

SOME LESSONS I HAVE LEARNED

AGE: A Model for School Development Through the Arts

The League of Cities produced a model for school improvement with the arts as both content and context. The model featured school-based planning, networking and collaboration as the chief strategies for implementation. This model has stood the test of time and transportability. In 1982 the New Orleans Public Schools used the first edition of this book to plan and install their Project Arts Connection, which is a direct descendant of AGE. They have managed the process without benefit of an active League or the technical assistance of the JDR 3rd Fund. It is interesting to ponder the differences, if any, that participation in the League would have made to the pace and shape of the program's development.

AGE provides the field with an ambitious and comprehensive model that describes an ideal whose fulfillment is probably an impossible dream. However, the philosophy, the rationale, the guidelines and criteria and many of the practices have been absorbed into programs, legislation and policy guidelines around the country. As Junius Eddy, an author and consultant and one of the elder statespeople in the field, commented about the contribution of the approach:

> "The concept of 'comprehensive planning' for arts education at all levels . . . has even worked its way into some state and national legislation and into the programs fostered by state and national organizations [such as the Kennedy Center's Alliance for Arts Education, the Arts in Education Guidelines for the New York State Council on the Arts, the National Endowment for the Arts' Arts in Education Program]."

I look forward to a time when educational reformers will include the arts on their agenda and recognize that they can serve as a powerful force for schoolwide change. I call their attention to a field-tested model—the AGE approach—that is available for study, research and further refinement.

Networking and Collaboration

Networking and collaboration have proved excellent strategies for AGE projects. My experience with AGE over the years has also confirmed other research findings: Networks and coalitions cannot survive without an administrative and coordinating hub—especially when their members champion causes that buck the status quo. Networks are particularly important delivery systems for members representing diverse schools or systems that cross geographic or jurisdictional boundary lines. The history of the

League of Cities (and the individual program networks within the League) and the Coalition of States are only two examples of this maxim that now verges on the cliché.

The Foundation as Technical Resource and Change Agent

In school improvement parlance, change agents are generally outsiders who are invited to provide a specific brand of technical assistance and intervene, not interfere, in the business of schooling. They may goad, prod, nurture, inspire and otherwise cajole school people to alter their behaviors, if not their most private thoughts and attitudes. John Goodlad likened the JDR 3rd Fund's role with the League of Cities and the Coalition of States as the "alternate drummer." We sounded a different call that beguiled the members—our partners—to march to a different beat. We had the cachet of the Rockefeller name, modest but sufficient resources, an honorable track record and an attractive mission to compel public attention and respect.

Unfortunately, the high rate of administrative, principal and teacher turnover forced us to do several cavalry-type rescue operations, lots of beating of the arts in education rhetorical drums and repetition of the rationale for the arts in the education of children to platoons of new faces. We also found that no matter how long we had been formal partners with a school system, at each changing of the guard, the demands on our time, patience and ability to improvise increased. So, while under certain very strict conditions (by invitation and as a resource) operating foundations can act as effective change agents, this should serve as fair warning that "success" is quixotic and ephemeral and some of the work is sheer drudgery.

The Arts, Not the Artist Alone, Can Change Schools

Artists, arts organization and arts agency personnel run serious risks when they perceive themselves as educational reformers. School personnel often become indignant when confronted with an artist's or an arts administrator's crusading zeal. They regard the outsiders warily, and if pushed too far, they will remind arts folk that they are not licensed teachers and that it is they, the school people, who are publicly accountable for their children's education.

Artists and arts administrators *can* serve as catalysts for *part* of the change process as long as they make a conscious and careful effort to understand the culture of the schools and the politics and dynamics of schooling. Their chief role is to act as resources to enhance curriculum, instruction and the school program.

When arts people behave as if they are senior partners in a joint venture and start telling the schools what to do and how to do it, they overstep the bounds of their authority and expertise and jeopardize their hard-earned credibility. If artists want to help the schools change and restructure themselves, their best bet is to hitch their energies and singular talents to the wagons of those principals and teachers in the vanguard of the change process. They will discover that they are most effective when they intervene by invitation, not interfere by divine inspiration.

Documentation and Dissemination

Innovative and exemplary arts-in-education programs and practices, or even those that show the faintest promise of having a usefulness beyond their immediate life or locale, must be documented and the results distributed to a wide audience. We also need to chronicle and share the failures and the disasters. Santayana's dictum still holds: those who do not know history are destined to repeat its mistakes. The field needs easily accessible resource banks, central clearinghouses of information that contain the catalogued and annotated materials that have been generated in abundance.

Think about it: The JDR 3rd Fund churned out quantities of information about its projects and networks and shipped it out in carloads. That is one reason for the formation of the League of Cities. I wrote a book ten years ago about the League's model for school change through the arts. That is one reason for Project Arts Connection. Our labors should not be kept secret; there are too many valuable lessons to be learned, warts and all.

The Arts in Education Field Has a Short, Spotty and Selective Memory

I was at a statewide conference recently and found a paper titled "Some Major Milestones in Arts Education" among the materials in the information packet. I was astonished to learn, according to the anonymous authors, that it all began in 1967 with Harvard University's Project Zero! The abstract mentioned the director, Dennis P. Wolf, but not Howard Gardner, one of the field's leading theoreticians, researchers and authors. Then, *nothing* of consequence happened for a decade, until the publication in 1977 of *Coming to Our Senses*, the findings of the Arts, Education and Americans Panel chaired by David Rockefeller, Jr. Things apparently began to pick up again in the seven years between 1982 and 1989 when the report ends.

Now, the roots of the arts in education field date back to the late 1950s, followed by a groundswell of innovative activity in the sixties and seventies. The conference paper mentions only *two* of them prior to the eighties—taking up no more than three inches of a nine-page paper! No wonder everyone keeps reinventing the wheel.

Of all the lessons I have learned over the years, perhaps the hardest is that the younger generation of arts in education professionals are unaware of their own rich, if checkered, history. I am even more troubled that no one seems to bother to do the research in the libraries we *do* have. Clearly, we can no longer rely on our increasingly fading memories and oral tradition to convey our legacy.

Determined to do something about the situation, I began to assemble material for a brief chronology of the field since its beginnings. I rooted through my library and found information scattered everywhere, in conference, project and research reports, *Coming to Our Senses*, my own magazine articles. I found nothing resembling a chart of the forty-year time span. To make sure I wasn't missing something, I checked with some of my historian colleagues.

I have decided to try to provide at least a temporary remedy and have prepared an annotated chronology that represents my perspective on important legislation, programs, events and publications in the developing history of the field. The listing may seem skewed or arbitrary to some, but it includes all those items that, as far as some of my colleagues and I can remember, have had a direct and indirect influence on the formative years of the arts in education. I refer you to the Appendix for the results for which I take full responsibility.

A CALL FOR ACTION:
A NATIONAL TASK FORCE ON
THE ARTS IN GENERAL EDUCATION

While there is a new patina of collegiality and a good deal of talk about common ground and the need for collaborative action, our relatively small but vociferous field is still fragmented by a persistent lack of trust and in some cases downright personal bickering and hostility. Unrelenting economic insecurity and financial threats of reduction of support or broadscale extinction do not create a climate conducive for burying hatchets.

Despite the formation of national ad hoc committees and working groups that have produced well-crafted resolutions and yet another concept paper for strengthening arts education in schools, and notwithstanding a spate of national, state and city summit meetings, symposia and task forces with their obligatory lists of recommendations, no meaningful or lasting consensus has been built that translates fluently across professional interests, commutes between the disciplines and passes freely between organizational boundaries. Worse, few of these words are transformed into practices that cascade or even trickle down into the field or over the threshold of the classroom door.

The field keeps advocating and preaching, almost smugly at times, to itself—the presumably converted. But no single agency or organization appears willing to position itself strategically and take the awesome responsibility for national, broad-based, non-sectarian programmatic action. No one seems to want to formulate a bold, comprehensive, long-range plan with a multi-year agenda. No one seems ready to try to corral the necessary funds to undertake the job for which some of us have clamored for what seems like eons. We do not need more words; we need strategic plans for deeds.

The AGE approach deserves renewed attention for its promise as an organizing principle. At the very least, it can serve as one of a number of points of departure for discussion by those willing to sit down together to design a comprehensive plan of action.

Throughout this book, I have identified some urgent needs. Among them are:

— Leadership training and professional development programs (academies, institutes, etc.) for current arts and education administrators, supervisors, teachers, artists and others who work in or with AGE programs
— AGE networks for teachers at the national, state and local levels
— Staff and curriculum development programs at the national, regional, state and local levels
— Orientation and training programs for artists
— Centralized resource centers and a network of technical assistance and information clearinghouses
— A comprehensive research and evaluation effort
— A similar documentation, dissemination and advocacy effort
— Money to plan, coordinate and operate all the above

Over the years, many people have laid the groundwork for these efforts. The talent bank of experienced practitioners and other authorities exists. The "raw material" for staff and curriculum development abounds. Programs are available for research, on-site study and documentation. The hunger for comprehensive and practical information is keen. Since the needs are as idiosyncratic as they are comprehensive, the grand design for meeting them must be equally flexible and encompassing.

I will end this edition with a new call to joint action by the secretary of the United States Department of Education and the chairs of the two national endowments. I ask them to lead a national task force on the arts in general education. I ask them to assemble and empower a nationally-representative group of education and arts professionals. These seasoned veterans and current practitioners should be charged to take national inventory and stock; examine the field for pressing needs and ripe opportunities, and travel the country to observe promising programs and practices. Give the task force the authority, the time, the support staff and a budget to do the research. Ask them to propose a comprehensive, collaborative long-range plan of action that suggests a series of effective and related strategies that can be implemented and evaluated at the national, regional, state, local and individual school building levels.

We have a good ten years of work ahead of us if we are to make a difference in education in the 21st century. It is not too soon to begin. We owe it to ourselves and to our schools. Our children deserve nothing less.

Jane Remer
August, 1990

A

Interpretive Chronology of Major Events in The Arts in Education

Focusing on the Period 1950 - 1990

"Don't trust anyone over thirty."

> Jerry Rubin, *yippie, in*
> *a popular slogan of the sixties*

"Those who cannot remember the
past are condemned to repeat it."

> George Santayana,
> *The Life of Reason*, 1905

BY WAY OF EXPLANATION

This chronology is a selective, personalized and interpretive account of
seminal events, landmarks and milestones in the field of the arts in education over the last forty years or more. It is not a scholarly work, nor does it
pretend to be objective or definitive. It is a framework for future efforts that
will perhaps fill in gaps, correct factual errors and smooth the feathers that
this version may ruffle. To my knowledge, it is the first comprehensive attempt of its kind.

My focus has been on those arts or education events—national, state
or local, public or private—that in my estimation helped make a positive dif-

ference to a significant number of schools, school people, school practices and school children. I have also thrown the spotlight on those people whose pioneering spirit and vision have plowed the fields in which so many of us continue to sow our own ideas and occasionally reap a bountiful harvest.

I had several reasons for undertaking what turned out to be a daunting task. First, nothing like it exists in one place in the field today. Second, not only scholars and graduate students, but the young people in leadership roles today (and tomorrow) stand to benefit from a sense of history and continuity so they can put their own work in proper perspective. Third, these young professionals and many of their elders in the field also deserve to discover that there *is* a substantial past from which they can learn some valuable lessons.

And finally, the general public needs to recognize that the idea of the arts in education has a pedigree and a solid track record of diligent field work behind it, all of which is marked by earnest intentions if not always spectacular results. In short, I want people to know that this field was not born yesterday, that patterns, trends, connecting threads emerge from the apparent crazy quilt if you stop a moment, step back and take the long view. It is refreshing, for example, to rediscover that the ideas of collaboration, partnerships and comprehensive planning have been around our field for quite a long time.

The need for a chronology has been on my mind for some time. The spark of inspiration was struck last fall when I was attending a state arts in education conference with national representation. A chronology of major events in the field was included in the information packet. The first entry was dated 1967 (Project Zero), the second entry skipped to 1977 for the publication of *Coming to Our Senses*, and the remaining eight-and-a-half pages contained somewhat randomly selected national, state and local events from 1982 to 1989.

"Goodness," I thought, "they have effectively wiped out about twenty years of the field's history and overlooked all the policies, all the legislation and all the people who were instrumental in its conception, birth and development! Something must be done!"

I searched through all my resource material hoping to find an off-the-rack piece to include in the appendix of this book. I discovered bits and pieces of information scattered about but no full accounting anywhere.

METHODOLOGY, GUIDELINES AND CRITERIA

I began by developing a grid of broad categories of events I thought worthy of inclusion:

— federal and state legislation, programs, projects and policies
— national conferences, summits, symposia, colloquia, seminars
— books, journals, publications, reports
— blue ribbon and other panels, task forces
— evaluation and research studies

Next, I jotted down a random list of major occurrences from memory and studied them to see if there were any emerging patterns on which I could base more formal guidelines and criteria. I ended up with the following context. Items were included or excluded on the basis of whether they:

— made a significant difference to the grassroots, non-sectarian people in the field, i.e., changed the way things work for the better for a substantial number of practitioners in *both* the arts and education [Note: I defined practitioners as state, district and school building supervisors and administrators, policy and decision-makers; generalist and specialist teachers; arts administrators and artists; researchers and evaluators.]

— made a significant impact on the teaching and learning process in the school program, generally, and in classroom practice, in particular

— had an immediate or long-range effect on arts in education theory that affected practice and, conversely, on practice from which emerged theory or patterns of recurring ideas;

— changed attitudes about the importance of the arts and their value to schooling

— helped create a climate more conducive to educational change and acceptance of the arts in the process

I deliberately omitted the qualifiers "lasting" or "enduring" when speaking of change or impact. I decided, for example, that a project (such as IMPACT in the early seventies) that had "only" a two-year lifespan should be included because its relatively brief duration did not, by itself, diminish its importance or its influence. In fact, examples such as these underscore some of the real hazards for long-range growth and development in the field of education.

Lastly, I have tried to follow the policy of inclusion when considering what I regard as important. For example, I have left to history or those who like to indulge in either-or, oppositionist struggles to settle the so-called controversy over who should teach the arts, which arts to teach and which approach (discipline-based versus experiential/creative/interpretive) is superior or preferable. My views on these issues tend toward the ecumenical and are addressed at some length in the preceding chapters, especially Chapter One, Chapter Seven and the Conclusion.

There is one major exception to the policy of inclusion which deserves mention: I have not attempted to list the myriad number of foundations, corporations and other benefactors nationwide that have contributed significant sums to arts in education projects of all shapes, sizes and descriptions since the sixties. While the magnitude of support has fluctuated over the years, a number of these institutions and individuals continue to provide critical and loyal support to several important efforts across the country. It is also worthy of mention that Grantmakers in the Arts, a national consortium of private and corporate donors, has held several conferences on the topic of the arts in education during the eighties.

ORGANIZATION AND CONVENTIONS

In searching for a "research design" for this project, I began with a matrix that listed decades down the left of the page grid and major categories or types of events across the top (programs and projects, research and development, publications, legislation, and the like). The result was a jumble because I found most events difficult to categorize, arbitrarily, under a single heading and to fit into a neat and tidy time frame. Since I planned on adding extensive descriptive and interpretive comment for each entry, a summary chart might be visually satisfying, but my instructive intent would be derailed. The uninitiated would probably be confused or bewildered by the myriad acronyms and other shorthand references such a graphic would require, and that would defeat the whole purpose of the effort.

I settled on a very straightforward approach and divided the chronology is into six "discrete" time sections:

— Pre-1930
— 1930 - 1960
— 1960 - 1970
— 1970 - 1980
— 1980 - 1990

I organized the welter of information I collected under these headings. Unfortunately, events in the field do not always fall neatly into these slots, especially in cases such as the National Endowment for the Arts, the United States Office of Education/Department of Education and other agencies and organizations whose history spans several decades.

Rather than make separate, disconnected and lengthy entries for each major event or turning point during the history of these agencies and organizations, I wrote one long description and entered it in the year the agency or organization was established. I then re-entered and cross-referenced a brief mention of only a few of what I deemed to be major occurrences in later sections under their historically-appropriate time slots. I hope this choice serves to illustrate the agency's or organization's total impact on the field as a whole as well as give context to the timeliness and timing of individual actions or initiatives.

A word about dates, program name changes and credits. In certain instances, finding definitive information for some of the entries was worse than looking for the proverbial needle in a haystack; it was more like the film*Rashomon* revisited. Reliable and conscientious sources often contradicted other equally reputable sources, and I found it was difficult but necessary for me to make final decisions.

SOURCES, RESOURCES AND A PUBLIC VOTE OF THANKS

I realize I have in large measure appointed myself as both judge and jury for this exercise, so, just for the record, a brief review of my credentials: I have worked as a teacher, an artist, an administrator, a programmer, a researcher, an evaluator and a writer in the arts and in education since the fifties. This means that I have been around, but not necessarily part of, a lot of what was and is happening across the country for about forty years. I have worked for or side-by-side with many of the country's philosophers, leaders and elder statespeople in both fields. I have a very good reference library and a pretty vivid memory. And I have a current, sure-footed working knowledge of the arts, artists, schools, school people and children.

All of this is well and good, but I know better than to go this one alone, so I showed an early draft to several veterans and colleagues who took the time to comment and add facts and information from their own memory storehouses and files. A few of them sent me precious "last copies" of out-of-print reports and other material. I am indebted to them for their help and encouragement, and where appropriate, I have inserted and credited verbatim quotes.

The reviewers included Junius Eddy, Charles Fowler, Harlan Hoffa and John McLaughlin. In addition to their long experience at the national and local levels, each of these gentlemen is a specialist in theater, music, the visual arts and dance—respectively. The first three lived through and helped to shape many of the exciting and formative days of the sixties and seventies. The last has done extensive research and work in the field as an arts educator and administrator. They are all writers and chroniclers of events in the field. Both Lonna Jones and Ted Berger helped me track down some elusive details, and David Bosca, the American Council for the Arts' library manager, found some precious archival material I had despaired of locating.

When I considered drawing up a list of all my source material, I realized that the entries would, for the most part, duplicate many of those in my bibliography. Furthermore, when I began the research, I had no idea that it would turn into a major sleuthing project, and I did not bother to keep track of every source or reference. I have decided not to take the time to retrace my tracks. In any event, and unfortunately, many of the sources I relied on most heavily are either out of print, scarce, or otherwise inaccessible to the general public. I have credited only those sources where I used their language verbatim; others are listed as "events" in the chronology itself; the balance are in the bibliography.

However, in the interest of comprehensiveness, I think it would be useful to list those magazines and journals that have, over the years, been important sources of information:

— *Association for Supervision and Curriculum Development Journal*
— *Cultural Affairs* (now defunct ACA magazine), especially Summer 1970
— *Design for Arts in Education*
— *Elementary and Secondary Principals Association Magazine*
— *Journal for Aesthetic Education*
— *Journal of Arts Management and the Law*
— *Phi Delta Kappan*
— *Vantage Point* (ACA magazine)

* * * * * *

While this chronology is long, it is only a beginning. It places some markers on the landscape and delineates some of the frontier territory of the arts in education field. It might be an interesting project for someone to study the entries and trace the pattern, frequency and lineage of recurring ideas and themes. Having completed the first phase of this archeological dig, I am content to leave that painstaking enterprise to other scholars in the field. At an age considerably beyond thirty, and having taken Santayana at his word, I hope I have made my contribution toward stopping at least one or two wheels from being reinvented.

Jane Remer
August 1990

The Chronology

PRE-1930

EARLY HISTORY OF ARTS EDUCATION: The 19th century was a period of expansion for the United States and later a period of invention and the beginnings of an industrial society. There was little time for the practice and enjoyment of the arts, let alone education in them. During this time, however, America saw its first music teacher. Lowell Mason volunteered to teach music free at the Hawes School in Boston during the 1937-38 school year. The following year the School Committee approved the hiring of music teachers (and funded them) and thus began the tradition of music specialists in the schools. At the end of the 1800s the country saw an interest in visual arts education, albeit for pragmatic reasons. In 1885 Isaac Edwards Clarke presented his report, "Art and Industry, Instruction in Drawing Applied to Industrial and Fine Arts," to the 46th Congress. [Entry by John McLaughlin.]

In 1864, Massachusetts was the first state to legislate a requirement for drawing in the school curriculum. "Art education in the public schools of the United States spans little more than a century [1870-1980]. Yet during this brief period of time it has sought to serve a number of different, often unrelated purposes. Art education has endeavored to train artisans and draftsmen for industry, to produce a moral citizenry, and aimed to promote creativity and self-expression." [Entry by Evan J. Kern, "The Purposes of Art Education in the United States from 1870 to 1980," in *The History of Art Education: Proceedings from the Penn State Conference*, The Pennsylvania State University College of Arts and Architecture School of Visual Arts,

Brent Wilson, Harlan Hoffa, eds. (National Art Education Association, 1985.) This paperbound book is an invaluable resource.]

THE GROWTH OF ARTS SPECIALISTS: The need for associations of arts professionals was coupled with a growth in the number of arts specialists in schools across the country. This growth was especially evident during the post-World War II era when parents sought to provide a full education for their children that would allow them to enjoy more fully all the benefits America had to offer. During the 1940s the professional associations— Music Educators National Conference (MENC), the National Art Education Association (NAEA) and the Alliance for Health, Physical Education, Recreation and Dance (AHPRED), which includes the National Dance Association (NDA)—were all divisions of the National Education Association. In 1972, these groups, because of the growing nature of the NEA as a union, formally separated and became independent associations. A few years later they moved to Reston, Virginia and, because of joint activities and concerns on behalf of art education and alliance with the theater education group, became known informally as the DAMT group (dance, art, music and theater.) During the time of this association activity, there was a growth in music and art in the schools. According to *Music and Art in Schools*, a 1963 research monograph from the National Education Association, the five-year period from 1958-1963 showed school districts across the country remaining the same or increasing their time allotment for art and music instruction. At this time, however, classroom teachers were responsible for most of this instruction. During the rest of the 1960s the number of specialists grew dramatically. This phenomenon is difficult to explain. Perhaps it resulted from the large number of union contracts that gave classroom teachers coverage or preparation time, necessitating other instruction and instructors for students during those periods. At any rate, this philosophy of using music and art specialists to "relieve" the classroom teacher is still evident today in many states such as Tennessee, for example, where the state level is funding re-instating specialists to provide release time for generalists. [Entry by John McLaughlin.]

MUSEUM EDUCATION PROGRAMS: The primary role of museums has been to collect and exhibit works of art and make them accessible and available to the general public. Their purpose, often part of their charters of incorporation, includes the education of the general public, and their activities encompass a number of educational services (broadly defined) for children and adults, such as interpretive exhibits, docent services, lectures and materials. Collaborative programs with schools (such as the training of public high school teachers) began as early as 1880 (at New York City's

Metropolitan Museum of Art, founded in 1870). In the early part of the 20th century, museum instructors began to served as guides to young students. These activities were soon followed by studio art classes and family programming at the art institution.

SYMPHONY ORCHESTRA EDUCATION PROGRAMS: Established for essentially the same reasons as museums. Beginning in the forties, many of them offered musical performances tailored for young people, such as Walter Damrosh's Young People's Concerts (on radio) and Leonard Bernstein, Aaron Copland, (both televised), Lorin Hollander and Thomas Scherman's/ Dino Anagnost's Little Orchestra Society.

1930 - 1960

While some of the following entries cannot be classified as strictly arts in education by my definition, I felt they were worthy of note. They chronicle activities that contributed to a general climate and attitude toward the arts and education that may help to set the stage for and explain or unravel the tangled web of many of the events to come.

COMMUNITY-BASED ARTS COUNCILS, PROGRAMS AND SERVICES

PROJECTS AND SERVICES OF THE ROOSEVELT NEW DEAL ADMINISTRATION'S WPA: Dance, theater, music, visual arts events, performances, exhibits and classes for community members primarily in the depression era of the early to mid-thirties.

LOCAL ARTS COUNCILS: Began to emerge in the late fifties, with Winston-Salem, North Carolina among the first to establish such agencies. The local councils grew in number and strength and eventually split off from their "parent" organization (National Assembly of State Arts Agencies, which had earlier broken away from the Associated Councils of the Arts, a former name of today's American Council for the Arts) to form their own association in the late seventies. Many of these agencies have a long and distinguished career of working as collaborators, partners and sponsors of arts in education programs.

AMERICAN SYMPHONY ORCHESTRA LEAGUE: Pioneer in arts management and education program guidelines and criteria. [Refer to *The Or-*

ganization, Administration and Presentation of Symphony Orchestra Youth Concert Activities for Music Educational Purposes in Selected Cities, Thomas Hill and Helen Thompson, U.S.O.E., 1968.]

ASSOCIATION OF JUNIOR LEAGUES: The Association of Junior Leagues (AJL) consists of over 231 chapters in which more than a hundred thousand trained members voluntarily participate in community affairs that include the arts and the arts in education. The AJL began its involvement with the arts in the 1930s, when it spearheaded the children's theater movement. After World War II, the Leagues initiated the community arts council movement in cities such as Vancouver and Winston-Salem.

The first volunteer museum docent program was begun by a Junior League at Kansas City's Nelson Gallery in 1936. Since then, Junior Leagues have started arts centers, festivals and museum programs and have assisted in symphony orchestra workshops and demonstrations for young people. [Author's note: Kathryn Bloom served for a number of years as consultant on the arts to the national association just prior to her assuming her post as director of the Office of Education's Arts and Humanities Program.]

In the early seventies the Junior League of Oklahoma City was in the advance guard when it worked as a partner with the school system to build the arts into the curriculum across the board. The League was deeply involved in the initial stages of planning and carrying out comprehensive arts in education programs with the school districts in Little Rock, Arkansas; Memphis, Tennessee; Winston-Salem, North Carolina; Seattle, Washington; and Birmingham, Alabama. Junior League services include research and development, fundraising, coordination and administration, long-range planning, documentation and evaluation. Efforts are generally of three-year maximum duration. An important publication, *Arts in Education Partners: Schools and Their Communities*, Nancy Shuker, ed. (JDR 3rd Fund, 1977), is an excellent source for additional information.

IN-SCHOOL PROGRAMS AND SERVICES

1952 YOUNG AUDIENCES, INC.: Young Audiences (YA) is a national membership organization that began in Baltimore, Maryland. Its original purpose was to educate future audience members by bringing chamber music lecture-demonstration programs to elementary age children in school assembly halls. It was the first nonprofit arts in education organization in the U.S. to bring professional artists into the classroom with presentations that combine performance, demonstration and participatory activities.

Operating in thirty-seven chapters and serving nearly five million public school children, YA presents a broad spectrum of participatory experiences and supporting services in the performing arts to children and their teachers. Services include in-school performances, classroom workshops, short and long-term residencies, and teacher training. Chapter programs now include music, dance, jazz, opera and theater among the art forms they offer to children and their teachers.

YA continues to explore innovative ways of broadening its arts education services. There are now special residencies for the handicapped, newly-designed programs for high school students and symphony partnership projects.

1960 LINCOLN CENTER FOR THE PERFORMING ARTS: The Lincoln Center Student Program began with a pilot series of in-school assembly performances and a series of events at Lincoln Center produced by its member organizations. Originally directed at New York City high school students, the center's later efforts extended to the tri-state area and included the "Resource Professional" artist in schools program (1967 to mid-1970s) as well as study guides and supporting educational materials. [Historical note: The center's artist-in-school's program preceded that of the NEA by a few years.]

The Lincoln Center Institute for the Arts in Education consolidated the center's earlier activities and introduced a new dimension: staff and curriculum development. Each summer, school teams of teachers and principals attend a series of professional arts events and workshops conducted by the center's artist-teachers who perform follow-up classroom services during the school year. The institute has served as a model and a technical resource for similar programs in New York State and nationally.

PUBLICATIONS

1934 *ART AS EXPERIENCE* BY JOHN DEWEY: Republished in New York, 1958, by Capricorn Books. Based on a series of lectures at Harvard University on the philosophy of art, this book explores the ways in which works of art enlarge human experience and help to deepen meanings through imagination. Indicates how the creative process of art makes connection with experience to intensify, clarify and enrich living. Dewey relates the practical and the fine arts and shows the aesthetic role that art can play in the formation of cultural attitudes. [Citation based on the annotated bibliography in *Arts and the Schools*, J. Hausman, ed., McGraw-Hill, 1980.]

1956 *EDUCATION THROUGH ART* **BY HERBERT READ**   Pantheon Books, New York (third revised edition). A classic work that promotes the conception of everyone as an artist in his or her own craft (doing something well). Argues for creative, aesthetic expression as the basis of education. Analyzes artistic activity in children using their own drawings as illustration. Sees teachers as sensitive, patient mediators, developing "sensibility" and "imagination." [Citation from *Arts and the Schools*, J. Hausman, ed. , McGraw-Hill, 1980.]

1960 - 1970

1960 AMERICAN COUNCIL FOR THE ARTS: (Originally founded as Community Arts Councils, Inc. and later known as Arts Councils of America and then Associated Councils of the Arts) began as a nonprofit membership and service organization headquartered in New York City. Its original objective was to assure the arts a higher place in the list of national priorities. It began as a forum for the country's emerging local and state arts agencies and other organizations and individuals concerned with the arts. The organization now serves as one of the nation's primary sources on legislative news affecting all the arts and acts as a leading advisor to arts administrators, arts patrons, educators, elected officials and the general public. While ACA has recently made arts education a priority, it has been actively supportive in the field for quite some time. Beginning in 1970, ACA sponsored a national conference on Youth, Education and the Arts in St. Louis; a conference on the Arts in the Schools in New Orleans in 1974; and another, "Coming to Our Senses: The Arts and Education" in Little Rock, Arkansas in 1978. [See individual entries for details about these conferences.]

1960 NEW YORK STATE COUNCIL ON THE ARTS: Established five years prior to the National Endowment for the Arts, and formalized in 1965. Its efforts in education began in a partnership with the State Education Department. Grants were made to arts organizations that provided arts programs and services to schools. State legislative financial support for the council's educational services diminished in the early seventies but was replaced by NEA Artists-in-Schools funds. In 1985, in a renewed partnership with the State Education Department, the council established the Arts in Education Program with money from the state legislature. Guidelines and criteria describe collaboratively planned and implemented programs and services that are the result of functional partnerships between arts providers and the schools. Both the arts organizations and the school partners are responsible for the grant application. [Historical Note: This initiative preceded the NEA Arts in Basic Education Grant guidelines.]

1963 "THE ARTS AND THE NATIONAL GOVERNMENT," BY AUGUST HECKSCHER: Report to the President [John F. Kennedy]. In March of 1962, President John F. Kennedy created a new White House staff position and appointed August Heckscher, a well-known supporter of the arts, as his special consultant on the Arts. Kennedy commissioned Heckscher to examine the state and status of the arts nationwide and to explore the potential for a leadership role by the federal government.

The study's policy recommendations paved the way for the establishment of the National Council on the Arts and the Endowments for the Arts and the Humanities. The study also encouraged a strong federal government role in the arts and noted that "the Office of Education . . . had until recently given little attention to the arts . . . . Further consideration [should] be given to increasing the share of the federal government's support to education which is concerned with the arts and the humanities . . . " It also pointed out the lack of arts education in the nation's public schools and the limited access of young people to professional arts experiences.

According to Harlan "Rip" Hoffa in the second chapter, "The Arts, Government and Education," of his invaluable (and out-of-print) 1970 final report to the U.S. Office of Education, Bureau of Research titled *Analysis of Recent Research Conferences in Art Education* (p.19 and 23):

> These two facts: Kennedy's unparalleled interest in the arts as an instrument and a responsibility of government and his uncommonly close relationship to [his then-recently appointed Commissioner of Education, Francis Keppel, who died in February 1990] are concomitant circumstances, and no evidence is available to suggest a direct relationship between them. Nevertheless . . . it seems unlikely that Keppel's support of the Arts and Humanities Program, in general, and of Kathryn Bloom, in particular, was entirely separate from the recommendations of the Heckscher Report and the overall support which the President evidenced for the arts . . . Harold 'Doc' Howe II [who followed Keppel as Commissioner] 'inherited' Kathryn Bloom as his Special Advisor on the Arts and Humanities, and . . . Howe's faith in Kathryn Bloom's judgment was amply demonstrated by the delegation of this authority to her.

Doc Howe was often called on to talk about the arts and, according to Hoffa (who was there), turned (as did Frank Keppel before him) to the Arts and Humanities staff to help prepare his speeches or other public statements. On June 13, 1967, Howe delivered a commencement address at Ohio State University in which he said in part:

I am not complaining here about a failure to educate battalions of poets and sculptors, nor am I urging that we teach every male to cry when he sees a daffodil. I am saying that beauty must not be the concern solely of the artist. It must be the concern of every citizen, for the presence of ugliness and shabbiness cheapens the quality of all our lives. *If we can cultivate a sensitivity to aesthetics in every student, we will produce a generation of businessmen, housewives, civil servants, computer programmers, journalists, veterinarians, radio-TV repairmen and dental technicians who can remake the face of America.* [Emphasis mine.]

1963-1974 ARTS AND HUMANITIES PROGRAM, BUREAU OF RESEARCH, U.S. OFFICE OF EDUCATION, DEPARTMENT OF HEALTH, EDUCATION AND WELFARE: Originally based in the Cultural Affairs Branch, Division of Library Services and Continuing Education in 1962, the Arts and Humanities Program ended up as the Arts and Humanities Staff under the new Department of Education in the late 1970s. The important work of the AHP began under the aegis of pro-arts Education Commissioners Francis Keppel and Harold (Doc) Howe. Keppel appointed Kathryn Bloom the first director in 1963 with the primary responsibility of administering a research program for the improvement of education in the arts and humanities. In 1967, Kathy joined the John D. Rockefeller 3rd Fund (JDR 3rd Fund) and worked with Mr. Rockefeller to establish its Arts in Education Program. She was succeeded at the Office of Education by Harold (Bud) Arberg in 1968.

In 1965, under the landmark Elementary and Secondary Education Act (ESEA), millions of dollars became available for research and development in arts education—primarily from Title IV. Under Kathy's leadership some basic research and mostly developmental (read: pilot demonstration) projects were supported. In addition, the program sponsored a series of ground-breaking "developmental conferences" on arts and humanities education-related issues. These conferences brought together the leadership from an array of disparate fields and stimulated proposals and programs.

(One of the better-known of these conferences was "The Arts and the Poor" held in Gaithersburg, Maryland in 1966, which according to Junius Eddy was in large measure responsible for the establishment of the NEA's Expansion Arts Program by then-Chairwoman Nancy Hanks. One of the better-known and important pilot efforts of the AHP was the four-year Educational Lab Theater Project in the mid-sixties. [For more about both, see entries below.])

In the late sixties and early seventies, AHP began to transfer money to the NEA's fledgling Artist in Schools efforts and was one of the sponsors of artists in the schools participating in Project IMPACT [see entry below].

According to Kathy Bloom, the AHP director's dual role of special advisor to the commissioner of education was crucial to the development of cooperative working relationships with the NEA and the NEH. This resulted in complementary and often subsidized efforts involving the scholarly community, artists, performers, arts agencies and educational institutions. [In my view, this also helped account for the close working relationship that developed between Kathy and Roger Stevens, the first chair of the NEA, and indirectly for her work with successive NEA chairs, including Nancy Hanks and Livingston Biddle.]

Junius Eddy confirms that the term "arts in general education" was coined by Kathryn Bloom during her tenure at the AHP. He also informs me that the program spent about $11 million dollars between 1963 and 1970.

A number of books and publications document this critical period in the development of the arts in education. Please refer to the bibliography for entries under J. Eddy, H. Hoffa, L. Jones and J. Murphy among others. [Authors note: Since many of these books and reports are becoming scarcer than the proverbial hen's teeth and are not available from any central library or clearinghouse, I think I detect a joint publication project for some enterprising research institution with NEA and DOE support. I got my hands on a lot of precious stuff "on loan" from my generous and trusting colleagues.]

1965 *THE PERFORMING ARTS: PROBLEMS AND PROSPECTS*: Published by McGraw-Hill 1965. A report produced by the Rockefeller Panel on the future of theater, dance and music in America. This is one of a series of reports funded by the Rockefeller Brothers Fund concerning various cultural, educational and socio-economic conditions in the country. The eight panel members included Chairman John D. Rockefeller 3rd, Nancy Hanks and August Heckscher.

In a chapter titled "Building Greater Appreciation," under the subheading "Education," the panel addresses the nature of the opportunities for young people to be exposed to and learn the value of the arts. Acknowledging that the performing arts institutions have a vital but far from exclusive role to play, the panel then turns its attention to the schools:

> While the performing arts have traditionally been a part of the school curriculum, the development of selective performing groups—bands, orchestras, and choruses—representing a relatively small segment of the total school population has generally been stressed. Only minor attention has been given to cultivating the artistic tastes of the large mass of students not engaged in performing organizations. Many school groups . . . devote too much time to . . . music and drama that is trivial and inconsequential. The objective often seems to be solely to entertain rather than to educate . . . .

We need more and better trained teachers in the arts, particularly at the elementary school level. School administrators need to be made more aware of the place of the arts in a balanced curriculum and the necessity for providing not only adequate time during the school day but also the materials and equipment needed for an arts program. Greater experimentation with newly developed teaching aids and materials should be sought. *School officials should be encouraged to make full use of the artistic resources of the community, both professional and amateur, in stimulating and enriching the education program in the arts . . . . The American school, in general, should show greater imagination, initiative and responsibility than it has in bringing art to the school and the child to art.* [Emphasis mine. Junius Eddy points out that this language, and the leadership of Cleveland Schools Superintendent Paul Briggs and Educational Facilities Laboratory President Harold Gores—who headed the task force that developed the ESEA Title III program—worked its way into the philosophy of that important program for the arts in education.]

While these examples of activity by the schools, by independent agencies and by the arts organizations themselves are heartening, it must be candidly admitted that they are but a fraction of what will have to be provided if the education of young people in the live performing arts is to be measurably broadened in our lifetime . . . . These same young people grow to become tomorrow's taxpayers and legislators, mayors and governors, corporation and foundation executives and labor and civic leaders. If the arts are to receive any substantial increase in support from any of these sources, it will be because we have leaders who are educated to an appreciation of art's value to the community.

The panel's recommendations on this aspect of the study concluded as follows: [It should be noted that the panel's findings were largely responsible for the establishment by Mr. Rockefeller of the Arts in Education Program at the JDR 3rd Fund and that these findings informed the work of the Fund over its twelve-year operational period.]

The effective exposure of young people to the arts is as much a civic responsibility as programs in health and welfare. Although the panel recognizes that the initiative for an expanded educational effort in the arts will generally come from individuals, success in the measure necessary will require the combined backing of the family and the school system. Also important are the encouragement of private organizations, local and state arts councils, and the cooperation of local governments and the federal Office of Education.

[Author's comment: I quote from this report at length as a reminder that the concerns expressed twenty-five years ago remain with us today. They were picked up in 1977 in *Coming to Our Senses*, at the NEA in the mideighties, and again in 1988 at the Interlochen Symposium, co-sponsored by the American Council for the Arts and the Music Educators National Conference. As we enter the nineties, they are alive and troublesome once more. They are being discussed by several state education departments, a number of state arts agencies and two special task forces convened to address policy and practice in the arts in education in New Jersey and New York.]

1965 ELEMENTARY AND SECONDARY EDUCATION ACT OF 1965: The Elementary and Secondary Education Act (ESEA) of 1965 (and succeeding amendments) was the landmark educational legislation of the "golden era" of the Great Society President Lyndon Johnson that supplied major resources for the arts in education. For the first time in the nation's history, arts services and artists were entitled to receive support by federal tax-levy, categorical and competitive funds—albeit in the service of other largely socio-economic purposes: Title I (compensatory education for the poor and disadvantaged, largely in basic skills acquisition, especially reading); Title II (texts, books, reference materials); Title III (innovative and exemplary programs, including the idea of partnership of arts organizations with schools as service providers primarily for cultural enrichment); Title IV (research, especially the Arts and Humanities Program under the direction of Kathryn Bloom); Title V (strengthening state education agencies).

Junius Eddy, in his two landmark reports to the Ford Foundation in 1970, states that hundreds of millions of dollars were spent for the arts but few programs originated with federal money survived once the federal dollar supply was cut off (usually after a three-year cycle). To my knowledge, the only such efforts that continue include the Washington State Cultural Enrichment Program; the Southwest Regional Education Lab; The Guggenheim/Title I Learning to Read Through the Arts; the Minneapolis Urban Arts Program; and the Providence Trinity Square Theater Project.

One of the major lessons learned from that period of relative opulence was that new ventures are fragile when they are perceived as add-ons without a secure institutional base or policy commitment. This is especially true in "peripheral" areas such as the arts, which were then regarded as supplemental, not basic, or to use the federal lingo, "cultural enrichment." Consequently, when "extra" money dries up, so do the programs. The moral is that arts in education projects should not depend on the massive infusion of start-up money from outside sources. In fact, unless there is a long-range plan in place when the cash starts flowing, large or small sums of outside funds can corrupt the intention, direction and health of many programs. [See also Eddy reports entry for 1970.]

These lessons are confirmed by a five-year study of the entire range of federal education projects seeking change or innovation that was released in 1977 and concluded: "The net return to the federal investment was the adoption of many innovations, the successful implementation of a few, and the long-run continuation of still fewer . . . . More money does not make a difference [because] it doesn't purchase the things that matter . . . more committed teachers, more effective project directors and more concerned principals. [Source: *Federal Programs Supporting Education Change*, vol.III, as cited in *Education Laws 1978: A Guide to New Directions in Federal Aid*, National School Public Relations Association.]

1965 NATIONAL ENDOWMENT FOR THE ARTS: The enabling legislation for the Endowment does not include a mandate for education that, until 1985, was a matter of institutional policy, not congressional law. The nature of and definition and support for arts education fluctuated, depending on Endowment leadership. Until the 1985 reauthorization, educational programs and initiatives were conducted largely at the discretion of the successive chairs (Roger Stevens, Nancy Hanks, Livingston Biddle, Frank Hodsoll and now John Frohnmayer). Under Hodsoll's leadership the arts in education became a priority at the Endowment.

The NEA's first foray into arts education can be traced back to efforts in 1966 when, under Chairman Roger Stevens, the agency helped to support artist services in the Laboratory Theater Project of the U.S.O.E.'s Arts and Humanities Program [see entry below]. The NEA's own education effort began with a pilot poet-in-the-schools program in St. Paul, Minnesota in 1968. In partnership with the Office of Education, the NEA established the Artists in Schools Program in 1969, expanding on the success of the pilot by adding a visual artists-in-school residency program in six states. The program grew to include a broad range of the arts and began to operate—in the early seventies—in all fifty states and special jurisdictions. In 1980 the program's name changed again to Artists in Education. Financial support, in addition to NEA money, came from U.S.O.E., the Bureau of Indian Affairs, state and local arts agencies and state and local education agencies.

The early history of these programs demonstrated an interest in providing employment for young artists rather than in the integration of the arts into the basic educational process. The 1985 reauthorization of the Endowment saw yet another change in direction and strengthening of language for arts education in the enabling legislation. This change set a new direction for funding and interest in making arts education a basic curriculum area of all schools.

During the eighties, the NEA conducted a study of the arts in education in the Northeast and in 1987, after extensive review of its history, policies and practices, it took the major step of changing its name to the Arts in Education Program and redirecting its support for artists in the schools to the support of comprehensive, rigorous and sequential programs that would give the arts a significant place in the curriculum. Current grant categories include the new Arts in Basic Education Grants (for comprehensive program planning and implementation with state arts agencies), support for State Arts Councils (including local artists-in-the-schools programs), and Special Projects (for innovative programming, curriculum and staff development; documentation and dissemination of information; research and evaluation, and the like). In addition, the agency is supporting the development of an instructional television series (with the Department of Education and the Getty Center for Education in the Arts) and the National Arts Education Research Center sites at the University of Illinois (Urbana-Champaign) and New York University.

In its early days, the Artists in Schools Program was a joint effort of the U.S. Office of Education and the NEA, which used millions of U.S.O.E. transfer funds to supplement the then-meager budget. The Endowment has steadily increased AIE funds, and the program now (1990) has a budget of $5.6 million. Funds for the arts in education have also been available from individual discipline programs (generally through the special projects category). More recently, and for the first time, guidelines for Challenge III grants specify two funding categories that support the arts in education: "Access" and "Appreciation." Grants range from $50,000 to $1,000,000.

The current guidelines for the NEA's Arts in Education Program include the following statement:

> As part of its mission of fostering artistic excellence and access to and appreciation of that excellence, the National Endowment for the Arts is concerned with arts education. In the May 1988 report to Congress, "Toward Civilization: A Report on Arts Education," the Arts Endowment recognized the need for all students in kindergarten through 12th grade to have a balanced education, one that includes comprehensive and sequential study in the three great branches of learning—the arts, humanities and sciences. The AIE Program, through its three categories (State Arts in Education Grants, Arts in Schools Basic Education Grants and Special Projects) has the overall goal of advancing the arts as part of basic education. It is a partnership program that is planned, administered and financed through cooperative efforts of the Arts Endowment, state arts and education agencies, local communities, and education, arts education, and cultural institutions and organizations.

1965 NATIONAL ENDOWMENT FOR THE HUMANITIES' SUPPORT OF ARTS IN EDUCATION: This program is largely directed to teacher training institutes (e.g. the Lincoln Center Institute for the Arts in Education), curriculum development and scholarly research and study. Some funds support the services and residencies of humanists in the schools.

1966 DEVELOPMENTAL CONFERENCE ON THE ROLE OF THE ARTS IN MEET-ING THE SOCIAL AND EDUCATIONAL NEEDS OF THE DISADVANTAGED: Held in November 1966 in Gaithersburg, Maryland, this arts and humanities conference resulted in Judith Murphy and Ronald Gross's interpretative report, *The Arts and the Poor: New Challenge for Educators*, published by the U.S. Department of Health, Education and Welfare, Office of Education, Bureau of Research in June 1968.

This was one of the better-known, action-oriented "developmental conferences" organized under the auspices of the Arts and Humanities Program (Kathryn Bloom, director). Among the distinguished participants were Elliot Eisner, Francis A. J. Ianni, Melvin Tumin, Edward Mattil, Jerrold Ross, Nina Perera Collier, Theodore Katz, Dorothy Maynor and Lloyd New Kiva. Also present were Harold (Doc) Howe II (then-Commissioner of Education), Roger Stevens (then-Chairman of the NEA) and Barnaby Keeney (then-Chairman of the NEH). At that time, Kathy's Arts and Humanities Program staff included: Harold Arberg, Irving Brown, Junius Eddy, Richard Grove, Harlan "Rip" Hoffa, Esther Nichols, Elizabeth Reuss and Lola Rogers.

According to Kathy in her introductory remarks to the 1968 conference report:

> The conference generated a number of new projects and programs which bear on the central issue: finding viable ways to relate the processes and techniques of the arts to the process of education in poverty-area schools . . . .The direct relevance of the arts to the learning process, their specific application to ghetto classroom teaching, and their motivational uses for school-based learning has only begun to be explored, let alone definitively researched and demonstrated. . . . The challenge [to teach children of poverty] is not to educators alone. Beyond the teachers and administrators— and utterly essential to any such enterprise—are those in all of the relevant fields and disciplines: the artists and performers, the arts educators, the poverty workers and the urbanologists, the sociologists and the educational researchers, the child growth and development experts and others.

1966-1970 EDUCATIONAL LABORATORY THEATRE PROGRAM: Supported jointly by the National Endowment for the Arts, U.S.O.E.'s Elementary and Secondary Education Act, Title III, and the Arts and Humanities Program.

According to Junius Eddy, "the Educational Laboratory Theatre was the brainchild of Kathryn Bloom [AHP] and Roger Stevens [NEA]." It was a major research and development effort that spent $6.4 million to determine ways to connect the work of repertory companies, the theater arts and literature to the ongoing instructional program in three cities: Los Angeles, New Orleans and Providence, Rhode Island.

Eddy continues: "It was (and probably still is) the single largest federally funded arts education project in the nation's history. It involved establishing new professional theaters in two major cities and using another that was already in place to provide three years of three to six productions a year, from a largely 'classics' repertoire, for all high school kids in grades ten through twelve in each metropolitan area—and in Rhode Island, for the entire state. Title III funds supported school activities. Title IV/AHP supported research, documentation and evaluation (at CEMREL), and the NEA funds covered the theater productions."

The project was thoroughly documented and evaluated by CEMREL in a four-volume set of reports under the overall title: *Final Report on the Educational Laboratory Theatre Project, 1966-1970* (out of print).

Among the important outcomes of this bold and imaginative project was the establishment of an arts in education program in the budget of the New Orleans School District under the direction of Shirley Trusty Corey. The comprehensive Project Arts Connection, which operates today in a network of almost twenty elementary schools, is the most recent manifestation of the ELT legacy.

1967 PROJECT ZERO, GRADUATE SCHOOL OF EDUCATION, HARVARD UNIVERSITY: A study of spatial intelligence centered in the arts, associated primarily with its co-director, Howard Gardner, and Research Associate Dennis Palmer Wolf. This project has been funded over the years by the U.S. Office of Education, the National Institute of Education and the Rockefeller Foundation. It is a long-range basic research program to study the varieties and interaction of human abilities, the nature of the tasks involved in the several arts and ways to develop those abilities. The project used psychological experimentation and clinical study of the brain as well as field work in schools to research the problems involved.

In 1985, with funding from the Rockefeller Foundation, Project Zero launched the ambitious and promising Arts PROPEL Project in collaboration with Educational Testing Service and the Pittsburgh Public Schools. [See entry below.]

1967-1979 ARTS IN EDUCATION PROGRAM OF THE JOHN D. ROCKEFELLER 3RD (JDR 3RD) FUND: The JDR 3rd Fund was an operating foundation whose Arts in Education Program staff worked cooperatively for twelve years with state education agencies, school systems and individual schools to develop and implement comprehensive arts in education programs. Its mission was to make all of the arts integral to the general, or basic, education of all students in entire school systems. Operating on a budget of $500,000 a year, its relatively modest grants supported comprehensive efforts or pieces of large-scale initiatives that were congruent with its main objective. In its last six years, more emphasis was placed on the staff's active involvement in and technical assistance to the planning and development of collaborative ventures rather than on making grants to isolated though complementary pilot projects.

Mr. Rockefeller and Kathryn Bloom conceived of and constructed the program essentially as a national research and development effort. It was concerned with the investigation of a particular concept and rationale. It had identified goals and specific objectives and chose to work closely and cooperatively with local and state education and arts agencies to determine whether and how successful practices could be developed and replicated in different settings. It documented and evaluated steps taken to reach its goals and deliberately built upon its experience (both successful and disappointing) and knowledge as it accumulated.

The Fund disseminated quantities of information about project outcomes as well as a series of working papers, monographs and other publications to a wide national audience. In addition, it served as a vocal and articulate advocate for the concept of "all the arts for all the children" for over a decade and provided free consulting and technical assistance to a broad range of practitioners in the field of the arts and education.

The Fund's early pilot projects were located in sites such as University City, Missouri; Mineola, New York; Oklahoma City, Oklahoma; and Jefferson County, Colorado. Later efforts included the coordination and support of two major national networks: the (AD HOC) Coalition of (Nine) States for the Arts in Education formed in 1975 [Arizona, California, Indiana, Massachusetts, Michigan, New York, Oklahoma, Pennsylvania, Washington] and the League of (Six) Cities for the Arts in Education, formed in 1976 (Hartford, Little Rock, Minneapolis, New York, Seattle, Winston-Salem). Members of these networks provided technical and consulting assistance to each other and to a broad national constituency that included the Office of Education, the two national endowments, foundations, professional arts associations, arts agencies and organizations, other school districts and state education departments.

In spite of its limited financial resources, the Fund often co-sponsored national events, conferences and studies on the arts in education, and its staff was invited to participate in the planning and development of national programs, legislation, research studies and evaluation designs.

The history of the Fund and case studies of some of its major initiatives are documented in *An Arts in Education Source Book: A View from the JDR 3rd Fund* (New York: The JDR 3rd Fund, 1980). The book is available from the American Council for the Arts, New York. The history of the

League of Cities for the Arts in Education and the documentation of its programs and practices may be found in this book.

1967-1975 CEMREL (CENTRAL MIDWESTERN REGIONAL EDUCATIONAL LABORATORIES):   St. Louis, Missouri. CEMREL was one of twenty national educational laboratories established to bridge the gap between sound educational research and its actual practice in the schools. Although concerned with mathematics as well as other disciplines, CEMREL was perhaps most closely identified with its Aesthetic Education Program (AEP), which was established with the Elementary and Secondary Education Act, Title IV funds and later supported in part by the National Institute for Education. Its chief purpose was to work cooperatively with schools, educational agencies and community representatives to develop guidelines for a curriculum in aesthetic education, kindergarten through high school.

Under the leadership of Stanley Madeja, the AEP designed and produced a comprehensive series of field-tested curriculum materials (boxes) in aesthetic education for kindergarten through seventh grades that were distributed nationally. These materials were designed to be used in classrooms by teachers who have little or no background in the arts. Content was organized around six major areas and examined the relationship of aesthetics to: the Physical World, Arts Elements, the Creative Process, the Artist, the Culture and the Environment. The instructional materials provided a major resource for students and classroom teachers who were able to use the arts—visual arts, language arts, music, dance and theater—as alternative approaches for learning in the schools. They were ultimately commercially produced and distributed nationally.

CEMREL also set up a network of eleven Aesthetic Education Learning Centers that were co-sponsored by local school districts, educational institutions and arts organizations. The centers were located in Long Island; New York City; Harrisburg; Memphis; Normal, Illinois; Oklahoma City; Jefferson County, Colorado; Oakland and Antioch, California; St. Louis; and Washington, D.C. The purpose of these centers was to provide services such as teacher and administrative training in effective curricular implementation and technical assistance in the development and evaluation of these efforts. Each center worked with three demonstration schools.

1967-PRESENT   SWREL (SOUTHWEST REGIONAL EDUCATION LAB): Although CEMREL's fifteen-year history in the field made it extremely visible in arts education thanks to its Aesthetic Education Program, a few of the other twenty government-funded educational laboratories demonstrated interest and developed projects in the field. The Southwest Regional Education Lab (SWREL), under the leadership of W. Dwaine Greer, produced a visual art curriculum that is discipline-based. This curriculum is in wide usage across the country. CAREL, the Central Atlantic Regional Education Lab, worked in the area of curriculum and teacher training for dance education.

1967-Present The Business Committee for the Arts: The Business Committee for the Arts is a national nonprofit business organization of chairmen, presidents and CEOs committed to encouraging and developing business involvement with the arts. BCA was founded in 1967 by David Rockefeller and a core of America's top business leaders who were concerned with the unprecedented growth in the number of arts organizations in the United States and with the growing need for business involvement with the arts. Mr. Rockefeller's concern was spurred by the findings of the 1965 Rockefeller Report (*Performing Arts: Problems and Prospects*—see earlier entry). In 1967, business gave an estimated $22 million to the arts. Today, this figure is estimated to exceed $1 billion annually.

Over the years, BCA has supported arts education and encouraged and recognized leadership activities in this area within the business community. In 1988, BCA published an *Arts Education Resource Guide* that provides an overview of the field for corporations and foundations interested in funding arts education projects. The guide contains information on current trends, historical perspectives, resources, a rationale for arts education and many practical "how-to" strategies. The guide also gives examples of and guidelines for successful arts education programs such as "Partnerships: Arts and the Schools," which was created and sponsored by the Metropolitan Life Foundation.

1970 - 1980

1970 Associated Councils of the Arts National Conference, "Youth, Education and the Arts": St. Louis. A significant three and one-half day conference in May 1970 gathered community leaders such as school and arts administrators, businessmen, politicians, parents, youth groups, philanthropists, journalists and academics. Funded in part by the U.S. Office of Education's Arts and Humanities Program, the conference was intended to bring these groups together with teachers and artists to make a collective commitment to the concept that "the arts must be a basic part of the general education of all children on the pre-school, elementary and secondary levels . . . . [However] the ideas, the talent, the facilities, the funds necessary to achieve this new dimension of arts education are neither present in nor available to the schools today."

The conference examined methods of introducing the arts into schooling through discussion, presentations, films and performances as well as case studies of promising programs. There were also sessions on instructional television, artist school residencies, film education and programs for the economically disadvantaged. Samuel B. Gould, chancellor of the State University of New York, presided as general chairman. Educator and author Harold Taylor served as chairman, and ACA's Joseph Farrell was conference director.

Topics covered included arts in the schools; arts in rural schools; government programs funding the arts (Arts and Humanities Program, U.S.O.E., NEA); environmental education; the anatomy of [educational] change; the role of state arts councils in arts education; arts careers; arts institutions as resources to schools. One session titled "A Study in Change: National and Local Implications" examined the University City, Missouri/ JDR 3rd Fund Arts in General Education Project and the role of the Aesthetic Education Program of CEMREL.

The conference generated a "Survey of State Arts Councils' and Commissions' Assistance to Arts Education for Youth," a selection of "Readings" by authors with pertinent comments on the arts and education, and a conference summary report by *New Republic* journalist Joseph Featherstone. It also generated the first of three "editions" of Junius Eddy's "The Upside-down Curriculum," published in the conference issue of ACA's *Cultural Affairs* magazine.

In an article describing the event in the September 1970 Music Educators Journal, Charles Fowler characterizes his feelings as "discouraged" and the event as disappointing because it did not include a sufficient number of artists, teachers and arts educators. He called then, as he does today, for unity in the field: "If we are to make the arts available to all, only the concerted effort of artists, educators and laymen working together will realize that goal. Let us forget rivalry and join together to solve the crisis in the arts."

1970 REPORTS TO THE FORD FOUNDATION BY JUNIUS EDDY: *A Review of Projects in the Arts Supported by ESEA's Title III* and *A Review of Federal Programs Supporting the Arts in Education* are two of the most useful and widely-quoted compendiums dealing with the origins of and federal support for the arts in education (for other critical sources of information, see bibliographical entries under Fowler, Hoffa, Jones and Murphy). They contain detailed, comprehensive and unique summaries of the disposition of millions of dollars for the arts in education during the golden days of the Johnson Administration. They focus primarily on the first five years of the Elementary and Secondary Education Act and Titles I and III of the legislation. They catalog just about every variety of cultural enrichment and arts exposure program imaginable and illustrate a number of ingenious ways in which arts organizations managed to justify their services to schools in order to be eligible for federal largesse.

1970 "The Upsidedown Curriculum," by Junius Eddy: Published in the summer issue of *Cultural Affairs* (a now-discontinued ACA magazine). Published twice since 1970 when it was distributed by ACA at its national conference on "Youth, Education, and the Arts," this short, prophetic article was subsequently reprinted in 1971 by the Ford Foundation which reportedly distributed some 20,000 copies nationwide. The last version was published ten years later by the Kennedy Center's Alliance for Arts Education in an annotated edition in 1981.

The title is taken from John Goodlad's also prophetic piece, "The Educational Program to 1980 and Beyond," which warned over twenty years ago that the omission of the arts from schooling was likely to produce a topsy-turvy, utilitarian value system:

> . . . in spite of an assumed "culture explosion," we continue to neglect art, music, drama, dance, sculpture, and, in fact, almost everything that smacks of being non-utilitarian. Ironically, we may discover not long after 1980 that, in the 1960's and 1970's we had an upsidedown curriculum, with what was considered then to be of most worth proving to be of little value to masses of the people. . . .

In his introduction to the 1981 AAE update, Eddy states:

> . . . Now, ten years later . . . it appears that most arts education advocates have made a solid assertion out of that somewhat venturesome question [should the arts become *fundamental* to the education of every American child?] . . . the fundamental questions persist, and much still remains to be done in our attempts to turn the upsidedown curriculum right side up at long last. . . .

It is now 1990, and almost ten years after its latest incarnation, the article and its thesis are still apt. The role of the arts in the general education of children in the nation's elementary and secondary schools is still peripheral. "There are noteworthy exceptions scattered across the land: in a handful of school systems . . . interesting, sometimes exciting, and often valuable things are going on . . . [but] *the arts, even 'Art' and 'Music,' are uneasy guests in the house of education.* [Emphasis mine.]"

1970-1972 Project IMPACT (Interdisciplinary Model Programs in the Arts for Children and Teachers):   Project Impact aimed at developing an arts-centered curriculum in five public school systems: Columbus, Ohio; Eugene, Oregon; Glendale, California; Philadelphia, Pennsylvania; and Troy, Alabama.

Funded by the U.S. Office of Education, Department of Health, Education and Welfare, the National Endowment for the Arts, and the JDR 3rd Fund, with support from the professional arts education associations, the objectives of the program were to:

— achieve a better balance between the arts and other instructional areas;
— upgrade the quality of the arts in the participating schools;
— conduct a variety of in-service programs and workshops;
— enhance and improve the quality and quantity of aesthetic education in the total school program; and
— enhance the quality of children's art experiences by drawing upon outstanding artists, performers and educators from outside the school system.

The project resulted in extensive evaluation reports and "Arts IMPACT: Curriculum for Change—A Summary Report," which was prepared by the Project Evaluation Team of the Pennsylvania State University and submitted to the Arts and Humanities Program, Office of Education, Department of Health, Education and Welfare, in March 1973.

1972 ALLIANCE FOR ARTS EDUCATION (AAE): Established as a joint program of the Kennedy Center for the Performing Arts and the Office of Education, AAE advances education in the arts for every U.S. citizen. This is accomplished through a network of nonprofit state organizations that work with other groups to create a dialogue about the value of education in the arts for young people. AAE has recently co-sponsored biennial National Summit Conferences on the Arts and Education. At the most recent summit (Fall 1989), AAE was joined by the NEA's Arts in Education Program, the Council of Chief State School Officers and the Getty Center for Education in the Arts, an operating program of the J. Paul Getty Trust. Attending were AAE regional and state representatives, state arts angencies' arts in education coordinators and state department of education supervisors of fine arts. Several sessions were held jointly with the National Assembly of State Arts Agencies.

[Historical footnote: Most of the following text is quoted verbatim from the 1974 JDR 3rd Fund Annual Report. It was written by Kathryn Bloom.]

In the early days of the program, Roger Stevens, Kennedy Center chair, asked Kathy Bloom and the JDR 3rd Fund staff to provide the center's education staff with technical and consulting assistance in the design and operation of the AAE program. "AAE encouraged the formation of committees in all of the states which helped to bring together the resources of state education departments and state arts councils and commissions for cooperative planning. Modest support was made available from the office of education to assist in planning and developing programs in a number of states. The characteristics of proposals for which financial assistance could be given were derived from the experience gained in arts in education projects supported by the JDR 3rd Fund which have demonstrated ways in which community arts organizations and artists can work with school systems to achieve high levels of quality and educational effectiveness."

The Kennedy Center sponsors national youth arts festivals (IMAGINA-TION CELEBRATION) across the nation. Kennedy Center education efforts include the American College Theater Festival, the Kennedy Center Theater for Young People, Educational Services and the National Symphony Orchestra Education Program. In addition, the center publishes a newsletter, *Interchange*, which is sent free of charge to Alliance members and others. *Interchange* is supported in part by the U.S. Department of Education.

1972 *ALL THE ARTS FOR EVERY CHILD: FINAL REPORT ON THE ARTS IN GENERAL EDUCATION PROJECT IN THE SCHOOL DISTRICT OF UNIVERSITY CITY, MISSOURI* : Written by Stanley S. Madeja (project director), with a foreword by Kathryn Bloom (JDR 3rd Fund, 1973), this landmark report documents the seminal JDR 3rd Fund comprehensive arts in general education project. Thousands of copies were distributed nationally along with other major dissemination materials prepared by the fund during the seventies. It describes the processes for establishing goals, staffing, developing units of instruction, observing in the classroom and creating complementary resources. It also describes the manner in which the project used the arts resources in the community and how the project was shaped through evaluation strategies.

Kathy's introduction sets the stage not only for this project but for much of the future work of the Arts in Education Program. It is interesting to trace the influence of the lessons learned at the Arts and Humanities Program and the manner in which they were applied in University City and in a number of the Fund's early pilot projects. [Author's note: out of print.]

1972 "THE HUNTING OF THE SQUIGGLE," A STUDY OF A PERFORMING ARTS INSTITUTION AND YOUNG PEOPLE: Conducted by Mark Schubart, director of the Lincoln Center for the Performing Arts' educational efforts, the study was funded by the Carnegie Corporation of America to examine Lincoln Center for the Performing Arts' history and its actual and potential role in the education of young people. The study paved the way for the establishment of the Lincoln Center Institute for the Arts in Education in the mid-seventies. [See entry below.]

1972-1977 PROJECT SEARCH (NEW YORK STATE DEPARTMENT OF EDUCATION): Project SEARCH (Search for Education Through the Arts, Related Content and the Humanities) was originally funded by the Elementary and Secondary Education Act, Title III and subsequently Title IV-C (for innovation), with assistance from the JDR 3rd Fund during the period 1972-1977. The project was initiated to provide an innovative curriculum model and establish an integrated humanities and arts program in six public school districts and one parochial school. SEARCH attempted to help students apply both intellect and feeling to the problems of living and to develop reasoning processes and means of expression that would lead to intelligent, responsible decisions.

Strategies were developed for integrating the skills in the arts with the skills in cognitive areas through a series of workshops using visual artists, actors, filmmakers and musicians from the community and its schools. The project developed a comprehensive evaluation plan and a set of teaching and resource materials that were used in all sites.

1972-1981 EMERGENCY SCHOOL AID ACT, SPECIAL ARTS PROJECT: ESAA/Special Arts Project provided $1 million a year for several years of U.S.O.E. dollars to state arts agencies and councils for arts projects and cultural services that supported desegregation efforts in individual schools and school districts. Grants up to $100,000 were made available to public agencies for projects designed to reduce minority group isolation in elementary and secondary schools by placing practicing artists representing various racial and ethnic groups in day-to-day contact with school children. Limited to schools with enrollments of no less than 20 percent minority-group students, the goal of the projects was to establish an environment in which students, teachers, artists and members of the community may communicate without racial and cultural barriers. Many programs in the League of Cities for the Arts in Education took advantage of this funding opportunity.

1972-1982 NATIONAL INSTITUTE OF EDUCATION (NIE): The NIE was established as a research agency within the Department of Health, Education and Welfare, but independent of the Office of Education. It provided major support for CEMREL's Aesthetic Education Program, Harvard's Project Zero and arts curriculum development in the Southwest Regional Education Laboratory (SWREL).

1972-PRESENT NATIONAL DIFFUSION NETWORK (U.S. DEPARTMENT OF EDUCATION): Established under the U.S. Office of Education, the National Diffusion Network (NDN) is a federally funded system that supports activities designed to recognize and further excellence in education throughout the nation. Public or nonprofit agencies, organizations and institutions that meet specific qualifications are eligible for awards, grants and contracts. In order to qualify for dissemination funding and adoption by schools, colleges and other institutions, model programs (Developer Demonstrator Projects) must be validated. They must meet with the approval of a panel of independent national education experts who determine, by a set of rigorous guidelines and criteria, whether a program, product or practice presents convincing evidence that it is innovative, exemplary and cost-effective, and that it can be successfully adopted in different settings. NDN approval provides no guarantee for adoption funding. Program priorities are determined every year by the Secretary of Education and funds are distributed to applicants accordingly.

Since its inception, very few arts programs (four, by my count) have received NDN validation. (I do not know how many have applied nor do I know how many dollars have been made available for the adoption process.) Among them are the Guggenheim Project, (developmental funding from ESEA Title I): Learning to Read through the Arts, which was validated in 1974 and is still operative today. The Minneapolis Public Schools Urban Arts Program (ESEA Title III) was also validated in the mid-seventies but is no longer on the NDN's active list. This program legitimized arts activities and services offered in and by the communitiy's arts studios and organizations for high school credit.

In 1983, Success Enrichment (ESEA Title III and IV-C), a program to enrich the education of intellectually, academically and creatively gifted students, was approved. This program provides special enrichment activities for students in grades 2-8 with exceptionally high ability in the areas of language arts and art. In 1988, the Getty Center for Education in the Arts (using its own funds for development) submitted its Discipline-Based Art Education approach and received national validation. DBAE is "a process for institutionalizing discipline-based art education is school systems through a combination of staff development, curriculum implementation and organizational change."

1972 - PRESENT THE ROCKEFELLER FOUNDATION: During the term of its arts program director, Howard Klein, with Junius Eddy serving as advisor, the foundation supported projects featuring teacher pre- and in-service education in the arts. It also joined the JDR 3rd Fund in support of the Arts Substudy of John Goodlad's comprehensive Study of Schooling. Today, under the leadership of Alberta Arthurs, the foundation continues its long-term support of the work of Howard Gardner and Dennie P. Wolf in Project

Zero and the Arts PROPEL project in Pittsburgh. It also sponsors and convenes various task forces and study groups on the arts in education.

1973 AMERICAN EDUCATIONAL RESEARCH ASSOCIATION PRE-CONFERENCE SEMINAR, NEW ORLEANS (AND 1974 CONFERENCE IN CHICAGO): The JDR 3rd Fund hosted a seminar on evaluation in the arts in education at the AERA convention in 1973. Assembled were national experts and practitioners in research and evaluation including Robert Stake, Frank Barron, Larry Braskamp, Leslie McLean and Jack Morrison. According to Kathy Bloom in the introduction to Stake's book, *Evaluating the Arts in Education: A Responsive Approach*:

> The purpose of the meeting was to test out Stake's concept of 'responsive evaluation' as an approach more amenable to the arts than anything we had seen so far . . . . In February 1973, Stake and Morrison co-chaired a meeting in New Orleans for about forty participants, some from JDR 3rd Fund projects and others interested in the evaluation of the arts in education . . . . At the April 1974 AERA meeting [in Chicago] (at a session entitled 'Developing Useful Techniques for Arts in General Education Programs'), Stake read a paper . . . to an overflow audience. Egon Guba of Indiana University and Michael Scriven of the University of California at Berkeley critiqued the paper.

These activities led to the Charles E. Merrill publication of the book and its unique annotated bibliography by Bob and Bernadine Stake in 1975. [Author's note: out of print.]

1973 *THE ARTS AND HUMAN DEVELOPMENT* BY HOWARD GARDNER: Published by John Wiley. Presents and integration of developmental theory and the artistic process. Uses Erikson's psychoanalytic view of development and Piaget's cognitive view to construct a schema for studying artistic development in children. [Citation from *Arts and the Schools*, J. Hausman, ed., McGraw-Hill, 1980.]

1973 "THE ARTS PROCESS IN BASIC EDUCATION" BY CHARLES FOWLER: For the Pennsylvania Department of Education in 1974 with funds from the JDR 3rd Fund and reprinted five times, this small (23-page) gem has been influential in making the case for the arts in the schools. It "promotes the infusion of the arts into the total curriculum, with responsibility for arts education shared by all teachers in order to expand the base for learning experiences for all students." [Citation based on the annotated bibliography in *Arts and the Schools*, J. Hausman, ed., McGraw-Hill, 1980.]

Ten true/false questions about the arts are followed by a rationale for focusing arts education on process. It also suggests how arts education and the arts process can serve as an ally to learning all subjects of "basic" education. The unique contribution of the booklet is the simple yet compelling way in which it presents the conceptual and functional linkages between the arts process and the learning process:

> In the educational environment the artist's modes of activity are translated into process. To become explorers, appraisers, transformers, communicators, and perfectors (or, in other words, to function as an artist) students need to experience perceiving, responding, understanding, creating, evaluating, and development of skills. Together these six components form a structure for learning in the arts that can be defined as 'the arts process.' These actions are interdependent, interrelated, nonsequential, intertwined.

Fowler illustrates the process with a diagram of six interlocking circles depicting developing skills (manipulating, perfecting); perceiving (awareness, associating, discerning); responding (simple, functional, complex); understanding (information gathering, empathetic); creating (active, expressive); and evaluating (editing, valuing, analyzing). Each of these actions is described in detail, and the potential for nineteen specific student outcomes as a result of the arts process are identified. A case is made for the place of the arts process as an integral part of basic education and central to the curriculum. The booklet concludes with another true/false questionnaire related to the school program, the roles and functions of teachers, specialists and community resources.

Now out of print, the book was circulated to a wide national audience in the mid-seventies. It has been used in a variety of ways: as an advocacy tool and particularly as a conceptual framework for curriculum and staff development in states such as Pennsylvania, Washington, New York and North Carolina, to mention only a few.

1973 FIVE SENSE STORE: AESTHETIC EDUCATION PROGRAM INSTRUCTIONAL MATERIALS,: Published by Comenius, Inc., Weston, Colorado. Multimedia for kindergarten through 7th grade. Each package contains ten hours of instruction in: "Aesthetics and the Elements," "Aesthetics and the Creative Process" and "Aesthetics in the Physical World." See also CEMREL's Handbook for *The Five Sense Store Exhibit: An Aesthetic Design for Education,* by Susan Ingham, CEMREL, St. Louis, Missouri. [Citation based on the annotated bibliography in *Arts and the Schools*, J. Hausman, ed., McGraw-Hill, 1980.]

1973 NATIONAL ART EDUCATION ASSOCIATION, NATIONAL CONFERENCE, SAN DIEGO: The NAEA national conference held in the spring of 1972 was an occasion to bring together in special session all the project directors and other key personnel of the U.S.O.E./NEA/JDR Project Impact and JDR pilot project sites to share information on problems, practices and prospects for the future.

1974 ASSOCIATED COUNCILS OF THE ARTS, NATIONAL CONFERENCE, NEW ORLEANS, "ARTS IN THE SCHOOLS":   This three-day seminar assembled 250 national, state and community leaders in the arts and education. Among the participants were artists, state and community arts council representatives, school superintendents and arts educators. The purpose of the conference was "to disseminate information about arts education programs that work, to suggest ways in which the schools may be persuaded of the importance of the arts, to work on criteria to follow in the design of arts-education programs and to consider the urgent but difficult problem of evaluation."

Learning from the experience of the 1970 conference in St. Louis, ACA President John Hightower, Vice President Michael Newton and a planning group designed an agenda that included sessions conducted by artists, case histories of programs that work, and arts activities for the delegates to learn, first-hand, "what arts in the schools is all about." Support for the seminar came from the William F. Donner Foundation, the National Endowment for the Arts, the New Orleans Public Schools and the Council of the Arts for Children.

Materials prepared for the conference included an annotated "Bibliography for Arts in the Schools Seminar" prepared by the JDR 3rd Fund and the American Dance Guild. Conference themes included school/community partnerships, the arts and teacher preparation, the roles of state arts agencies and state education agencies in planning cooperative programs, ideal conditions for artist-in-schools programs, and strategies for integrating the arts into other disciplines. Final sessions dealing with reasonable expectations and criteria for arts in education programs as well as standards for program evaluation produced heated debate.

1974 COMPREHENSIVE ARTS PLANNING AND DEVELOPMENT PROJECT, KENNEDY CENTER (WASHINGTON, D.C.):   Sponsored by the National Council of State Supervisors of Music and Art and funded by the National Endowment for the Arts with assistance from the JDR 3rd Fund's Arts in Education Program, 165 arts educators, artists, community arts leaders, state arts council leaders, U.S.O.E. officials and officers from the major arts education organizations (MENC, NAEA, ATA, etc.) met for four days to develop plans for comprehensive arts programs.

Forty-two state departments of education including Hawaii and Alaska participated in a series of comprehensive arts planning and development workshops at the John F. Kennedy Center for the Performing Arts in

Washington, D.C. The agenda included general sessions, state team cluster work sessions, state team writing sessions and job-alike group meetings (state department-art and music, state arts councils and the Alliance for Arts Education, state education agencies, school districts, colleges and universities, community arts organizations). JDR 3rd Fund comprehensive planning documents were among the materials distributed.

At the final general session, a panel of distinguished experts addressed the question of "The National Implications of Comprehensive Arts Plans." Those presenting included Russell Getz, Junius Eddy, Kathryn Bloom, Stanley Madeja, John Mahlmann, Charles Mark and Forbes Rogers. Charles Fowler was responsible for the conference report.

The conference was a landmark in comprehensive planning and brought together a wide group of arts in education practitioners who were able to share ideas, approaches, practices and workable strategies. Specific state and local plans emerged for implementation. [Entry based on material supplied by Charles Fowler.]

1974 *HARVARD PROJECT ZERO: BASIC ABILITIES REQUIRED FOR UNDER-STANDING AND CREATION IN THE ARTS*: Published by Harvard University's Graduate School of Education. Final report by Nelson Goodman, David Perkins and Howard Gardner for the U.S. Office of Education, Project No. 9-0283. A long-range basic research program [continues to this day (1990)] to study the varieties and interaction of human abilities, the nature of the tasks involved in the several arts and ways to develop those abilities. Used psychological experimentation and clinical study of the brain as well as field work in schools to research the problems involved. [Citation from *Arts and the Schools*, J. Hausman, ed., McGraw-Hill, 1980.]

1974-1981 TITLE IV-C, 1974 EDUCATIONAL AMENDMENTS TO THE ELEMENTARY AND SECONDARY EDUCATION ACT (ESEA) OF 1965: In 1974, various funding authorizations (for science and related fields in the National Defense Education Act, in ESEA for library books and other instructional materials, guidance and counseling, strengthening state education agencies, health and nutrition for poor children, dropout prevention and innovation) were consolidated into Title IV. In other words, Part IV-C of the amendments was the successor to the original Title III in that it included funds for "innovation." The major (and significant) difference was that decision-making was decentralized and funds were distributed to states based on their numbers of school-age children. Innovative funds covered the whole spectrum of education, including the arts. Many arts in education projects received funding under this title nationwide.

MID-1970s COMPREHENSIVE EMPLOYMENT TRAINING ACT (CETA):
CETA funds from the Federal Department of Labor were made available to
address the issue of underemployment of the unskilled and untrained.
These funds were often used to support artist services and administrative
positions for arts in education programs nationwide.

1975 *EVALUATING THE ARTS IN EDUCATION: A RESPONSIVE APPROACH:*
Edited by Robert Stake, with assistance from the JDR 3rd Fund and published by Charles E. Merrill. This unique book proposes an alternative to
"preordinate" evaluation: using program activities, portrayals (case
studies), testimony and audience comprehension. Natural rather than formal communication methods are used, such as classroom observation and
documentation of issues. Suggestions are made to improve reliability of observation and opinion-gathering, and a twelve-point scheme (in the shape
of a clock) is offered for responsive evaluation. Other chapters deal with accountability, judging school as a place conducive to art, the consumer's
viewpoint and an extensive annotated bibliography. [Citation based on the
annotated bibliography in *Arts and the Schools*, J. Hausman, ed., McGraw-
Hill, 1980. See also earlier entry on AERA New Orleans and Chicago conferences.]

1975-80 THE AD HOC COALITION OF STATES FOR THE ARTS IN EDUCATION:
A national network of the JDR 3rd Fund, the purpose of the Ad Hoc Coalition of States for the Arts in Education was:

> To promote the arts as a means for improving the quality of educa-
> tion for all students by establishing a network of state education
> agencies working cooperatively to provide mutual assistance and
> support to local, state and national agencies in the planning and
> development of comprehensive arts in education programs.

Beginning with the Pennsylvania Department of Education in 1973, the
JDR 3rd Fund's Arts in Education Program developed cooperative working
relationships with nine state agencies and agreed to provide technical and
consulting services to each. Although a few grants were made for developmental purposes, most of the operating costs were born by the reallocation
of existing funds within the budgets of the education agencies. The nine
states included Arizona, California, Indiana, Massachusetts, Michigan, New
York, Oklahoma, Pennsylvania, Washington.

By the spring of 1975, a significant amount of experience had been accumulated, and at the invitation of Pennsylvania's Commissioner of Basic
Education, chief state school officers and their curriculum and instruction
teams attended a meeting in Chicago. The delegates agreed to form a net-

work, designated a steering committee of one representative from each state to carry on its work and asked the JDR 3rd Fund to coordinate its activities.

Comprehensive Arts Planning (The JDR 3rd Fund, October 1975) is a manual describing the process by which each of the nine states in the coalition arrived at its stage in the development of a design for including the arts in education in all of its schools. Additional information about the coalition can be found in *An Arts in Education Source Book: A View from the JDR 3rd Fund* . (JDR 3rd Fund, 1980; available from the American Council for the Arts.)

1975-1981 ARTS EDUCATION PROGRAM, (U.S. OFFICE OF EDUCATION, DEPARTMENT OF EDUCATION: The Arts Education Program began as a joint effort of the U.S.O.E. and the Kennedy Center's Alliance for Arts Education and was authorized by the Education Amendments (to the Elementary and Secondary Education Act) of 1974. The AEP served as grants and national program administrator and made over 350 planning, development and "saturation" grants to state education departments and city school districts. Planning and development grants originally ranged from $2,000 to $10,000. Saturation grants were a maximum of $50,000. Some salary and expense monies were used in 1975 to conduct regional "awareness" conferences and workshops at which Roger Stevens (then Kennedy Center chair), Forbes "Buck" Rogers (AAE's first director) and Sidney Marland (commissioner of education) assisted sites in planning for comprehensive arts educational programs.

The AEP promoted the idea nationally that the arts should be an integral part of elementary and secondary school programs. The JDR 3rd Fund and members of the Coalition of States and the League of Cities for the Arts in Education were asked to help develop the "regs" (federal guidelines and criteria) for AEP grants.

The 1979 Department of Health, Education and Welfare publication, *Try a New Face* (A Report on HEW-Supported Arts Projects in American Schools, Charles Gary, project coordinator), sums up the era of the Harold "Bud" Arberg stewardship and the AHP staff at the time. Among the contributors to the report were Junius Eddy, Charles Fowler and Harlan Hoffa.

1976 "THE ECOLOGY OF EDUCATION: THE ARTS": Special issue of *The National Elementary Principal*, vol. 55, no. 3, January/February. For the first time in its history—indeed, to my knowledge, in the history of any professional education association—the National Association of Elementary School Principals decided to devote an entire issue to the arts in education as part of a series intended to point up a new relationship between the school and society.

The editor of the magazine approached the JDR 3rd Fund's staff for assistance in the design and content of the issue. Articles by practicing professional artists and educators, several of whom were associated with Fund projects, discuss topics such as the status of the arts in education, comprehensive program planning, the arts in the curriculum, artists in educational settings and evaluation. In addition, there are brief reports on federal, state and local programs and practices, the Kathy Bloom/Jane Remer "Rationale for the Arts in Education" and an annotated bibliography.

1976-1980 THE LEAGUE OF CITIES FOR THE ARTS IN EDUCATION:
A network of the JDR 3rd Fund's Arts in Education Program, formed in April 1976, the mission of the League of Cities for the Arts in Education was to support and facilitate the efforts of its members as they seek to improve the effectiveness of education and the quality of life for all children and youth by incorporating all the arts in the teaching-learning process and to make results available to others.

In its Declaration of Intent, members of the League stated:

The following cities—Hartford, Little Rock, Minneapolis, New York, Seattle, and Winston-Salem, in collaboration with the JDR 3rd Fund— have begun to plan and implement comprehensive school-development programs in order to reach the common goal of 'all the arts for all the children.' These cities have found it useful to meet together regularly under the auspices of the Fund to share information, resources and effective strategies for planning and implementing comprehensive arts in general, or basic, education programs.

The League intends to enable participating school districts to:

— raise the level of awareness of schools and communities about the value and effectiveness of the arts as a vehicle for school change, tools for living and learning and areas of study in their own right

— demonstrate how the total climate, environment and organization of a school can be changed through the arts so that it becomes a place conducive to better teaching, learning and living

— make better use of the arts, artists and the arts process as one of several ways to achieve educational excellence in individual schools and throughout school systems

— avail themselves of existing human, material and financial resources to support program planning, development and operation

— take advantage of the leadership and other specialized knowledge and skills possessed by members of the League. As consultants and technical assistants to each other,

League members can help design and assess strategies for program planning and for staff, curriculum and school development

The League of Cities further intends to develop and disseminate a position paper defining what we mean by the arts in education. We also intend to produce a notebook describing and illustrating the components and strategies for the school and school district development process through the arts based on our experience. Further, the League will make available to its members and others pertinent documents and materials related to the arts in general, or basic, education and school development through the arts.

Additional information about the League can be found in *An Arts in Education Source Book: A View from the JDR 3rd Fund* (JDR 3rd Fund, 1980. Available from the American Council for the Arts) and in *Changing Schools Through the Arts: How To Build on the Power of An Idea* (ACA Books, 1990).

1977 *The Art Museum as Educator: A Collection of Studies as Guides to Practice and Policy* : Published by the University of California Press, Berkeley. An eighteen-month study conducted by Barbara Y. Newsom and Adele Z. Silver into visual arts education programs in schools, museums, universities and community centers. Part II develops comprehensive lists of programs for school children in museums and other sites; visual arts programs for high school students; and teacher training programs and classroom materials available. [Citation based on the annotated bibliography in *Arts and the Schools*, J. Hausman, ed., McGraw-Hill, 1980.]

1977 *Arts in Education Partners: Schools and Their Communities* : Edited by Nancy Schuker and published by JDR 3rd Fund, 1977. An illustrated handbook developed from the proceedings and conclusions of the task-oriented symposium in Oklahoma City in 1976 that was jointly sponsored by the Junior League of Oklahoma City, the Arts Council of Oklahoma City, Oklahoma City Schools, The Association of Junior Leagues and the JDR 3rd Fund. The conferees—all practicing professionals—addressed the question: How can a community and its school district cooperate to initiate, develop and maintain an arts in general education program?

The impetus for the venture came largely from the Oklahoma City Public Schools arts program "Opening Doors," which uses community cultural agencies as educational resources as well as projects in Seattle, Little Rock, Memphis and Birmingham. The conference report offers guidelines for working together in problem areas and for setting priorities; brings perspectives to goals of arts in education; cites case studies; presents the Bloom/Remer JDR 3rd Fund rationale for the arts in education and has a useful bibliography.

1977 *COMING TO OUR SENSES: THE SIGNIFICANCE OF THE ARTS FOR AMERICAN EDUCATION:* Originally published by McGraw-Hill and reprinted by ACA Books in 1987. This is the landmark report of the Arts, Education and Americans Panel. Sponsored by the American Council for the Arts in Education and chaired by David Rockefeller, Jr., a national panel of distinguished artists, educators and concerned citizens was convened to assess the state of the arts in education as it had developed since 1965.

The twenty-five distinguished members of the panel and a staff of professional researchers examined the role educational institutions, community agencies and the public at large can play when the arts become important to the education of all young people. The report made ninety-seven recommendations under fifteen general categories on how these and other groups can work cooperatively to integrate the arts in education. Three basic principles undergirded these recommendations:

1. The fundamental goals of American education can be realized only when the arts become central to the individual's learning experience, in or out of school and at every stage of life.
2. Educators at all levels must adopt the arts as a basic component of the curriculum deserving parity with all other elements.
3. School programs in the arts should draw heavily upon all available resources in the community: the artists, the materials, the media and the total environment—both natural and man-made.

The report communicated the panel's belief in the arts and their potency for improving the quality of schooling. Arts education is seen as learning *in* the arts, *about* the arts, and *through* the arts and as an essential part of "basic education," since the arts are basic to individual development. They are also seen as vehicles for extended learning through the integration of the arts with other studies. In addition to a valuable historical overview, the report discusses the role of federal legislation and provides statistical information concerning the status of aesthetic instruction.

Coming To Our Senses, probably more than any other single publication, has had a profound and often controversial impact on the field. It was republished by ACA in 1987 with a companion book by Charles Fowler, *Can We Rescue the Arts for America's Children?: Coming to Our Senses—10 Years Later.*

Following the initial publication of the report, David Rockefeller, Jr. established Arts, Education and Americans, Inc., a not-for-profit agency, to continue the panel's work. AEA published a series of ten monographs about planning, implementing and financing arts in education programs, began to assemble a national library and clearinghouse of information and continued to advocate for the idea. AEA has closed down but its library has been absorbed by the American Council for the Arts and is available to the public. [See entry for AEA below.]

1977-1978 *REPORT OF THE TASK FORCE ON THE EDUCATION, TRAINING AND DEVELOPMENT OF PROFESSIONAL ARTISTS AND ARTS EDUCATORS:* Prepared by Charles Fowler, staff writer and consultant for the National Council on the Arts, National Endowment for the Arts, December. In 1977, NEA Chair Nancy Hanks established a task force "to find ways to encourage ample opportunities for the training and development of professional artists and arts educators and through them extend knowledge and appreciation among all citizens." Livingston Biddle, the succeeding NEA chair, continued the work of the task force, a cooperative effort of several federal agencies including the Humanities Endowment and the Office of Education. Under Biddle, a panel of distinguished artists, educators, foundation representatives and government personnel assembled to define their tasks. They based their conclusions on an assessment of urgent needs as expressed by professionals and practitioners who were interviewed by panel subcommittees or presented papers and statements before the panel in open hearings.

Several of the premises on which the task force based its recommendations relate directly to the arts in education:

> To occupy a central place in American life, the arts must figure in education at all levels and in all forms. To develop a more discerning audience, all Americans must be continuously exposed to the best in the arts in a multiplicity of ways. Beginning in pre-school and elementary school, the arts must be seen as an essential rather than a peripheral part of the curriculum.

> The preparation of artists and arts educators is a common effort with common goals . . . . The artistic talent of teachers and the teaching potential of artists must be nurtured throughout their careers.

The task force made a series of recommendations regarding interagency cooperation and the appointment of a senior person in the Endowment who would be given responsibility for program development, liaison with the Office of Education and other agencies and overview Endowment efforts. [Historical note: in 1978, and for the first time in federal history, Commissioner of Education Ernest Boyer had appointed an arts education coordinator. Boyer's stay in Washington was relatively brief and the coordinator's position was not continued.] Another series of recommendations was made regarding the needy, the artistically gifted and talented, support for traditional and non-traditional training institutions and basic and applied research into the nature of learning in the arts and the processes for identifying and developing artistic talent.

For the purposes of this chronology, and in consonance with the position I take in this book, the most significant observations and recommendations fell in the category of "The Education, Training and Development of Arts Educators." I am tempted to cite, verbatim, pages 26 through 41 of the report, but will instead pick out only the highlights:

> TEACHERS: Exceptional teaching like exceptional artistry requires great talent. Such teaching talent must be cultivated through preparation and continuous development. This involves pre-service and in-service training and development *for four general kinds of arts educators: (1) arts specialists, (2) artists, (3) general classroom teachers, and (4) non-traditional teachers and aides.* [Emphasis mine.]

The report continues with an examination of the roles of each of the four arts educators and recommendations for action and sources for support. Under the heading of Institutions, the report focuses on the elementary and secondary schools, colleges and universities, and arts institutions and organizations outlining their responsibilities. Finally, Curricula and Research are addressed:

> Aesthetic education, composite programs embracing several arts and infusion of the arts into other subjects are significant recent additions to the curriculum. The interrelatedness of the arts should be appreciated . . .

> To assist artists and teachers, there must be continuous inquiry into the nature of learning in and through the arts. Curriculum development, evaluation, dissemination, and audience development deserve steady attention . . . . The results of this research should be made available through a clearinghouse to assist with arts education advocacy, planning and decisions at all levels and by all constituents . . .

It is interesting to note that it has taken twelve years for the important work of this task force to bear some fruition at the Endowment, if not across the board at the national level. The dream of broad-based interagency cooperation with strong and significant financial investment from the Department of Education has still not materialized. However, there is renewed support for the identification of the artistically gifted and talented in the new Javits legislation (see entry below), and the NEA's Arts in Education and Challenge Programs have taken meaningful steps in the direction of fulfilling the panel's recommendations in each of the categories listed above, notably in the creation of the National Arts Education Research Center. (See entry below.)

1977-MID-1980S ARTS, EDUCATION AND AMERICANS, INC. : Established by David Rockefeller, Jr. as a nonprofit advocacy organization following the publication of *Coming to Our Senses.* AEA was designed to help carry on the work started by the panel. As a private organization, it would seek to create links with the public sector and foster the development of a national program for strengthening the role of the arts in education at all levels from kindergarten through college. It would:

— organize half a dozen regional conferences, in which there were opportunities to discuss the report, to develop specific plans for local or regional implementation and to make recommendations toward the national plan

— maintain a Speakers Bureau that would include members of the current panel and others connected with the report

— establish a central communications center in the New York office, that would receive reactions to the report and answer questions about it

— promote distribution of the report, along with McGraw-Hill [the publisher]

— participate in developing a national plan for the arts in education

AEA published a series of ten monographs on arts in education programs and issues. [See also entry in the same year under *Coming to Our Senses* and under AEA, 1980-81, both below.]

1978 AMERICAN COUNCIL FOR THE ARTS NATIONAL CONFERENCE , LITTLE ROCK, ARKANSAS: "COMING TO OUR SENSES: THE ARTS AND EDUCATION" A three-day national conference took place in March focusing on the theme derived from the Arts, Education and Americans Panel report published a year earlier. The event represented the first time four leading organizations concerned with the place of the arts in American education collaborated on a major national meeting. Co-sponsors were: The Alliance for Arts Education (AAE); the American Council for the Arts (ACA); Arts, Education and Americans Inc. (AEA) and the Department of Arkansas Natural and Cultural Heritage. ACA President Michael Newton convened a planning committee of representatives from the sponsoring organizations and the JDR 3rd Fund. [The Fund underwrote travel and related costs for certain conference delegates.]

Approximately 300 delegates representing both arts and education interests met in small group sessions to discuss thirty major recommendations of the Rockefeller report. In addition, thirty-two model arts-in-education programs at the state and local levels were examined. [A third of the model programs were JDR 3rd Fund project sites or members of the Coalition of States and the League of Cities for the Arts in Education.]

Among the materials distributed for the conference were several thousand copies of JDR 3rd Fund documentary materials and a booklet prepared by AAE titled "Programs that Work" and organized according to the sessions scheduled for the conference. A report on the proceedings, "An Unprecedented Conference: Arts and Education at Little Rock," was written by the Pennsylvania Department of Education's Christine Crist and published by ACA.

The conference had three overall purposes: to foster the advocacy and growth of arts education; to assist current efforts for outlining local and state needs as perceived by those in the field of the arts and education; and to obtain grassroots reactions to *Coming to Our Senses*.

Ann Timberman, AAE assistant director and conference program coordinator, spelled out four goals: to assist states in developing and implementing comprehensive state plans for arts in education; to increase the involvement of state arts agencies and community arts councils in the arts programming activities in local schools; to arrive at a message to Washington about legislation and national policy for the arts in education based on discussion of selected recommendations from *Coming to Our Senses*; and to focus national attention on arts and education programs that had been developed in Arkansas.

Obstacles to these goals were identified (the same list as ten years before and fifteen years hence), as were strategies recommended for overcoming them. Junius Eddy spoke of a "Decade of Change" in a keynote address and outlined pertinent issues: strategies for increasing federal and state support; training and retraining of teachers; leadership development; the curriculum (disciplinary, interdisciplinary, for all children, the gifted); the tension between arts professionals and professional arts educators; research; the nature of the planning process.

1978 THE ARTS IN EDUCATION ACT OF 1978, AN AMENDMENT TO THE ELEMENTARY AND SECONDARY EDUCATION ACT (ESEA) OF 1965: The act authorized a program of federal grants and contracts to "encourage and assist state and local educational agencies and other public and private agencies, organizations and institutions to establish and conduct programs in which the arts are an integral part of elementary and secondary school curricula."

1980 - 1990

1980 *ARTS AND THE SCHOOLS*: Edited by Jerome J. Hausman, assisted by Joyce Wright and published by McGraw-Hill. A substudy of John Goodlad's *Study of Schooling in the United States*, this book focuses on the teaching of the arts in schools and was supported by grants from the JDR 3rd Fund and the Rockefeller Foundation. There are chapters by John Goodlad, Jack Morrison, Dennie Wolf and Howard Gardner, Nancy R. Smith, Bennett Reimer, Junius Eddy and Lillian Drag. Especially useful and illuminating are Reimer's chapter, "Designing Effective Arts Programs," and Goodlad's "Beyond the Rhetoric of Promise." The annotated bibliography is excellent.

1980 *AN ARTS IN EDUCATION SOURCE BOOK: A VIEW FROM THE JDR 3RD FUND:*   Written by Kathryn Bloom, Junius Eddy, Charles Fowler, Jane Remer, and Nancy Shuker, edited by Charles Fowler and published by the JDR 3rd Fund. This book provides a comprehensive review of the twelve-year history and major developmental activities of the Arts in Education Program. Part I includes the first six years during which the task and mission were defined and pilot projects were launched, illustrated by two case studies (Jefferson County, Colorado; University City, Missouri). Part II focuses on school districts and the formation of the League of Cities for the Arts in Education, with case studies on New York City and Winston-Salem. Part III concentrates on the formation of the Coalition of States for the Arts in Education with illustrative case studies on Oklahoma and Pennsylvania. The Appendix includes the Fund's grant history, a series of working papers, a program rationale with guidelines and criteria and a bibliography.

1980 UNITED STATES DEPARTMENT OF EDUCATION: Direct and indirect Department of Education support for the arts in education has diminished rapidly and dramatically during this decade and in the early eighties, especially as state funding was consolidated into block grants with no federal guidelines or priorities for the arts and no categorical funds earmarked for them. With the current trend to consolidation, the old and often successful practice of "piggybacking" arts in education proposals for funds earmarked for other purposes has also fallen into disuse.

In the 1960s, hundreds of millions of federal education funds were spent on the arts; in the 1970s, between twenty to thirty million. Recent DOE support has been confined to certain joint efforts with the National Endowment for the Arts (television project, National Research Center for the Arts); the Very Special Arts (formerly National Committee, Arts for the Handicapped) organization that develops programs that integrate the arts into the general education of children with disabilities and the lives of adults with disabilities; and the Kennedy Center's Education Program. Funds for these activities have stayed in the $3.5 million range. In 1988, the Jacob K. Javits Gifted and Talented Students Education Act of 1988 (Title IV, B of the Elementary and Secondary Education Act of 1965 as amended) authorized the Gifted and Talented Program. The program funds research, demonstration projects, training and similar activities to help build a nationwide capability in elementary and secondary schools to identify and meet the special educational needs of gifted and talented students. The definition of gifted and talented includes language such as "creative" and "artistic," and several arts education efforts have received multi-year grants averaging $250-300,000 per year.

1981 *CHANGING SCHOOLS THROUGH THE ARTS: THE POWER OF AN IDEA* **BY JANE REMER:** First edition published by McGraw-Hill. One of the few case studies available for increasing understanding of the processes of school improvement using the arts as both vehicle and content for systemic and system-wide change. The book examines the concept of school development through the arts and, defining the characteristics of the process, offers guidelines for the planning and installation of arts in general education (AGE) programs. In addition, it presents specific examples of schools and districts that are putting the idea into practice. It discusses the strategies of networking and collaboration, identifies the people and assesses the support systems needed for effectiveness—including leadership training, financing, staff and curriculum development, research, evaluation, documentation and dissemination. A unique and valuable feature of the book is a detailed account tracing the history of a successful program aimed at school change and development as it evolved over a ten-year period. It serves as a college and university text and a reference manual for the field.

1981 **THE EDUCATION CONSOLIDATION AND IMPROVEMENT ACT:** Part of the Omnibus Budget and Reconciliation Act of 1981, this act folded a number of small discretionary grants programs, including those authorized by the Arts and Education Act of 1978, into a basic block grants program giving the states full discretion on how funding should be reallocated. The legislation sounded the "death knell" of the era of federal education categorical and competitive funds for the arts and the arts in education.

1980-81 **ARTS, EDUCATION AND AMERICANS, INC.:** Published a Monograph Series of ten reports addressing pertinent arts in education issues and topics written by authorities and practitioners in the field. Topics included:

— *People and Places: Reaching Beyond the Schools*
by Judy Murphy
— *Your School District and the Arts: A Self-Assessment*
by Junius Eddy
— *Local School Boards and the Arts: A Call for Leadership*
by Richard Lacey
— *Ideas and Money for Expanding School Arts Programs*
by Diane Reische

— *Method and the Muse: Planning a School Arts Program*
    by Ralph Burgard
— *Developing Financial Resources for School Arts Programs*
    by Alan Green, Nancy M. Ambler
— *The Case for the Arts in Schools*
    by Junius Eddy
— *Arts in the Curriculum*
    by Ruth Weinstock
— *Creative Collaborations: Artists, Teachers, and Students*
    by Mary Bliss, Nancy Ambler, Barbara Strong
— *Arts in the Classroom: What One Elementary Teacher Can Do*
    by Nancy Ambler and Barbara Strong

1981-1984 ROCKEFELLER BROTHERS FUND AWARDS IN ARTS EDUCATION:
This national program was designed to recognize schools with excellent
and effective arts programs. Awards up to $10,000 were to be made to no
more than ten public elementary and secondary schools a year for a five-
year period. A total of thirty-three grants were made in twenty states.
Through the program, the Rockefeller Brothers Fund (RBF) hoped to enhance the quality and quantity of students' engagement with the arts by encouraging schools to sustain and expand outstanding programs and by
making those programs widely known. The program, originally envisioned
as a five-year effort, was discontinued after four years largely as a result of
a lack of qualified applicants.

Schools applying for the awards were self-selected; they were asked
to identify themselves in response to general mailings, posters and other
means for disseminating information about the program opportunity. Each
school was required to complete a comprehensive and detailed report
describing its arts in education efforts. RBF assembled a review committee
of authorities in the field and knowledgeable RBF staff, augmented occasionally by consultants. The committee reviewed school submissions,
visited certain schools for a day and made final decisions based on its consensus about what constitutes excellence in arts education.

The awards had both a negative and positive impact. In a few cases,
the recognition of one school and the attention showered on it prompted
local resentment and envy. In others, the award gave the school and its
hardworking practitioners visibility and legitimacy. In several, the money
was invested as an "endowment" fund, the proceeds of which were to be
used exclusively for arts education purposes.

Mid-way through the program, a one-week "retreat" was held for
thirty-one arts teachers chosen by the review committee from actual and
potential award sites. Guest speakers were invited and participants were

immersed in arts and social events. According to RBF's Benjamin Shute, "The event was designed to study the special qualities and talents of the group of singular arts teachers; promote exchange of insights; and help obtain broad perspectives on arts education." This event, among others, indicated, Shute believes, that "in most instances, although the awards program recognized schools, the excellence seemed to be attributable to outstanding teachers or groups of teachers, not programs or curricula per se." What an interesting opportunity that would have been for establishing another self-identified national network!

1982 THE GETTY CENTER FOR EDUCATION IN THE ARTS, JOHN PAUL GETTY TRUST, LOS ANGELES: "In the belief that the arts are fundamental to every child's educational development, the center is dedicated to contributing to the improvement of the quality and status of arts education in the nation's schools." (Newsletter, Summer 1988). The center's long-range mission is to enable students to acquire an informed understanding of art. The center's main strategy has been to focus its efforts on the development and implementation of an approach to teaching art they call discipline-based art education (DBAE). Its content consists of the four major disciplines of art: studio art, art history, art criticism and aesthetics. The approach has been validated for replication by the Department of Educations National Diffusion Network.

The center's activities are in five program areas: advocacy of DBAE and the value of art in education through national conferences, publications, research studies and reports, occasional papers, partnerships with other agencies; professional development of teachers; demonstration programs supported by grants to local school districts, universities, art museums etc.; DBAE theory development by the scholarly community; and curriculum development through the sponsoring of a Curriculum Development Institute that will produce prototype DBAE units for elementary, middle and secondary grades.

The center spends several million dollars a year in support of these nationwide activities. Staff participate in national conferences and other efforts related to the center's purpose. The Getty has served as a lightning rod and a catalyst for national attention to the arts in education. It has stimulated useful discussion and debate and has enlisted the services and support of several authorities in the field of art education who are contributing to the knowledge base for the arts. The center's presence on the national foundation scene, especially since the demise of the JDR 3rd Fund, the Arts, Education and Americans, Inc. and the RBF Awards program, serves an important function.

1982 NATIONAL OPERA INSTITUTE COLLOQUIUM, "LITTLE LEAGUES, SCIENCE CLUBS AND OPERA: THE ROLE OF PRODUCTION COMPANIES IN EDUCATION FOR LIFE," WASHINGTON, D.C.: This colloquium was one of a series of eight sponsored by the National Opera Institute, a service and grant-making organization for the field of music theater. The agenda focused on comprehensive planning for school-based arts in general education programs and examined the role of opera companies (and other community cultural resources) in the endeavor. A report on the event was written by Junius Eddy.

1982 *THE MUSIC CAME FROM DEEP INSIDE: A STORY OF ARTISTS AND SEVERELY HANDICAPPED CHILDREN* BY JUNIUS EDDY: Published by McGraw-Hill and revised and reissued in 1989 by Brookline Books, Cambridge, Mass. Originally an evaluation/documentation of the first (and so far, the only) project of any consequence to explore the role of the arts in meeting the social and educational needs of severely and profoundly handicapped youngsters. It was funded by the Department of Health, Education and Welfare through the National Committee, Arts for the Handicapped. The book describes the year-long venture and follows the work of professional artists with the children and teachers at three special education schools across the country. The revised version includes a new introduction on developments in this special aspect of arts with the disabled and a section updating what has happened to the people of the project (the artists, teachers and especially the children) ten years later.

1983 *A PLACE CALLED SCHOOL: PROSPECTS FOR THE FUTURE* BY JOHN I. GOODLAD: Published by McGraw-Hill. A restructuring of the nation's schools, by such means as smaller schools, education beginning at age four and the elimination of "tracking" students by ability are among recommendations in this final volume of a comprehensive study of American education by John Goodlad, former dean of the UCLA Graduate School of Education. Goodlad spent more than eight years on the study and concluded that problems facing education today are of such crippling proportions that the whole system is nearing collapse. He criticized the schools as "emotionally flat," with too much "teacher talk" and "no broad agreement" on what students should know. "Curriculum planning is a conceptual swamp," he observed. In his comments on the arts, Goodlad states:

> ... most arts classes in our sample ... did not convey the picture of individual expression and artistic creativity toward which one is led by the rhetoric of forward-looking practice in the field. A funny thing happens to the arts, too, on their way to the classroom .... There was a noticeable absence of emphasis on the arts as cultural expression and artifact .... The impression I get of the arts programs ... is

that they go little beyond coloring, polishing and playing . . . . What does not come through in our data is much if any indication that the arts were being perceived as central to personal satisfaction in a world rich in art forms, processes, and products. To grow up without the opportunity to develop such sophistication in arts appreciation is to grow up deprived.

Tracing Goodlad's comments on the state of the arts in American education over a thirty-year span, one is led to the inescapable conclusion that very little significant, systemic change has occurred.

1983 GETTY CENTER FOR EDUCATION IN THE ARTS - INSTITUTE FOR EDUCATORS ON THE VISUAL ARTS, LOS ANGELES: First institute held by the Getty consisting of a staff development program for elementary school teachers and principals, a seminar for school superintendents and a seminar for board of education members.

1983 *HIGH SCHOOL: A REPORT ON SECONDARY EDUCATION IN AMERICA*, BY ERNEST L. BOYER: Published by the Carnegie Foundation for the Advancement of Teaching. Boyer believes that the core of common learning should include the arts, foreign language and literature.

1983 *A NATION AT RISK*: A report from the National Commission on Excellence in Education, published by the U.S. Department of Education. Recommends that the arts be included in the curriculum during the "crucial" eight grades leading to high school. (The arts are not mentioned on the list for high school subjects.)

1984-1985 GOAL STATEMENTS FOR 1990 BY MENC, NAEA AND NASAA: During these two years, all three organizations adopted strong statements about the arts in education. MENC urged "that [by 1990], every student, K-12, have access to music instruction in school; that every high school require at least one Carnegie unit of credit in the arts for graduation; and that every college and university require at least one Carnegie unit of credit in the arts for admission."

The NAEA called for a sequential program of art instruction in all elementary and secondary schools; the completion of at least one year of credit in one of the fine arts as a requirement for high school graduation; and at least one year of credit in visual art as a requirement for admission to a college or university [also by 1990].

NASAA endorsed seven recommendations pertaining to arts education that were adopted in 1982 by the National Conference of State Legislatures.

1985 *ACADEMIC PREPARATION IN THE ARTS: TEACHING FOR TRANSITION FROM HIGH SCHOOL TO COLLEGE* : Written principally by consultants Dennie Palmer Wolf and Thomas Wolf for the Educational EQuality Project of College Entrance Examination Board in 1985, the "Red Book" holds that the arts are a basic subject. It maintains that course work in the arts, like courses in the other basic subjects, contributes to the development of the Basic Academic Competencies identified in the 1983 CEEB publication, *Academic Preparation For College: What Students Need to Know and Be Able to Do*, known as the "Green Book." According to the Wolfs:

> The Green Book outlined the knowledge and skills students need in order to have a fair chance at succeeding in college . . . . It sketched learning outcomes that could serve as goals for high school curricula in six Basic Academic Subjects: English, the arts, mathematics, science, social studies, and foreign languages . . . . It also identified six Basic Academic Competencies on which depend, and which are further developed by, work in these subjects. Those competencies are reading, writing, speaking and listening, mathematics, reasoning, and studying.

One of a series of six books compiled through the use of national advisory committees, the preface to the Red Book by the Arts Advisory Committee states "this is an idea book. It offers curricular ideas, teaching strategies, rationales for arts learning, and explorations of other, related issues." It also offers an important chapters on "Courses in the Arts" and "The Arts and the Basic Academic Competencies."

The final chapter, "Toward Further Discussion," is a gem. It raises and addresses timely and timeless issues: How to achieve excellence; moving beyond production and performance; which arts?; assessment; breadth versus depth; the arts and other subjects; the use of outside artists and arts organizations; seeing arts courses as basic; overcoming the vulnerability of arts programs.

The College Board is a nonprofit membership organization that provides tests and other educational services for students, schools and colleges.

1985 *ARTS, EDUCATION, AND THE STATES*, **COUNCIL OF CHIEF STATE SCHOOL OFFICERS, WASHINGTON, D.C.** : A survey of state arts education policies and practices, this publication is an important resource.

1985 ARTS PROPEL: A PROJECT OF HARVARD UNIVERSITY'S PROJECT ZERO: With funding from the Rockefeller Foundation, Project Zero launched the ambitious and promising Arts PROPEL Project in 1985. Designed as a collaborative effort between Educational Testing Service, the Pittsburgh Public Schools and Project Zero, its goal is to create fresh approaches to artistic learning and assessment in programs involving middle and senior high school students.

The project is particularly interested in the nature of creative thinking and how it can be taught to a full range of students. Project staff is also examining the opportunities and obstacles to aesthetic learning in three domains: music, imaginative writing and visual arts. They are monitoring a series of skills that underlie achievement in the arts: production, reflection and perception.

Arts PROPEL uses the concepts of projects, portfolios and interviews as assessment methodologies. It is working closely with a number of teachers and students of varying ability and is trying to help educators establish common standards and values for measuring artistic quality and achievement.

According to Project Director Dennie Palmer Wolf in the December/January 1988 issue of ASCD's *Educational Leadership* (page 29), "there are larger suggestions about why it's worth bothering with what is obviously an ambitious project. First, the term 'artwork' is no mistake. What these students show us is that, even during high school, the production or performance of a work involves not just interest, intuition or gift, but problem finding, pursuit, choice, and reflection. *In other words, involvement in the arts can constitute an extraordinarily worthwhile part of schooling.*" [Emphasis mine.]

1985 *BEYOND CREATING: THE PLACE FOR ART IN AMERICA'S SCHOOLS*: Published by the Getty Center for Education in the Arts, Los Angeles, California. The Center's first publication that presents the case for the Getty "discipline-based" approach to art education and its component parts: art history, art criticism, aesthetics and production. It contains important articles by Ernest Boyer and Elliot Eisner.

1985-PRESENT STATE ARTS AGENCY ARTS IN EDUCATION PROGRAMS: Also includes the Arts in Education Program of the New York State Council on the Arts. [See also 1960 entry, above]. Largely (but not exclusively) as a result of the shift in emphasis of funding priorities at the NEA's Arts in Education Program, a number of state arts agencies began to take important initiatives in comprehensive planning and implementation of curriculum-related program in the arts. An *Arts & Education Handbook: A Guide to Productive Collaborations*, Jonathan Katz, ed., was published in 1988 by the National Assembly of State Arts Agencies (of which Katz is executive director.) The contents include chapters titled "Opportunities for Cooperative Efforts" (Charles Fowler); "Working Effectively with Schools" (Terry

Baker); "How to Get the Most Out of State and Local Arts Agencies" (Robert Lynch, Anne Jennings and Katz); and a useful appendix of resources.

1986 *FIRST LESSONS: A REPORT ON ELEMENTARY EDUCATION IN AMERICA*: Written by William Bennett, Secretary of Education, and published by the United States Department of Education, Washington, D.C. Includes a statement about the importance of the arts in basic education.

1986 THE HOLMES GROUP: "TOMORROW'S TEACHERS": A report published in East Lansing, Michigan. The Holmes Group is a professional organization that consists of about one hundred major research universities across the country. Named after a dean at Harvard University, the group holds national and regional meetings addressing the question of teacher training. Issues include content, methodology, curriculum relevancy to school needs, minority and ethnic concerns including the recruitment of teachers. In the view of several arts educators, the Holmes Group represents an opportunity for arts professionals to enter into useful dialogue and perhaps affect national policy and practice.

According to Kathryn A. Martin and Jerrold Ross in the paper "Developing Professionals for Arts Education" that they presented at the arts education symposium co-sponsored by ACA and MENC in Interlochen in 1987:

> The Holmes Group is a consortium of approximately one hundred research universities. [It is investigating issues of teacher education and in-service training in the arts], and it endorses many of the provisions of the report of The Carnegie [Commission] Task Force on Teaching as a Profession . . . which proposes a National Board for Professional Teaching Standards and which would establish minimum standards for the certification of teachers. The Holmes Group approves of the National Board, the use of 'lead' or 'master' teachers, a specific degree (Master of Teaching) that lead teachers would have to hold, and continuing education offered by school districts or schools of education. The Holmes Group also supports a three-tiered system of teacher licensing, including master teachers.

Martin and Ross continue with a timely recommendation:

> . . . to capitalize on the 'reform' movements, this might be the time for arts education groups to insist on increasing the numbers of art, music, dance or theater teachers to support the notion of quality promulgated by Holmes and Carnegie and to ensure that arts educators be just as eligible as others for the upward professional mobility provided for in the recommendations for teacher licensing. (*Toward A New Era in Arts Education*, J. McLaughlin, ed., ACA Books, 1988)

In his introduction to *The Challenge to Reform Arts Education: What Role Can Research Play* (ACA Books, 1988), David Pankratz adds: "Arts educators have written responses to these ideas [Carnegie and Holmes] and formulated proposals that consider the unique requirements and conditions of teaching in the arts." Pankratz goes on to point out that various promising research opportunities exist for the field.

1986 "THE PHILADELPHIA RESOLUTION": This document was drafted by the Ad Hoc National Arts Education Working Group, a body of thirty-one organizations (arts education associations, arts advocacy groups, arts service organizations) originally co-convened by the American Council for the Arts and the Music Educators National Conference. [Author's note: The group formalized its activities in 1988 and is now known as the National Coalition for Education in the Arts.] The resolution expresses the group's consensus on common values in arts education and has since been ratified by their parent and other organizations.

The group also developed an eleven-point document titled "Concepts for Strengthening Arts Education in Schools" that puts forth specific guidelines for the improvement of arts education that can be applied to every aspect of the schooling process. It worked with former Secretary of Education William Bennett to ensure the mention of the arts in his 1986 report, *First Lessons*. Ideas are also included in the NEA report, *Toward Civilization*. Both the resolution and the concept paper were endorsed by the participants at the symposium at Interlochen in 1987.

1987 ARTS IN EDUCATION PROGRAM, NATIONAL ENDOWMENT FOR THE ARTS: (See NEA 1965 entry above.)

1987 THE NATIONAL EDUCATION RESEARCH CENTER AT NEW YORK UNIVERSITY AND THE UNIVERSITY OF ILLINOIS, URBANA: Established at two university sites by the NEA and the DOE to improve the kind and quality of arts education in American schools, this is the first significant research effort (other than the National Institute of Education's support for Gardner's work in Project Zero and the Aesthetic Education Program of CEMREL] to focus on theory and practice in the arts in education since the Office of Education's Arts and Humanities Program in the 1960s. [See entry above.] The center's purpose is to study effectiveness in teaching the arts, to reform arts curricula in the schools and ultimately to improve instruction in the arts. The center has been funded on a yearly basis for an initial period of three years ending in 1990.

1987 *TOWARD A NEW ERA IN ARTS EDUCATION*: Edited by John T. McLaughlin and published by the American Council for the Arts. This book is a report of the November 1987 symposium held at the Interlochen Center for the Arts in Michigan. The invitational conference was sponsored by ACA and the Music Educators National Conference, and several papers on important issues in the field were prepared for discussion by the assembled group. Participants called upon the schools "to provide arts education for all students every day and to recognize that the arts are essential to every child's education." Participants also recognized that to reach this goal, research is needed to improve the quality of teaching and learning in the arts. The conferees endorsed the Philadelphia Resolution and made a set of recommendations for strengthening arts education nationwide.

1988 *CAN WE RESCUE THE ARTS FOR AMERICA'S CHILDREN?: COMING TO OUR SENSES—10 YEARS LATER* BY CHARLES FOWLER   Published by ACA Books. Fowler's 1987 retrospective, assesses what has happened to the status of arts education and concludes that the arts are still in a perilous state in the nation's schools. Fowler believes we face a catastrophe in the making and that their "possible significance in the education of America's youth is largely unrecognized, often ignored, generally underrated. Access to this vast treasury of American and world culture is denied to many American children, with the result that their education is incomplete, their minds less enlightened, their lives less enlivened."

Fowler discusses such basic topics as whose culture shall be taught, who should teach the arts and just how academic the arts should become. Two final chapters discuss the changing landscape of arts education, including the expanding role of the NEA, the need for additional funding, the mechanisms for establishing policy and the necessity for advocacy.

1988 JACOB K. JAVITS GIFTED AND TALENTED STUDENTS EDUCATION ACT OF **1988:**   (Title IV, B of the Elementary and Secondary Education Act of 1965 as amended) This act authorized a new and more broadly-based gifted and talented program than had previously been enacted. The program funds research, demonstration projects, training and similar activities to help build a nationwide capability in elementary and secondary schools to identify and meet the special educational needs of gifted and talented students. The legislation is particularly concerned with the identification of those children (the poor, the handicapped, those without competency in the English language) who are normally overlooked as potential participants in G&T programs.

The definition of gifted and talented includes very specific language about the arts such as "creative" and "artistic," and several major arts education organizations, including New York City's ArtsConnection, have received multi-year grants averaging $250,000-300,000 per year for innovative projects in this area. [Historical note: Until the seventies, gifted and talented programs did not include the arts in the profile or definition of eligible children.]

1988 THE METROPOLITAN LIFE FOUNDATION, "PARTNERSHIPS: ARTS AND THE SCHOOLS":   This program has awarded a total of $75,000 for arts education programs that serve students, kindergarten through high school, in the public schools. Grants of up to $15,000 were given for the expansion of existing arts education programs or the planning or implementation of new programs and projects. The primary objectives of the Partnerships Program are to foster collaborations between public schools and local arts organizations that support the arts in the curriculum and that can be replicated in other locales. [Author's comment: The first edition of my book, *Changing Schools Through the Arts*, served as a primary resource for the development of the guidelines for this program.]

1988 NEA CHALLENGE III GRANT GUIDELINES: For the first time, the guidelines include major project support for the arts in education under the categories of "appreciation" and "access." [See entry under 1965, NEA above.]

1988 *TOWARD CIVILIZATION: A REPORT ON ARTS EDUCATION* :   The National Endowment for the Arts' report, mandated by Congress, characterizes the current state of arts education in the country. Recommendations, many of which are directed at federal, state and local education agencies, are made for policy in the areas of curriculum, assessment, research, teachers and leadership. Recommendations are also made concerning a future education agenda for the NEA. Arts included are: dance, creative writing, music, visual arts and design, architecture, theater and opera/musical theater, film, television, radio. This is only the second status report of its kind in over a hundred years. [Congress mandated the first study in 1879-1880.]

This report has had a powerful impact on the field and, in spite (or, as I believe, because) of inevitable controversy, provides an important road map for future action. Brent Wilson of Pennsylvania State University was the report's principal author and former Chairman Frank Hodsoll the final editor.

1989 CENTER FOR POLICY AND EVALUATION STUDIES IN THE ARTS, PENNSYLVANIA STATE UNIVERSITY: Under the direction of Dr. Brent Wilson, head of the art education program at Penn State's School of the Visual Arts, a group of faculty members and scholars will be developing information through research and analysis that will help legislators, educators and arts managers make policy decisions for the arts. The two associate directors are Dr. Harlan Hoffa, former associate dean of the College of Arts and Architecture, and Clyde McGeary of the Pennsylvania Department of Education.

The center's primary purpose will be to undertake a comprehensive, organized and cooperative analysis of arts and arts education policy and to evaluate programs related to the arts. The need for the center was determined by the recognition that many arts institutions are so concerned with survival that they rarely have time to pay attention to long-term policy considerations. Initial studies will focus on issues such as government funding policies, practices and beliefs of state arts consultants; politicians' priorities; the social, artistic and aesthetic consequences of funding decisions; arts advocacy efforts; audiences for the arts; arts in higher education; and testing policies and practices in arts education. Administrative support for the venture is provided by the University, and funding will be secured from external grants and contracts.

[Author's note: Wilson was the principal researcher and author of *Toward Civilization*, the National Endowment for the Arts' 1988 report to Congress; Hoffa is a past president of the National Art Education Association and was a member of Kathryn Bloom's Arts and Humanities Program staff at the U.S. Office of Education in the sixties; McGeary is division chief for the arts and sciences in the Pennsylvania Department of Education and was an important partner in several JDR 3rd Fund projects, including the Coalition of States for the Arts in Education. All three are professional art educators.]

1989 *THE CHALLENGE TO REFORM ARTS EDUCATION: WHAT ROLE CAN RESEARCH PLAY,* Edited by David B. Pankratz and Kevin Mulcahy, and published by ACA Books. An American Council for the Arts report on a seminar held in February 1988 at the University of the Arts in Philadelphia following the Interlochen symposium. The seminar examined past and current research in arts education as undertaken by the NEA, the Getty Center and the National Center for Research in Arts Education. The seminar also identified the need to broaden the scope of arts education research and for new sponsors in the field.

1990 *CHANGING SCHOOLS THROUGH THE ARTS: HOW TO BUILD ON THE POWER OF AN IDEA* **BY JANE REMER:** Published by ACA Books. Revised, updated and expanded—and with a slightly different subtitle—this book serves as a guide to strategic and comprehensive long-range planning for educational improvement with the arts as the catalysts and substance for change. New to this edition are guidelines and criteria for identifying a broad category of arts educators (including arts specialists, classroom teachers, artists and community volunteers) and defining their roles and responsibilities in instructional programs. There are also a series of new frameworks for school-based arts program planning and for artist-residency programs. The second edition includes, for the first time anywhere, an interpretive chronology of the major events in the arts in education field over the last forty or more years. [See also entry under 1981, above.]

B

State of the Field: A Summary Response to My Questionnaire

In July 1989, in anticipation of the revision of this book, I mailed approximately one hundred questionnaires to colleagues in the arts in education across the country. I wanted their perspectives on the events of the last decade and specific information about the status of League and other programs. I also wanted a reality check on my interpretation of the state of the field and my opinions on prospects for the future.

I received forty or more completed questionnaires, phone calls, letters, copies of speeches, publications and other written materials. They came from the then-chairman-elect to the NEA; executive directors of state arts agencies; heads of schools, and professors in colleges and universities; directors of arts organizations; commissioners of state education departments; school system administrators and principals; foundation executives; and independent arts and education authors, journalists and consultants. I also heard from at least one person in each of the League sites.

Here are the questions, my summary of the most frequent responses, and some representative quotes from the respondents.

I. IN THE DECADE BETWEEN 1980 AND 1990, WHAT DEVELOPMENTS IN THE ARTS IN EDUCATION DO YOU CONSIDER TO BE SIGNIFICANT AND WHY:

A. AT THE FEDERAL, STATE AND LOCAL GOVERNMENT LEVELS

B. AT THE NATIONAL AND/OR REGIONAL LEVEL (FOUNDATIONS, CORPORATIONS, ALLIANCES, CONSORTIA, ETC.)

C. AT THE LOCAL LEVEL (SCHOOLS, DISTRICTS, ARTS ORGANIZATIONS)

Significant developments include the Department of Education's "abdication of responsibility for arts education"; the NEA's shift of focus from artists in schools to the arts in the curriculum and support of strategies (such as teacher training) to get them there; NEA basic grants to state arts agencies to work with state education departments on comprehensive plans; the establishment of the Getty Center for Education in the Arts; state education and arts agency collaborations; national reports calling for more arts in the curriculum; state legislation for arts instructional requirements and arts teachers; and uneven implementation at the local district level.

> Governmental agencies have generally defaulted on school improve-
> ment during the eighties . . . the challenge was to tie the arts in educa-
> tion to the basic education movement . . . if principals can be
> reached, if parents see the need and if there are teachers trained and
> interested in the process, arts in education can become a reality . . .
> the problem is to find the key players at each local level to take the
> necessary steps.
>
> *(Paul Hoerlein, former Seattle*
> *School District Administrator,*
> *now at Seattle Pacific University)*

> From my perspective, the most significant (and lamentable) develop-
> ment in arts education on the part of governmental agencies during
> the 1980s is that nothing has happened. More importantly, much of
> the deeply rooted optimism of the prior two decades has slowly
> eroded as a result of that drift toward nothingness . . . The
> Washington scene now seems very much as I remember it before
> Kathy [Bloom] whipped the USOE [United States Office of Educa-
> tion] Arts and Humanities Program into shape a quarter century
> ago. In some ways the situation is now even more grim than it once
> had been because of the loss of arts supervisory positions in most
> cities and in many states and the resultant loss of both visibility and
> leadership.
>
> *(Harlan Hoffa, Associate Dean*
> *for Research and Graduate*
> *Studies, Pennsylvania State*
> *University)*

> One of the strongest influences on arts in education came from the
> initiative taken by the National Endowment for the Arts in estab-
> lishing the Arts in Basic Education Program. In the absence of
> strong arts education leadership from the Department of Education,
> the NEA has formed education partnerships through the research
> centers and at the state levels with state departments of education.
> This has occurred primarily in states that have received funding in
> this new NEA category; however, through this funding and through
> the report *Toward Civilization*, the Endowment has had an impact on
> the way arts education is viewed in this country.
>
> *(Bennett Tarleton, Executive*
> *Director, Tennessee Arts*
> *Commission)*

The circumstances requiring attention to the arts in schools probably are worse today than when you and your associates in the Fund were doing your good work. The governors' slogan, "Better Schools Mean Better Jobs," does not leave much room for the arts. I would say that the situation has declined, particularly in middle- to upper-middle-class school districts where parents are so geared to achievement test scores and getting their children into the best colleges and universities . . . In brief, there clearly is a need for your book.

(John Goodlad, Professor and Director, Center for Educational Renewal, University of Washington)

[The emergence of the Getty Center for Education in the Arts] "with its sole focus on improving the quality and status of arts education in America's schools . . . . The number of school districts across the country which are implementing a more comprehensive approach to teaching art, including schools in Oregon, California, Utah, Ohio, Tennessee, Nebraska, Minnesota, Florida and Texas, to name just a few.

(Leilani Lattin Duke, Director, Getty Center for Education in the Arts)

I think the focus on collaboration is essential, but it brings arts people into the larger context of defining education. Many don't yet realize this, but our current focus will lead us into larger educational arenas [and] even greater contact with educational "authority" will be needed . . . . It seems to me that foundations and corporations still have no idea what to do with AIE.

(Andrew Ackerman, Director, Arts in Education Program, New York State Council on the Arts)

Lack of arts specialists in the elementary schools [in many of our largest cities, where vast numbers of our future citizens are being denied adequate access to their cultural heritage.] in these systems means that elementary teachers, already overburdened, must take on responsibility for the arts, if any are to be taught. These teachers just might find that the AGE approach would help them provide a more effective educational program all around, but they simply do not have the knowledge and, therefore, the ability or incentive to put such an arts curriculum in place. AGE requires arts specialists, a fact that has escaped those who champion "discrete only" arts curricula. The resources of a strong arts program and the expertise of arts specialists are essential to an AGE program.

(Charles B. Fowler, Writer and Consultant in the arts)

There are more and more districts asking for help in re-educating teachers in the effective use of the arts, i.e., AGE. A goodly percentage of the people going through our AGE Masters Program at Seattle

Pacific University are becoming effective change agents in their various school districts . . . . Over ninety people have been through the program since it began in 1983, and they are recognized as a leadership cadre throughout the state . . . . We use your book, *Changing Schools Through the Arts* as a text . . . . It's clear, concise and based on actual experience.

(Ray Thompson, former Music and Performing Arts Supervisor in the Seattle Schools, currently Professor at Seattle Pacific University)

[Advances on the local level include:] focus on in-service teacher training, arts programs that are integrated into the curriculum, and meaningful and longlasting partnerships between arts organizations and schools . . . . Regarding foundation and corporate giving, it appears to have gotten much tougher to get their support. I think there are more arts in education organizations and less federal support.

(JoAnn Forman, Director of Education, Metropolitan Opera Guild)

II. **HAVE YOU (OR YOUR COLLEAGUES) HAD OCCASION TO USE *CHANGING SCHOOLS THROUGH THE ARTS* AS A TEXT, A PLANNING TOOL, A REFERENCE OR IN ANY OTHER MANNER? IF SO, PLEASE DESCRIBE THE CIRCUMSTANCES.**

Generally, yes—in schools, colleges, universities, arts agencies and organizations, foundations—with administrators, teachers, board members, interns, artists.

III. *FOR JDR 3RD FUND PROJECT AND NETWORK MEMBERS (AND OTHERS WHO WISH TO COMMENT):* **WHAT INFLUENCE OR IMPACT, IF ANY, BOTH DIRECT AND INDIRECT, DO YOU SEE IN THE FIELD AS A RESULT OF THE FUND'S ARTS IN EDUCATION PROGRAM AND THE WORK OF THE COALITION OF STATES AND THE LEAGUE OF CITIES? (E.G., LEGISLATION, RATIONALE, OTHER PROGRAMS, ATTITUDES, ADVOCACY, RESEARCH, EVALUATION, ETC.)**

The impact has been both direct and indirect; on the whole, it has been great, although the field has a short memory and prefers to "reinvent the wheel." "[It is] an old idea whose time comes again and again".

1. as a model for such collaboration

2. as an on-going and long-lived example of collaboration and program design in New York City. I don't know about other cities. I have often heard of the project in other cities, but usually referred to in the past tense.

3. Kathryn Bloom is revered and cited frequently as a trend-setter and guide. Some have suggested the need for a biography of her to inspire and inform a badly-informed new generation of teachers and administrators.

(Terry Baker, Professor, Hofstra University, New York)

In my opinion, the original concept of the JDR 3rd Arts in Education Program has now become a model for the State Basic Education Program. Dance, music and arts are now provided to the State of North Carolina as an integral part of the curriculum. Therefore, literally hundreds of artists are now in the school system in those areas . . . . Our ABC Program also had a great influence in the direction of the statewide program.

(C. Douglas Carter, recently-retired Assistant Superintendent, Winston-Salem/Forsyth County Schools)

One carry-over from the JDR 3rd days is that each Minneapolis school was encouraged (not required) to establish an arts committee to develop an annual arts plan. Local funds were to be assigned from the school budget (on a per-pupil basis) and these would be matched by district and foundation grant monies. A great incentive— which not all schools accessed!

(Elmer A. Koch, Jr., former Minneapolis School District Administrator and currently Director of General Studies, Torah Academy, St. Louis Park, Minnesota)

I think the influence has been profound, all things considered; if the various grants didn't ever really *prove* anything, the consciousness has been effectively raised nationally, I think—especially attitudinally. The phrase "arts *in* education," for example, is omnipresent these days — and yet most of the new folks have no idea about its derivation (Kathy Bloom coined it at the USOE as shorthand for "arts in the general education of all children"); I think, too, that probably its greatest legacies are in the "coalition-building" strategies it fostered early on at the state and big-city levels—this and the concept of "comprehensive planning" for arts education at all levels; this last has even worked its way into some state and national legislation and into the programs fostered by national organizations. JDR 3rd wasn't the *only* place where theses strategies could be found (nor were its staff members the *only* advocates. . .) but it always managed to keep those ideas relatively central to its overall mission. The loss of the fund and Kathy Bloom's retirement from the scene, were crucial blows to the movement's continuing momentum.

(Junius Eddy, Author and
Consultant, Rhode Island)

[AGE] continues as an example.

(Jack Morrison, Author,
Consultant and former Associate
Director, JDR 3rd Fund)

For League members, I included an addendum to the questionnaire, the answers to which I will also summarize:

1. **DOES THE AGE (OR YOUR VERSION OF IT) PROGRAM AND NETWORK STILL EXIST, AND IF SO, IN WHAT FORM, WITH WHAT PURPOSE, WITH HOW MANY MEMBERS ETC.?**

With the exception of Seattle and New York City, it no longer really exists. Where it does exist, it does so in bits and pieces, or in a severely altered form. As of this writing, both the Seattle and New York programs are in jeopardy. Here is Ray Thompson's (Seattle) response:

The AGE program, as it existed during the League years, does not exist. The entire curriculum Department was disbanded in 1982 and has only gradually been restored. Judith Meltzer [former JDR 3rd administrative fellow] is virtually all that is left. [She survived yet another budget cut this summer when the arts community clamored for her reinstatement and warned the school district that, without her presence on staff, they would not continue their arts grants for the schools.] However, her knowledge of the League structure and the functions of a good AGE program have helped her to nourish those schools that continue to function, and she has done a superb job of bringing the arts community into the schools on a regular basis. She has done about all one person could do under the circumstances. From the mid-sixties to the present, the student population in the Seattle schools fell from 99,000 to 41,000, almost a 60 percent drop. In the past decade, there have been five superintendents and who knows how many assistant and associate superintendents. . . . What exists now are a few committed principals whom Judith tries to assist and a very close working relationship with the local arts commission and the general arts community.

2. **IF THE PROGRAM NO LONGER EXISTS OR HAS CHANGED DRAMATICALLY IN FORM, FOCUS AND MEMBERSHIP, PLEASE DESCRIBE THE CIRCUMSTANCES THAT CONTRIBUTED TO THE CHANGE.**

The primary reason given was loss of education and outside funding attributed to the loss of commitment and leadership from local decisionmakers. Other factors were turnover in school board membership, district superintendents, school principal leadership and the teaching staff—all or most of whom were replaced by people who did not know or care about the educational value of the project and who had little sympathy for the arts. In addition, initial sponsors such as community organizations (Junior Leagues, foundations) quickly or gradually withdrew their support and commitment.

Several people with whom I spoke preferred not to be quoted directly. They told me that without the League of Cities network as a support system or the JDR 3rd Fund "forces" to respond to frantic rescue calls, help shore up the faltering morale and commitment of beleaguered administrators and rekindle dwindling community enthusiasm, the program just could not survive the competition for scarce education resources and general apathy towards the arts.

3. ARE YOU CURRENTLY ACTIVE IN THE ARTS, IN EDUCATION, IN THE ARTS IN EDUCATION? WHETHER YES OR NO, PLEASE EXPLAIN.

Just about everyone is still involved in education or the discrete arts disciplines in one way or another, but only a few are still active in the arts in education.

New York State Council on the Arts
Arts in Education Guidelines[1]

The Arts in Education Program is a collaboration between the Council and the State Education Department (SED), with the Council as the administering agency.

The Council and SED believe that the arts are essential to every child's education and that education is a primary responsibility of the State's cultural institutions. Toward this end, the Council encourages cultural institutions and schools to form partnerships to create programs which improve or enhance the study of the arts and environmental science (hereafter referred to collectively as the arts), and other curriculum areas through the arts, for the students of New York State. The intent of the program is to involve teachers, artists and arts professionals in collaborative efforts which will result in direct, active arts experiences for children.

Because children learn more about the creation and interpretation of art as a result of long-term instruction, the Council will support projects which provide *in-depth* experience for students in the process of creating and/or understanding art. Proposed activities must be conceived, planned and implemented by teachers, artists and arts professionals working together to utilize the resources of a cultural organization(s) within the context of a school or district's curriculum. Projects must be designed to supplement and not supplant existing school programs.

Because collaboration is integral to this process, cultural organizations are required to apply with an educational partner. Educational partners may be an individual school, group of schools, a district, a BOCES or urban Board of Education. In most cases, cultural institutions and educational partners are required to fill out separate program descriptions for the same project. The educational partner should describe how the proposed program fits into specific areas of school instruction and should identify learner outcomes for students. This should complement the description by the cultural institution, which should describe the overall goals and activities of the project and how the program will utilize the resources of the applying cultural organization. Proposals should clearly describe how the proposed

---

[1] From the New York State Council on the Arts' Program Guidelines.

project will achieve results which would be difficult for the school or district to accomplish without collaboration with a cultural organization.

Projects may focus on an art form as a discipline or the infusion of the arts into other academic disciplines. In general, greater emphasis will be placed on the quality of the *process* through which children learn in and through the arts than the quality of a finished *product*, such as performance or exhibition.

The long-range goal of the AIE program is to enable schools and cultural organizations to define and implement comprehensive courses of study in the arts for children from pre-K through grade 12. Thus, the Council will give priority to those projects which are developed within a school or district's arts or arts in education plan and which are designed as part of a plan which extends over many grade levels.

Project components may include, but are not limited to, planning meetings, artists-in-residence, study trips to cultural institutions, teacher in-service seminars or workshops, the development of curriculum materials, the use of consultants, performances and artist training.

Applications in all categories should have:

— clearly articulated *goals*;

— specific *learner outcomes* and educational *needs* to be met;

— evidence of collaborative *planning*;

— specific *activities* planned for students;

— precise information about the *number of children served, grade levels and subject areas*;

— evaluation plans which should identify the issues and broad questions to be addressed and should reflect and analysis of how effective the program was in meeting the stated goals;

— resumes for key personnel and outlines for publications, curricula or videotapes *must* be provided. Outlines may be submitted as an appendix to the application on 8 1/2" x 14" paper.

Eligibility

Nonprofit cultural and environmental organizations based in New York State may submit applications. Under State law, public schools and BOCES may not apply directly to the Council.

Programs in all arts disciplines are encouraged: architecture and design, audio and video, computer arts, dance, film, folk art, literature, music, radio, television, theatre, and visual art. Environmental science and local history projects which utilize the resources of arboreta, historical societies, nature centers and zoos are also eligible; interdisciplinary projects are encouraged. Programs for students in grades pre-kindergarten through 12th grade are eligible for funding. Programs for children during non-school hours are not eligible for AIE funding. Applicants interested in family, intergenerational or after-school programs should refer to the guidelines of other Council programs.

Evaluative Criteria

Applications in all categories are evaluated according to the following criteria: (Note that these criteria are not in priority order.)

— artistic quality, expertise or background of the proposed artists and professionals;

— clarity and appropriateness of the proposed goals and the specific activities and learner outcomes associated with each goal;

— commitment of the educational partner, as evidenced by cash contributions toward the project and the commitment of staff time to the collaborative process;

— cost effectiveness of the program;

— creative use of the resources of cultural organizations with special emphasis on the quality and quantity of contact time between students and artists or students and original works of art;

— depth of the proposed activities, as evidenced by the number of contact hours between artists or arts professionals and students;

— how well the program strengthens existing arts syllabi or curricula or an existing arts education plan; quality of the collaboration between the cultural organization and educational partners, as evidenced by the depth of planning and the clarity of the roles for each of the participating professionals; and

— degree to which the proposed program fits into a specific curriculum area and the overall instructional plan of a school or district. Applications which contain specific descriptions of how the proposed program fits into a multi-year sequence of arts or non-arts instruction will be given special consideration.

Program Priorities

The Council will give special consideration to those applications which:

— address the needs of students in rural areas of the State;

— develop programs in new or emerging art forms, such as media arts, contemporary American music, dance and theatre, or in areas traditionally undeveloped in the schools, such as fold arts and architecture and design;

— develop programs relating to the arts and culture of individuals who are Black, Hispanic, Asian and Native American. Priority will be given to those programs which utilize artists or professionals with expertise in the above fields who are representatives of the culture being studied.

Number of Requests per Applicant

Applicants may submit up to two requests to the AIE program, except as noted below. Requests may be in two separate categories or both within the Implementation, Planning or Special Projects categories. A third request may be submitted in one of the two incentive categories: Evaluation and Research or Long-Term

Projects. General Operating Support applicants may submit a second request for a new project (in Planning, Implementation or Special Projects) or in one of the Incentive Categories.

Funding Restrictions

The Arts in Education Program will not fund:

— arts exposure programs or programs which are solely assembly programs or one-time visits or performances;

— programs which do not take place during the school day;

— programs which appear to substitute for or replace arts specialists;

— more than 50% of the direct expenses of individual projects; and

— programs which are exclusively teacher training.

FUNDING CATEGORIES

Institutional Support

GENERAL OPERATING SUPPORT

It is now Council policy that any organization that is eligible for General operating Support must apply for it and must request three-year multi-year support. Organizations that have not previously received General Operating Support MUST contact the Arts in Education Program staff BEFORE applying for such funds. Refer to page 8 the Introduction for further information about multi-year support. Requests will usually be considered at the June Council meeting.

To be eligible for funding in this category and organization must:

— have arts in education as its primary mission;

— be funded by the AIE program for three consecutive years; and

— have at least one full-time paid staff member.

Organizations will be evaluated according to the specific criteria used for all AIE applicants as stated above. In general, this means that organizations whose primary mission is arts in education, but who do not conduct in-depth collaborative programs as a major portion of their activities will not be likely GOS candidates.

General Operating Support applicants may submit a request in another category if the proposed project is for new programming or a limited special project. GOS organizations are encouraged to apply in one of the two incentive categories.

Program Support

PLANNING

Multi-year support is not available in this category, although applicants may receive single year support for more than one year. Requests will usually be considered at the October Council meeting.

Planning grants enable cultural organizations and their educational partners to assess needs, identify resources, develop an ongoing planning process among educators, artists and arts professionals, explore program opportunities and pilot program ideas.

Planning support may be used to:

— begin an arts in education program within a cultural organization;

— develop a new collaborative project with a different educational partner, a different grade level, or a different subject;

— assess the activities of a cultural organization in light of their overall institutional mandate and local school needs; or

— conduct regional planning activities—even if they are ongoing—which are coordinated by a cultural organization.

Eligible planning expenses include consultants' fees, artists' fees, travel expenses, expenses associated with a pilot project and administrative costs.

IMPLEMENTATION

Support in this category is available for one, two or three years. Applicants who have received prior Implementation grants must apply for multi-year support. Requests will usually be considered at the June and August Council meetings.

The intent of this category is to support programs where students are actively involved in the creation and\or interpretation of art or the study of art in the context of another discipline. Projects submitted in this category must have explicit goals, activities and learner outcomes and a clear definition of the specific roles of teachers, arts specialists, artists and arts professionals. Projects should be collaboratively planned, address specific needs within a curriculum area in a school or district and utilize the resources of a cultural institution and artists in creative ways. It is expected that programs will be consonant with State syllabi and local curricula and will involve arts specialists and district arts coordinators.

Projects may include the commissioning of new works of art by an artist or by an artist working with children. In either case, the applicant must demonstrate how the commissioned work will be used within an AIE collaborative project.

SPECIAL PROJECTS

Requests will usually be considered at the October Council meeting.

This category is intended for four types of projects:

— programs which take place in non-traditional settings, such as hospitals or prisons, which, if on-going, must be for two or three years of support;

— services to the field, such as conferences, publications, and films, which benefit AIE practitioners;

— training for artists to work in school settings; and

— projects which do not meet the requirements of other categories.

In general, proposals in this category will be reviewed according to the general AIE criteria and those in the Implementation category.

Incentive Programs

The following two Incentive categories target specific areas of concern for the Council and the State Education Department. The Council expects to support relatively few projects in each category at significant funding levels for an extended period of time. Initial requests must be for only one year, subsequent requests must be for three years of funding; with the Council reserving the right to award one, two, or three years of support.

Applicant in Incentive categories should contact AIE staff before completing an application. Both categories will be considered at the October or December Council meetings.

EVALUATION/RESEARCH

Through this category, the Council intends to:

— support projects which contribute to a more sophisticated body of research about how children learn in and through the arts; and

— support projects which evaluate the effectiveness of specific arts in education programs.

In general, it is up to the applicant to determine the most effective and appropriate research design or evaluation tool for their project. It is expected that all projects will yield results which lead to a better understanding of learning in the arts and which will lead to more reflective practitioners in the field. Applicants to this category may apply to *plan* or to *implement* a research or evaluation study.

Requests must include resumes of key researchers and evaluators and a detailed study design or evaluation tool. This must include a clear definition of what is to be evaluated or a clear statement of the goals of the research. Detailed activities must be articulated, including the names of the personnel responsible for each phase or component. Applications must also include plans for publication and dissemination.

Priority will be given to longitudinal studies which follow the progress of children over a number of years. It is expected that most applications will represent a collaborative effort by a cultural organization, a school or district and a college or university.

LONG-TERM PROJECTS

During the past five years, a great number of successful collaborative programs have been established in New York. Frequently, these programs are endeavors between one cultural organization and a handful of schools, and focus on a particular grade or subject. This has resulted in a strong foundation of programs to supplement and expand the ongoing instruction offered by teachers and arts specialists.

At this point in time, few schools or districts have integrated individual programs into a comprehensive educational place for the arts. Thus, many individual programs operate in isolation within a school or district and are usually not planned as part of a multi-grade sequence. Such isolation also hinders efforts by cultural organizations to define when their resources can be used most effectively.

The Council and State Education Department believe that schools must move toward more comprehensive planning in the arts and that cultural organizations can play a pivotal role in such planning. Through this category, the Council will support projects which develop specific goals and activities in the arts for a minimum of three grade levels in a school district. Projects must demonstrate how arts education builds from grade to grade and must articulate the learner outcomes for each grade and the overall program.

Because several organizations may work with the same school or district, a consortium or organizations may be formed, with one organization as the formal applicant on behalf of all the participants. If a consortium is formed, the role of each organization in the consortium must be clearly stated. The consortium must demonstrate how each organization's programs complement one another to form a coherent plan for a sequential long-term project.

Applicants may request support for a year of *planning* or to *implement* a long-term project. All first time applicants to this category must apply for single-year support, for either planning or implementation. Following one year of funding for implementing a long-term project, applicants must apply for multi-year support.

Strong requests will include:

— detailed sequential goals and activities for each grade;

— a programmatic and financial commitment by the educational partner to at least a three grade program;

— a commitment by cultural organizations to rethink and, in some cases, revamp educational programs in light of programs offered by other cultural organizations and the school's comprehensive arts education plan.

Proposed programs may focus on the teaching of an arts discipline, the infusion of the arts into other academic disciplines or a combination of the two. In all cases, the primary objective is to set forth a course of study for children which will make the arts a basic curriculum area and not an isolated unit of study. Projects which are developed within the framework of statewide initiatives, such as Community Schools, or local initiatives, such as the Corridor Program in New York City, are encouraged.

SPECIAL APPLICATION INSTRUCTIONS

Generally, cultural organizations are required to apply with an educational partner for all funding categories in AIE. All applicants must complete the entire Council Application Form. In addition, the educational partner must complete a separate Project Support Insert B (project description and budget). Together, the applicant and the educational partner answer the 11 questions which comprise the application supplement. In cases where there are more than two educational partners, the applicant should contact the staff for guidance. The applicant is responsible for assembling all or the requested materials from the educational partners and submitting the complete application on or before March 1.

Project Budget

The cultural partner (applicant) is required to submit a complete and detailed Project Budget for each request. This budget will include an itemization of the income and expenses of both the cultural and the educational partner(s).

The project budget should reflect the financial commitment of both partners to the project by:

— demonstrating that 50% of the project expenses will be met by unearned and earned revenues;

— detailing the cash contributions of the educational partner(s) and the cultural organization.

Each educational partner must submit a separate budget indicating the source of its cash contribution, expenses, and in-kind contributions. Strong applications will include a significant cash contribution by each educational partner. Only funds committed for new expenses are considered income; reallocations of existing budget lines are considered in-kind. As a general guideline, each educational partner should demonstrate a cash financial commitment of at least 15% of total project expenses.

The extent and nature of the educational partner's commitment may vary based on the number of educational partners and the specific project. Contact AIE staff in cases where the 15% guideline may be inappropriate.

INCOME ON THE PROJECT BUDGET   Indicate each funding source and the amount on a separate line so that each partner's sources are clearly identified. Do not include in-kind contributions.

EXPENSES ON THE PROJECT BUDGET   Each line must be fully itemized. For example, specify under artist's fees the number of artists and the rate of payment. Also, itemize specific costs of all materials to be used. Allowable costs include but are not limited to: artistic and technical fees; program and administrative salaries and appropriate fringe benefits (for cultural partners only); supplies and materials; justifiable equipment needs; travel and transportation costs (including costs for busing of students to and from cultural activities); space or equipment rental fees; outside professional services; building maintenance or service costs for the cultural partner; and release time for teachers. Do not include in-kind expenses.

NYSCA REQUEST   This amount may be up to 50% of the total project expenses. Requests may not exceed the difference between the project expenses and income.

IN-KIND CONTRIBUTIONS ON THE PROJECT BUDGET   In-kind contributions are donated services, materials, or facilities. In-kind contributions are not considered to be part of the project expenses and income and cannot be part of the project request. The total of the estimated costs of the in-kind contributions from all partners should appear at the bottom of the project budget, after the request amount. Although in-kind contributions are not part of the project budget, and are not a requirement, the Council considers in-kind contributions a further demonstration of each partner's commitment to the project.

The Application Supplement

All applicants are required to complete an application supplement for each request, regardless of the category. The supplement is to be submitted as part of the application on or before March 1.

The Council DOES NOT provide a special form for the supplement. Every applicant and educational partner should complete the supplement together by responding to all eleven questions on 8 1/2" x 14" paper, typed single-spaced on one side. No more than three separate sheets of paper may be used.

In cases where there are more than one educational partner for one request, the applicant should contact the staff for guidance on how to complete the supplement.

1. Provide the name, address, and telephone number of the educational partner along with the *signatures* of the superintendent, principal and project director for the educational partner. Applications without signatures will be considered incomplete.

2. Indicate whether the educational partner is a school, district, BOCES, local board of education, or other type of educational partner.

3. Provide the B.E.D.S. (Basic Education Data System) number as assigned by the State Education Department.

4. Provide the number of students at each grade level who will be served directly and the number of teachers who will participate.

5. Provide the number of elementary, junior high and high schools which will be directly served by this project.

6. Indicate how many full-time and part-time art, music, dance or theatre teachers work in the district or school. Please indicate number in each discipline. How many will be involved in this project?

7. Describe the ongoing arts instruction provided by the school for the students involved in this project.

8. Does the district have an arts in education coordinator and a formal arts in education plan and/or advocacy program? If yes, identify the coordinator and attach appropriate materials.

9. Describe the relevant skills and experience that make the project team (artists, teachers, administrators, consultants, professionals) appropriate for this project. Specify responsibilities for each member of your team.

10. Work Plan: This is intended to be an outline of the special activities which will be undertaken during the grant period. Because it is a part of the application which the panel evaluates carefully, it should include as much detail as possible about activities children and professionals will be engaged in during the project.

11. Describe your plans for evaluation. Projects may be evaluated with regard to student achievement, use of cultural resources in an effective manner, appropriateness of a project to a school or district's overall arts in education plan or as part of a specific curriculum. In all cases, the evaluation should be directly tied to the goals of the project and should detail the issues and broad questions to be addressed.

APPLICATION ASSISTANCE

If you have any questions concerning your request to the Arts in Education program or need assistance in filling out the application form, call the Arts in Education Program at (212) 614-2975.

Bibliography

The Arts, Education and Americans Panel. *Coming to Our Senses: The Significance of the Arts for American Education*. New York: ACA Books, 1988. (Originally published, New York: McGraw-Hill, 1977.)

The Association for Supervision and Curriculum Development. "A New Design for Education in the Arts" in *Educational Leadership: Journal of the Association for Supervision and Curriculum Development*, Vol. 45, No. 4, December 1987/January 1988.

Baumol, William J., and William G. Bowen. *Performing Arts: The Economic Dilemma*. New York: The Twentieth Century Fund, 1966.

Bentzen, Mary M. *Changing Schools: The Magic Feather Principle*. IDEA Reports on Schooling, a Charles F. Kettering Foundation Program. New York: McGraw-Hill, 1974.

Bloom, Kathryn. *The Arts in Education Program: Progress and Prospects*. New York: The JDR 3rd Fund, 1976.

———. *Arts Organizations and Their Services to Schools: Patrons or Partners?* New York: The JDR 3rd Fund, 1974.

———, and Jane Remer. *A Rationale for the Arts in Education*. New York: The JDR 3rd Fund, 1975.

———, and Jane Remer. *Community Arts Programs and Educational Effectiveness in the Schools*. New York: The JDR 3rd Fund, 1975.

———, Junius Eddy, Charles Fowler, Jane Remer, and Nancy Shucker. *An Arts in Education Source Book: A View from the JDR 3rd Fund*, ed. Charles B. Fowler. New York: The JDR 3rd Fund, 1980. (Distributed by the American Council for the Arts, New York.)

Chapman, Laura H. *Instant Art, Instant Culture: The Unspoken Policy for American Schools*. New York: Teachers College Press, 1982.

———. *Approaches to Art in Education*. New York: Harcourt Brace Jovanovich, 1978.

The College Board. *Academic Preparation For College: What Students Need to Know and Be Able to Do*. New York: The College Board, 1983. (known as "The Green Book")

Dewey, John. *Art as Experience*. New York: Capricorn Books, 1958. (First published in 1934.)

Dobbs, Stephen M., ed. *Arts Education and Back to Basics*. Reston, Va.: National Art Education Association Publications, 1979.

Eddy, Junius. "A Review of Projects in the Arts Supported by ESEA's Title III," and "A Review of Federal Programs Supporting the Arts in Education." New York: The Ford Foundation, 1970.

————. *A Report on the Seattle School System's Arts for Learning Project*. Seattle: Seattle Public Schools, 1978.

————. *Arts Education 1977—In Prose and Print: An Overview of Nine Significant Publications Affecting the Arts in American Education*. Washington, D.C.: The Arts and Humanities Program, Office of Education, U.S. Department of Health, Education and Welfare, Publication 260-934/2044, 1978.

————. *The Music Came From Deep Inside: A Story of Artists and Severely Handicapped Children*. Cambridge, Ma.: Brookline Books, 1989. (First edition, New York: McGraw-Hill, 1982.)

————. "Toward Coordinated Federal Policies for Support of Arts Education: A Position Paper of the Alliance for Arts Education." Washington, D.C.: The Alliance for Arts Education, 1977.

————. *The Upsidedown Curriculum*. Washington, D.C.: Alliance for Arts Education (J.F. Kennedy Center for the Performing Arts), 1981. (Revised reprint of the Ford Foundation booklet, *Cultural Affairs*, Summer 1970.)

Eisner, Elliot W. *Cognition and Curriculum: Deciding What to Teach*. New York: Longman, 1982.

————. "Can Educational Research Inform Educational Practice?" in *The Art of Educational Evaluation: A Personal View*. London: The Falmer Press, 1985.

Fowler, Charles B. *The Arts Process in Basic Education*. Harrisburg, Pa.: Pennsylvania Department of Education, 1973.

————. *Can We Rescue the Arts for America's Children: Coming to Our Senses—10 Years Later*. New York: ACA Books, 1988.

————. *Dance as Education*. Washington, D.C.: The National Dance Association, an Association of the American Alliance for Health, Physical Education and Recreation, 1977.

Gardner, Howard. *Art, Mind, and Brain*. New York: Basic Books, 1982.

————. *The Arts and Human Development: A Psychological Study of the Artistic Process*. New York: Wiley, 1973.

———— . *Frames of Mind: The Theory of Multiple Intelligences*. New York: Basic Books, 1983.

Gary, Charles L., ed. *Try a New Face*. Washington, D.C.: Office of Education, U.S. Department of Health, Education, and Welfare Publication (OE) 79-7305, 1979.

Getty Center for Education in the Arts. *Beyond Creating: The Place for Art in America's Schools*. Los Angeles: Getty Center for Education in the Arts, 1985.

Goodlad, John. *A Place Called School: Prospects for the Future*. Final report of the Study of Schooling in the United States. IDEA Reports on Schooling, a Charles F. Kettering Foundation Program. New York: McGraw-Hill, 1984.

———— . "Beyond the Rhetoric of Promise" in *Arts and the Schools*, ed. Jerome J. Hausman. New York: McGraw-Hill Book Company, 1980.

———— . *The Dynamics of Educational Change*. IDEA Reports on Schooling, a Charles F. Kettering Foundation Program. New York: McGraw-Hill, 1975.

———— . *What Schools Are For*. Phi Delta Kappa Educational Foundation, 1979.

———— , with M. Frances Klein and Associates. *Behind the Classroom Door*. Worthington, Ohio: Charles A. Jones Publishing Company, 1970.

Hausman, Jerome J., ed., assisted by Joyce Wright. *Arts and the Schools*. New York: McGraw-Hill, 1980.

Hoffa, Harlan. *An Analysis of Recent Research Conferences in Art Education: Final Report*. Washington, D.C.: Bureau of Research, Office of Education, U.S. Department of Health, Education and Welfare, December 1970.

House, Ernest R. *The Politics of Educational Innovation*. Berkeley, Ca.: McCutchan Publishing Corporation, 1974.

The JDR 3rd Fund. *Annual Report*. New York: The JDR 3rd Fund, 1963-1977.

Joel, Lydia. *The Impact of Impact: Dance Artists as Catalysts for Change in Education*. DanceScope, Vol 6., No. 2, Spring/Summer 1972.

Jones, Lonna. *The Arts and the U.S. Department of Education: A List of Funded Projects and Activities, U.S. Department of Education, 1978*. Washington, D.C.: U.S. Department of Education, 1979.

Katz, Jonathan, ed. *Arts & Education Handbook: A Guide to Productive Collaborations*. Washington, D.C.: National Assembly of State Arts Agencies, 1988.

Koch, Kenneth. *Wishes, Lies and Dreams: Teaching Children to Write Poetry*. New York: Random House, 1971.

Langer, Susanne K. *Feeling and Form: A Theory of Art*. New York: Charles Scribner's, 1953.

————— . *Philosophy in a New Key*. Cambridge, Ma.: Harvard University Press, 1957.

Laybourne, Kit, ed. *Doing the Media—A Portfolio of Activities and Resources*. New York: The Center for Understanding Media, 1972.

Lopate, Phillip. *Being With Children: A Highly Spirited Personal Account of Teaching Writing, Theater and Videotape*. New York: Doubleday & Co., 1975.

Madeja, Stanley S. *All the Arts for Every Child*. New York: The JDR 3rd Fund, 1973.

————— , ed. *Arts and Aesthetics: An Agenda for the Future*. St. Louis, Mo.: CEMREL, Inc., 1977.

————— , ed. *The Arts, Cognition, and Basic Skills*. St. Louis, Mo.: CEMREL, Inc., 1978.

————— , ed. *Curriculum and Instruction in Arts and Aesthetic Education*. St. Louis, Mo.: CEMREL, Inc., 1980.

McLaughlin, John, ed. *Toward a New Era in Arts Education: The Interlochen Symposium*. New York: ACA Books, 1988.

Morrison, Jack. *The Maturing of the Arts on the American Campus: A Commentary*. Los Angeles, Ca.: University Press of America, 1985.

————— . *The Rise of the Arts on the American Campus*. Carnegie Commission on Higher Education series. New York: McGraw-Hill, 1973.

Murphy, Judith, and Lonna Jones. *Research in Arts Education: A Federal Chapter*. Washington, D.C.: Office of Education, U.S. Department of Health, Education, and Welfare Publication (OE) 76-02000, 1978.

————— , and Ronald Gross. *The Arts and the Poor: New Challenge for Educators*. Washington, D.C.: Bureau of Research, Office of Education, U.S. Department of Health, Education and Welfare, June 1968.

Music Educators National Conference. "The Arts in General Education" in *Music Educators Journal*, Vol. 64, No. 5, January 1978.

————— . *Try a New Face*. A Report on HEW-Supported Arts Projects in American Schools. Arts and Humanities Staff, Office of Education. Charles L. Gary, Projects Coordinator (in cooperation with the American Theatre Association, National Art Education Association, National Dance Association. Reporters include Sara A. Chapman, Junius Eddy, Charles B. Fowler, Charles L. Gary, Harlan Hoffa, Araminta Little). Washington, D.C.: U.S. Department of Health, Education and Welfare, 1979.

————— , and CEMREL, Inc. *Toward an Aesthetic Education*. Reston, Va.: The Music Educators National Conference and CEMREL, Inc., 1970.

National Endowment for the Arts. *Report of the Task Force on the Education, Training and Development of Professional Artists and Arts Educators*. Washington, D.C., December 1978.

————. *Toward Civilization: A Report on Arts Education*. Washington, D.C.: U.S. Government Printing Office, 1988.

National School Boards Association. *The Arts in Education: Research Report 1978-2*. Digest of the report by the Arts, Education and Americans Panel. Washington, D.C.: NSBA, 1978.

Newsom, Barbara Y., and Adele Z. Silver. *The Art Museum as Educator: A Collection of Studies as Guides to Practice and Policy*. Berkeley, Ca.: University of California Press, 1977.

New York City Board of Education. *All the Arts for All the Children: A Report on the Arts in General Education, New York City, 1974-1977*. New York: New York City Board of Education, 1978.

————, Division of Curriculum and Instruction. *Architecture: A Design for Education*. New York: New York City Board of Education, 1979.

————, Division of Curriculum and Instruction. *Arts in General Education: An Administrator's Manual*. New York: New York City Board of Education, 1979.

The New York State Education Department. *RITA: Reading Improvement through the Arts*. Albany, N.Y.: The New York State Education Department, Division of Federal Educational Opportunity Programs, Title 1, ESEA, and the Division of Humanities and Arts Education, 1979.

Oklahoma State Department of Education. *A New Wind Blowing: Arts in Education in Oklahoma Schools*. Oklahoma City: Oklahoma State Department of Education, 1978.

Reimer, Bennett. "Designing Effective Arts Programs" in *Arts and the Schools*, ed. Jerome J. Hausman. New York: McGraw-Hill, 1980.

Pankratz, David B., and Kevin V. Mulcahy. *The Challenge to Reform Arts Education: What Role Can Research Play?* New York: ACA Books, 1989.

Pennslyvania State University. *Arts IMPACT: Curriculum for Change—A Summary Report*. Prepared by the Arts I(nterdisciplinary) M(odel) P(rograms) in the A(rts) for C(hildren) and T(eachers) Project Evaluation Team and submitted to the Arts and Humanities Program, Office of Education, U.S. Department of Health, Education and Welfare. University Park, Pa.: Pennslyvania State University, March 1973.

"The Ecology of Education: The Arts," in *The National Elementary Principal*, Vol. 55, No. 3, January/February 1976.

Read, Herbert. *Education Through Art*. (3d. Revision.) New York: Pantheon Books, 1956.

Reimer, Bennett. *A Philosophy of Music Education*. Englewood Cliffs, N.J.: Prentice-Hall, 1970.

Remer, Jane. *Networks, the Arts and School Change*. New York: The JDR 3rd Fund, 1975. (Revised and expanded for The National Elementary Principal. The Ecology of Education: The Arts. Vol. 55, No. 3, January/February 1976.)

———. *The Identification Process for Schools Participating in the New York City Arts in General Education Project Network*. New York: The JDR 3rd Fund, 1975.

———. *Considerations for School Systems Contemplating a Comprehensive AGE Program*. New York: The JDR 3rd Fund, 1977.

———. *The League of Cities for the Arts in Education*. New York: The JDR 3rd Fund, 1977.

———. *Changing Schools Through the Arts: The Power of An Idea*. New York: McGraw-Hill, 1982.

———. "Arts Policy in Public Education" in the *Journal of Arts Management and Law*, Vol. 13, No. 1, Spring 1983.

———. "Quo Vadis Arts Education: A National Agenda" in *Design for Arts in Education*, Vol. 89, No. 2, November/December 1987.

Rockefeller Panel. *The Performing Arts: Problems and Prospects*. New York: McGraw-Hill, 1965.

Sarason, Seymour B. *The Culture of the School and the Problem of Change*. Boston: Allyn and Bacon, Inc., 1971. (Seventh printing, 1974.)

Shapiro, Stephen R., Richard Place, and Richard Scheidenhelm. *Artists in the Classroom*. Hartford, Conn.: Connecticut Commission on the Arts, 1973.

Shuker, Nancy, ed. *Arts in Education Partners: Schools and Their Communities*. Jointly sponsored by the Junior League of Oklahoma City, the Arts Council of Oklahoma City, Oklahoma City Public Schools, the Association of Junior Leagues, and the JDR 3rd Fund, 1977. (Distributed by the American Council for the Arts, New York.)

Silberman, Charles. *Crisis in the Classroom: The Remaking of American Education*. New York: Random House, 1970.

Smith, Ralph A. *Aesthetic Concepts and Education*. Urbana: University of Illinois Press, 1970.

Spolin, Viola. *Improvisation for the Theatre: A Handbook of Teaching and Directing Techniques*. Evanston, Ill.: Northwestern University Press, 1963. (Republished as the *Theater Game File*, consisting of index cards packaged in a box, CEMREL, St. Louis, Mo., 1976.)

Stake, Robert E. *Evaluating the Arts in Education: A Responsive Approach*. Columbus, Ohio: Charles E. Merrill, 1975.

Tye, Kenneth A., and Jerrold M. Novotney. *Schools in Transition: The Practitioner as Change Agent*. IDEA Reports on Schooling, A Charles F. Kettering Foundation Program. New York: McGraw-Hill, 1975.

Weinstein, Gerald, and Mario D. Fantini. *Toward Humanistic Education, A Curriculum of Affect*. New York: Praeger University Series, 1970.

Wenner, Gene C. *Comprehensive [State] Arts Planning: The Ad Hoc Coalition of States for the Arts in Education*, ed. Kathryn Bloom. New York: The JDR 3rd Fund, 1975.

————. *Dance in the Schools: A New Movement in Education*. New York: The JDR 3rd Fund, The City Center of Music and Drama, and the National Endowment for the Arts, 1974.

Wilson, Brent, and Harlan Hoffa, eds. *The History of Art Education: Proceedings from the Penn State Conference*. University Park: The Pennsylvania State University, College of Arts and Architecture, School of Visual Arts, 1985.

Wolf, Dennie Palmer, and Thomas Wolf. *Academic Preparation in the Arts: Teaching for Transition from High School to College*. New York: College Entrance Examination Board, 1975. (known as "The Red Book")

Wolf, Thomas, ed. *The Arts Go To School: An Arts-in-Education Handbook*. New York: New England Foundation for the Arts and American Council for the Arts, 1983.

ABOUT THE AMERICAN COUNCIL FOR THE ARTS

The American Council for the Arts (ACA) is one of the nation's primary sources of legislative news affecting all of the arts and serves as a leading advisor to arts administrators, educators, elected officials, arts patrons, and the general public. To accomplish its goal of strong advocacy of the arts, ACA promotes public debate in various national, state and local forums; communicates as a publisher of books, journals, *Vantage Point* magazine and *ACA Update*; provides information services through its extensive arts education, policy and management library; and has as its key policy issues arts education, the needs of individual artists, private-sector initiatives and international cultural relations.

BOARD OF DIRECTORS

ABOUT THE AUTHOR

JANE REMER   is an author and free-lance consultant in education, the arts and the arts in education. She does strategic long-range planning, designs and evaluates programs, writes for national publications and edits curriculum and other educational materials. She is also Grants and Program Director for the Capezio/Ballet Makers Dance Foundation.

Ms. Remer has worked for over 25 years with public and private arts and education agencies at the federal, state and local levels. She was Associate Director of the John D. Rockefeller 3rd Fund's Arts in Education Program, Special Assistant to the Director of Curriculum and Instruction, New York City Public Schools, and Assistant Director of Education at Lincoln Center for the Performing Arts. She is the author of *Changing Schools through the Arts: How to Build on the Power of an Idea*, which was first published by McGraw-Hill in 1982 and has been substantially revised for publication by the American Council for the Arts in 1990.

Ms. Remer has a B.A. from Oberlin College and an M.A. in Teaching (French) from Yale University. She attended Yale Law School and has been a dancer, choreographer, musician and theater artist.